Cilia

CASEBOOK SERIES

SHAKESPEARE: *Early Tragedies* Neil Taylor & Bryan Loughrey
SHAKESPEARE: *Hamlet* John Jump
SHAKESPEARE: *Henry IV Parts I and II* G.K. Hunter
SHAKESPEARE: *Henry V* Michael Quinn
SHAKESPEARE: *Julius Caesar* Peter Ure
SHAKESPEARE: *King Lear* (Revised) Frank Kermode
SHAKESPEARE: *Macbeth* (Revised) John Wain
SHAKESPEARE: *Measure for Measure* C. K. Stead
SHAKESPEARE: *The Merchant of Venice* John Wilders
SHAKESPEARE: *'Much Ado About Nothing'* & *'As You Like It'* John Russell Brown
SHAKESPEARE: *Othello* (Revised) John Wain
SHAKESPEARE: *Richard II* Nicholas Brooke
SHAKESPEARE: *The Sonnets* Peter Jones
SHAKESPEARE: *The Tempest* (Revised) D. J. Palmer
SHAKESPEARE: *Troilus and Cressida* Priscilla Martin
SHAKESPEARE: *Twelfth Night* D. J. Palmer
SHAKESPEARE: *The Winter's Tale* Kenneth Muir
SPENSER: *The Faerie Queene* Peter Bayley
SHERIDAN: *Comedies* Peter Davison
STOPPARD: *'Rosencrantz and Guildenstern are Dead'*, *'Jumpers'* & *'Travesties'*
T. Bareham
SWIFT: *Gulliver's Travels* Richard Gravil
SYNGE: *Four Plays* Ronald Ayling
TENNYSON: *In Memoriam* John Dixon Hunt
THACKERAY: *Vanity Fair* Arthur Pollard
TROLLOPE: *The Barsetshire Novels* T. Bareham
WEBSTER: *'The White Devil'* & *'The Duchess of Malfi'* R. V. Holdsworth
WILDE: *Comedies* William Tydeman
VIRGINIA WOOLF: *To the Lighthouse* Morris Beja
WORDSWORTH: *Lyrical Ballads* Alun R. Jones & William Tydeman
WORDSWORTH: *The 1807 Poems* Alun R. Jones
WORDSWORTH: *The Prelude* W. J. Harvey & Richard Gravil
YEATS: *Poems 1919–35* Elizabeth Cullingford
YEATS: *Last Poems* Jon Stallworthy

Issues in Contemporary Critical Theory Peter Barry
Thirties Poets: 'The Auden Group' Ronald Carter
Tragedy: Developments in Criticism R.P. Draper
The Epic Ronald Draper
Poetry Criticism and Practice: Developments since the Symbolists A.E. Dyson
Three Contemporary Poets: Gunn, Hughes, Thomas A.E. Dyson
Elizabethan Poetry: Lyrical & Narrative Gerald Hammond
The Metaphysical Poets Gerald Hammond
Medieval English Drama Peter Happé
The English Novel: Developments in Criticism since Henry James Stephen Hazell
Poetry of the First World War Dominic Hibberd
The Romantic Imagination John Spencer Hill
Drama Criticism: Developments since Ibsen Arnold P. Hinchliffe
Three Jacobean Revenge Tragedies R.V. Holdsworth
The Pastoral Mode Bryan Loughrey
The Language of Literature Norman Page
Comedy: Developments in Criticism D.J. Palmer
Studying Shakespeare John Russell Brown
The Gothic Novel Victor Sage
Pre-Romantic Poetry J.R. Watson

Hardy

The Tragic Novels

The Return of the Native
The Mayor of Casterbridge
Tess of the d'Urbervilles
Jude the Obscure

A CASEBOOK

EDITED BY

R. P. DRAPER

Revised Edition

MACMILLAN

First edition 1975
Reprinted eight times
Revised edition 1989
MACMILLAN PRESS LTD
Houndmills, Basingstoke, Hampshire RG21 2XS
and London
Companies and representatives
throughout the world

ISBN 0–333–53363–1 hardcover
ISBN 0–333–53364–X paperback

A catalogue record for this book is available
from the British Library.

10   9   8   7   6   5   4   3
02   01   00 99 98 97 96 95

Printed in Hong Kong

FOR ANNE, ISABEL AND SOPHIA

CONTENTS

ACKNOWLEDGEMENTS

The author and publishers wish to thank the following, who have kindly given permission for the use of copyright material: Kristin Brady for 'Tess and Alec: Rape or Seduction?' from *Thomas Hardy Annual* No. 4 (1986), ed. Norman Page, pp. 127–45, by permission of Macmillan Publishers Ltd; Jean Brooks for extract from *Thomas Hardy: the Poetic Structure* by permission of Paul Elek Ltd, and Cornell University Press; Peter J. Casagrande for extract from *Unity in Hardy's Novels* (1982), pp. 127–43, by permission of Macmillan Publishers Ltd; R. P. Draper for '*Jude the Obscure*: A Novel of the Comically Tragic' from *Critical Essays on Thomas Hardy: The Novels*, ed. Dale Kramer (1990), by permission of G. K. Hall Ltd; D. H. Lawrence for extract from 'Study of Thomas Hardy' from *Phoenix*, by permission of Laurence Pollinger Ltd, and the Estate of the late Mrs Frieda Lawrence; David Lodge for 'Tess, Nature and the Voices of Hardy' from *Language of Fiction*, by permission of Routledge & Kegan Paul Ltd, and Columbia University Press; F. Manning for *Novels of Character and Environment*, by permission of *Spectator*; Robert Schweik for 'Character and Fate in *The Mayor of Casterbridge*', © 1966 by the Regents of the University of California, reprinted from *Nineteenth-Century Fiction*, vol. 21, no. 3 (December 1966), pp. 249–62, by permission of the Regents; Elaine Showalter for 'The Unmanning of the Mayor of Casterbridge' in *Critical Approaches to the Fiction of Thomas Hardy*, ed. Dale Kramer (1979), pp. 101–14, by permission of Macmillan Publishers Ltd; Rosemary Sumner for extract from *Thomas Hardy: Psychological Novelist* (1981), pp. 165–82, by permission of Macmillan Publishers Ltd; Tony Tanner for 'Colour and Movement in Hardy's *Tess of the d'Urbervilles*'; Raymond Williams for extract from *The English Novel from Dickens to Lawrence*, by permission of Chatto & Windus Ltd, and Oxford University Press, Inc, New York; Virginia Woolf for 'The Novels of Thomas Hardy' from *The Second Common Reader* by permission of the Author's Literary Estate, The Hogarth Press Ltd, and Harcourt Brace Jovanovich, Inc. The publishers have made every effort to trace the copyright-holders, but if they have inadvertently overlooked any they will be pleased to make the necessary arrangement at the first opportunity.

GENERAL EDITOR'S PREFACE

The Casebook series, launched in 1968, has become a well-regarded library of critical studies. The central concern of the series remains the 'single-author' volume, but suggestions from the academic community have led to an extension of the original plan, to include occasional volumes on such general themes as literary 'schools' and genres.

Each volume in the central category deals either with one well-known and influential work by an individual author, or with closely related works by one writer. The main section consists of critical readings, mostly modern, collected from books and journals. A selection of reviews and comments by the author's contemporaries is also included, and sometimes comment from the author himself. The Editor's Introduction charts the reputation of the work or works from the first appearance to the present time.

Volumes in the 'general themes' category are variable in structure but follow the basic purpose of the series in presenting an integrated selection of readings, with an Introduction which explores the theme and discusses the literary and critical issues involved.

A single volume can represent no more than a small selection of critical opinions. Some critics are excluded for reasons of space, and it is hoped that readers will pursue the suggestions for further reading in the Select Bibliography. Other contributions are severed from their original context, to which some readers may wish to turn. Indeed, if they take a hint from the critics represented here, they certainly will.

A. E. DYSON

INTRODUCTION

'Wanted: Good Hardy Critic' is the title of a review article by Philip Larkin in the *Critical Quarterly* (Summer 1966). The obvious retort is that there are many good Hardy critics; but it is true that there is no single critic who seems to have taken the full measure of his subject and whose book one could recommend to the newcomer to Hardy as *the* critical account. But in this respect Hardy is no worse served than certain other major writers, D. H. Lawrence, for example, and it is perhaps even a relief that there is no established, 'authoritative' view of him, no stone that has to be rolled away from the tomb before one can start looking for oneself at the embalmed corpse. The body still breathes, and at any moment will walk, run, spring upon us, or hide, with all the elusiveness and unpredictability of life.

Until comparatively recently there was, however, a special problem connected with Hardy in that he often struck readers as somehow being greater than there was any apparent cause for him to be. E. M. Forster, the most engagingly frank of literary critics, illustrates this reaction in *Aspects of the Novel* (1927), where he comments that Meredith knows better how to combine plot and character, but 'the work of Hardy is my home and that of Meredith cannot be'. This would seem to be the cue for a generous appraisal of Hardy's achievement as a novelist, but most of what Forster has to say proves to be on the negative side: Hardy's characters are dominated by plot. They 'are ordered to acquiesce in its requirements'. The sense of a tragic fate is strong, but 'fate above us, not the fate working through us'. He is more successful in *The Dynasts* where the great engine of Fate is really seen working out the destinies of his characters. In the novels, however, with the one exception of the character of Tess, who 'conveys the feeling that she is greater than destiny', the machine works, but 'never catches humanity in its teeth'. And of *Jude the Obscure* Forster says, 'there is some vital problem that has not been answered, or even posed in the misfortunes of Jude the Obscure'. His misgivings are summed up in the remark that Hardy 'has emphasized causality more strongly than his medium permits'. This adds up to something like a statement of failure. Yet one senses that all these comments are made against the grain, as if Forster feels himself bound by some external commitment (possibly the fact that he is giving a lecture on 'Plot') to expose the inadequacies of Hardy's novelistic technique, while feeling that all this is fundamentally irrelevant to the deeply moving poetic effect which Hardy's novels have upon him. The most telling comment is: 'Hardy seems to me essentially a poet . . .', a tacit admission that the greatness of Hardy is not explicable in the usual terms of novel criticism.

Though never a literary *enfant terrible* or leader of an artistic revolution Hardy was from the first in uneasy relationship with the publishing practices and reading public of his day. His first attempt at novel-writing, *The Poor Man and the Lady*[1] written supposedly 'By the Poor Man', is described in *The Life of Thomas Hardy* (nominally by Florence Emily Hardy, Hardy's second wife, but now recognised to be, in effect, the work of Hardy himself) as 'a striking socialistic novel'. In 1869 it was read, among others, by George Meredith, then publisher's reader for Chapman and Hall, who thought it was too outspoken for a young man's first novel. The meeting between the new and the already established author is described in the *Life*:

Meredith had the manuscript in his hand, and began lecturing Hardy upon it in a sonorous voice. No record was kept by the latter of their conversation, but the gist of it he remembered very well. It was that the firm were willing to publish the novel as agreed, but that he, the speaker, strongly advised its author not to 'nail his colours to the mast' so definitely in a first book, if he wished to do anything practical in literature; for if he printed so pronounced a thing he would be attacked on all sides by the conventional reviewers, and his future injured.[2]

The reference to 'conventional reviewers' is ominous, though it was conventional readers who were to pose the more serious problem for Hardy.

Meredith further suggested that Hardy should 'attempt a novel with a purely artistic purpose, giving it a more complicated "plot" than was attempted with *The Poor Man and the Lady*'. As can be seen in his next, but first published novel, *Desperate Remedies* (1871), the young writer, whose wish to do something 'practical in literature' included a legitimate hope for a modicum of reputation and financial success, bent his will to this advice; nevertheless his *prédilection d'artiste* (to borrow the phrase used by D. H. Lawrence in his 'Study of Thomas Hardy') for romantically uncompromising characters and his instinctive sense of the falsity of conventional values asserted itself in forms that increasingly disturbed his efforts to write for the market, and particularly alarmed the editors of magazines to which Hardy tried to sell the serial rights of his novels.

Problems of this kind arose more especially with the later work, i.e. with *The Return of the Native* (1878) and subsequent novels.[3] As a result of editorial pressures various details, and some whole episodes, were bowdlerised to satisfy the moral prejudices of the late Victorian reading public. For example, from the manuscript version of *The Return of the Native* it would appear that Hardy originally intended Thomasin to go through an illegal marriage ceremony with Wildeve and be away from home for a whole week – a more compromising experience than her merely returning the same day because the licence is found to be invalid. At the same time Hardy's revisions suggest that his own imagination was increasingly fired by the unconventional character of Eustacia, who became a more 'Promethean' figure, and that the world of the novel grew less 'pastoral' in the manner of such earlier successes with the public as *Under the Greenwood Tree* (1872) and *Far From the Madding Crowd* (1874), and through increased mythological reference acquired the aura of 'the more comprehensive world of classical Greece'.[4] In the serial versions of *The Mayor of Casterbridge* (1886) and *Tess of the d'Urbervilles* (1891) further steps were taken to appease the Mrs Grundys of the magazines: Lucetta's Jersey affair with Henchard was glossed over as a marriage undertaken in the belief that Henchard was now a free man; and in the case of *Tess* two episodes, described by Hardy as 'more especially addressed to adult readers', were excised from the text and printed separately (though they were restored to the book version) in presumably more 'adult' periodicals. These episodes were Tess's seduction by Alec (chapters 10 and 11 of the book), which were published in a Special Literary Supplement of the *National Observer* (14 November 1891) under the ironic title of 'Saturday Night in Arcady', and her unorthodox baptising of her illegitimate baby (chapter 14), published in the *Fortnightly Review* (May 1891). In the serial version of *Tess* the hoary device of a seemingly legal marriage was used yet again, and towards the end of the novel, in the crucial episode of Alec d'Urberville and Tess at the Sandbourne boarding-house, a feeble attempt was made to suggest that the couple were simply staying there as 'friends'. Silliest of all was the change of detail in chapter 23 so that Angel could wheel the dairymaids in a barrow instead of actually carrying them in his arms over the flooded lane.

More serious problems were encountered with *Jude the Obscure* (1895). Serialisation, in *Harper's New Monthly Magazine*, was agreed in principle in 1893 on condition that the story should be 'in every respect suitable for a family magazine', and Hardy said that 'it would be a tale that could not offend the most fastidious maiden'. But it did not work out that way, and several adjustments had to be made for the serial version. For example, Arabella's false-pregnancy device for tricking Jude into marriage was softened into the innocuous pretence that a former sweetheart was offering to marry her, with a letter being produced to 'prove' the point. Jude's night with Arabella in Aldbrickham was made quite inoffensive by their being packed off to separate lodgings, and Sue and Jude were likewise put in separate, though contiguous, houses. Again, in the serial version Sue was never allowed to give in to Jude sexually, as she does in the book when she fears the rivalry of Arabella; a mere promise of marriage was substituted. Above all, Sue's confiding in Little Time about the coming baby was omitted from the serial, thus sparing the 'young person' reader a blush, but simultaneously destroying a vital element in the tragedy.

All this is perhaps mainly illustrative of the queasy morality governing late Victorian magazines and their readers; but that Hardy should have written scenes so unacceptable to contemporary taste, while still wishing to benefit from serialisation, is an indication not, as Mary Ellen Chase would suggest, of his lack of integrity as an artist,[5] but rather of the strength of his imaginative compulsion to express the truth even in the forbidden territory of sexual relations.

The reviews of Hardy's work, though they were by no means uniformly unfavourable, and his reactions to them, once again indicate the uneasiness of his relationship with his contemporaries. As might be expected, the two novels which most aroused the moral indignation of propriety-conscious reviewers were *Tess* and *Jude*. In *The Life of Thomas Hardy* the intemperate outbursts of a 'maiden lady' critic of *Jude* are quoted, including such comments as 'I thought that *Tess of the d'Urbervilles* was bad enough, but that is milk for babes compared to this. . . . Aside from its immorality there is coarseness which is beyond belief. . . . When I finished the story I opened the windows and let in the fresh air.'[6]

At the beginning of chapter 24 of the *Life* it is suggested that misrepresentations of this sort 'wellnigh compelled [Hardy], in his own judgement at any rate, if he wished to retain any shadow of self-respect, to abandon at once a form of literary art he had long intended to abandon at some indefinite time', and turn to poetry. But how seriously such hostile attitudes (and by no means all reviews of *Tess* and *Jude* were bad) influenced Hardy's decision to abandon novel-writing it is difficult to say. The implication of 'had long intended to abandon at some indefinite time' is that he was already prepared to make the change from fiction to poetry before he read the reviews. The likelihood is that such factitiously moral diatribes were no more influential than they were true criticism; but it is worth paying attention to them since they further exemplify the uncongenial publishing conditions in which Hardy had to work. He was a man who wished to be on good terms with his readers yet felt he could not trust the moral judgement of many of them. This becomes evident in the tone of the later novels, and not least in the title page of *Tess*. Hardy asserts that the sub-title, 'A Pure Woman', was an afterthought, inserted after he had read the final proofs, 'as being the estimate left in a candid mind of the heroine's character – an estimate that nobody would be likely to dispute'. To which he caustically adds, 'It was disputed more than anything else in the book.'[7] However, it must be said that this is somewhat disingenuous. The sub-title is a deliberate defiance of conventional opinion, reinforced by the words 'Faithfully Presented' and the appending of a quotation from *The Two Gentlemen of Verona*: '. . . Poor wounded name! My bosom as a bed/Shall lodge thee.' If these additions were made to ensure a correct interpretation of Hardy's intentions, they also seem to indicate the expectation of misinterpretation.

Saner and more penetrating criticism came from men like Havelock Ellis, R. H. Hutton, William Watson and Edmund Gosse.[8] These praised Hardy while adding strictures, which, though in the end one may have to reject them, started a critical debate of an altogether more serious kind, to be continued by the authors of books and articles produced at greater leisure and after time had been given for the sifting processes of reflection and discussion. Thus Hutton begins to raise the whole issue of Hardy's pessimism and

Watson and Gosse begin to question whether his style is perhaps too clumsily pedantic.[9] Havelock Ellis, on the other hand, takes up the vexed problem of moral censorship and argues for a more enlightened attitude in a way that must have given Hardy great satisfaction.

Hardy was now beginning to achieve recognition as a major writer whose work was not only to be reviewed, but to be given in-depth study. Prior to the publication of *Jude the Obscure*, Lionel Johnson had published a book with the deferential title *The Art of Thomas Hardy* (1894), which, as shown in the extract printed here, combined thoughtful disagreement with Hardy's 'general sentiments, about the meaning of the unconscious universe, or of conscious mankind' with judicious admiration for his imaginative powers and skill as a writer. Johnson's list of the characteristics of Hardy's work, including concentration on Wessex, the choice of powerful characters set off by others less powerful and their clash with men of 'more modern experiences', focus on erotic love, and preference for a certain tragic curve in the development of his plot, still provides a useful summary of the leading features of Hardy's work. Likewise, F. Manning, in his article on 'Novels of Character and Environment' (1912), pays Hardy the compliment of making a serious assessment of his achievement so far. He identifies tragedy as the central preoccupation of Hardy's later novels, and while deploring the passivity which he attributes to a character like Tess, on the grounds that it diminishes the sense of free will on which the ennobling effect of tragedy depends, he recognises quite clearly that the special tragic power of Hardy's work derives from 'the depth and richness of his emotional nature' which finds its fullest expression in *Tess of the d'Urbervilles* and *Jude the Obscure*.

From this point onwards the feeling that Hardy is great in spite of being in some way curiously wrongheaded becomes a widespread critical reaction. D. H. Lawrence, however, is more confident than most in defining what he believes is right and what is wrong. For him tragedy in Hardy's work is associated with characters who answer the call of individual fulfilment instead of submitting to 'the comparative imprisonment' of society's conventional standards of behaviour, but in so doing are destroyed. He senses Hardy's dislike of conformity but is impatient because Hardy does not, in his opinion, go far enough in asserting it. The comment is often made that the 'Study of Thomas Hardy' tells us more about Lawrence than it does about Hardy, and there is some truth in the suggestion that the interpretation of tragedy which Lawrence attributes to Hardy is really a reflection of Lawrence's own impatience with the inhibitive force of convention. Hardy, along with Tolstoy, is condemned by Lawrence for making his characters submit to the dictates of society, or to a morality which is socially induced, instead of allowing them to assert, and live by, their own innate vitality. Nevertheless, Lawrence is acutely sensitive to the presence of that vitality in characters like Eustacia and Tess and, rather surprisingly, Arabella as well; and in his comments on *The Return of the Native* he shows full awareness of the importance in Hardy of the relationship between the human and the natural. He also gives an original analysis of Egdon Heath which initiates a long series of attempts to account for the peculiarly evocative power of Hardy's descriptions of it.

For Virginia Woolf, too, man in the tragic context of Nature is the special subject of Hardy and, like Forster, she finds the poet at work in the novels, though in her view poet and novelist are not at odds with each other, but join their forces together: 'In short, nobody can deny Hardy's power – the true novelist's power – to make us believe that his characters are fellow-beings driven by their own passions and idiosyncrasies, while they have – and this is the poet's gift – something symbolical about them which is common to us all.'

A rather different kind of emphasis is given to the poetic element by one of Hardy's more recent critics, Jean Brooks. Acknowledging the truth of the sentence just quoted from Virginia Woolf, she none the less goes on to argue that 'the poetic structure' informing Hardy's work, not simply the presence of the 'poet's gift' in parts of his work, demands central critical attention, for this explains and justifies, as other critical approaches do not, the tensions and seeming contradictions of his art. The 'poetic' principle as thus understood is the more or less explicit assumption on which many recent studies of particular novels are based. Examples in this collection are the studies of *Tess of the d'Urbervilles* (the Hardy novel which most seems to invite this approach) by Tony Tanner and David Lodge. Tanner uses a favourite method of modern critics, the selection and analysis of significant images, to show that Hardy's poetic impressionism depicts in Tess a type of human life drawn out from Nature, but doomed to be destroyed by Nature, and 'a universe of radical opposition, working to destroy what it works to create . . .'.

Lodge, on the other hand, studies the details of Hardy's style, taking up the well-tried theme of its unevenness and attempting to establish with greater precision where it is successful and where it fails.

The poetic approach may not be the definitive approach to Hardy, but it has the great merit of concentrating attention on the words that Hardy wrote and their evocative power. It largely invalidates the preoccupation of earlier critics with such matters as the supposedly deterministic philosophy of Hardy and his excessive use of chance and coincidence. If Hardy is not seeking to present a fictional imitation of character and circumstance as they actually interact in observable day-to-day existence, if he is not, that is to say, a realist (and he certainly denied that he was), such offences against plausibility are no more to be held against him, as Virginia Woolf suggests, than the similar offences of the Elizabethan drama-tists. The appropriate question to ask, then, with regard to Hardy's fiction is whether characters, setting, plot and language combine in an imaginatively effective whole. The novels must be judged by their inner coherence as works of art rather than by their faithfulness in reflecting the real conditions of the external world.

However, no sooner is this said than it appears to be an overstatement. In the 'General Preface to the Novels and Poems', written for the 1912 Wessex Edition of his works, Hardy speaks of the trouble he has taken to authenticate the detail of his presentation of 'Wessex' (at once the actual, and yet also a fictional version of south-western England) 'in order to preserve for my own satisfaction a fairly true record of a vanishing life'. Much of the background, he says, 'has been done from the real – that is to say, has something real for its basis, however illusively treated'.[10] Such a juxtaposition of 'real and 'illusively' may seem confusing, but it probably springs from Hardy's quite legitimate desire to retain the freedom of the artist creating a work of fiction while keeping as close as possible to the 'feel' of the experiences which he himself had had as boy and young man in the region of which he writes. Moreover, the attitudes and habits of 'Wessex' touched him all the more keenly as he appreciated the quality of the social and intellectual forces which were detaching him from that life. As a result there is also an entirely justifiable biographical and sociological strain to be found in some Hardy criticism. This, in its turn, has generated a reaction. The historical accuracy, for example, of Douglas Brown's suggestion that the tragic novels, and *The Mayor of Casterbridge* in particular, are about the agricultural tragedy of 1870–1902[11] is questioned by J. C. Maxwell in his essay 'The "Sociological" Approach to *The Mayor of Casterbridge*'.[12] Maxwell reminds us that Hardy's 1912 Preface to that novel alludes to an earlier period, involving 'the uncertain harvest which immediately preceded the repeal of the Corn Laws',[13] and while conceding that the struggle between Henchard and Farfrae does reflect in a general manner the conflict between old and new styles of life, he shows that Farfrae cannot seriously be identified with the new financial methods and cold ruthlessness of modern enterprise encroaching on the warm, passionate ways of old Wessex. The essence of Brown's argument remains, however. For him all the later novels are permeated by Hardy's 'sensuous understanding' of the organically integrated agricultural life and a tragic sense of its decay; though in some ways it is *Tess of the d'Urbervilles* rather than *The Mayor of Casterbridge* which best illustrates this thesis. His deep feeling for 'Wessex' makes Tess at once a very real woman and a representative, almost at times a mythic figure: 'For Tess is not only the pure woman, the ballad heroine, the country girl: she is the agricultural community in its moment of ruin'.[14]

If we are in danger, by following this train of thought, of losing once more the elements of immediate knowledge which Hardy draws upon to create his Wessex world – one should remember that it is Angel to whom Tess appears as 'a visionary essence of woman' (*Tess*, chapter 20); she herself prefers to be taken as simply 'Tess' the milkmaid – Raymond Williams' chapter on Hardy in *The English Novel from Dickens to Lawrence* is another salutary reminder of Hardy's grasp of the complex reality. The particular vantage point given him by his background (he was neither of the agricultural labouring class nor of the farmers and landowners, but the son of a builder, and himself trained to a professional career as an architect) enabled Hardy to write about 'Wessex' as 'both the educated observer and the passionate participant', and an important consequence of this combination of detachment and sympathy was that he could represent the pressures to which his characters were subjected as 'pressures from within the system of living, not outside it'.

To some extent all criticism proceeds by disagreement and qualification compelling a return to whatever text is being considered for renewed impressions and reappraisal. The question of the realism or ultra-realism of Hardy's fiction can in this light be seen as a fruitful contradiction resulting from shifting critical points of view. The essays in this volume on *The Return of the Native* by John Paterson and Peter J. Casagrande are further examples of such fruitful variation. Paterson's researches into the making of *The Return* bring out for him the double, and to some extent self-contradictory, theme of the romantic enlargement of the novel in the process of revision and the pretentiousness of its too explicit claims to tragic grandeur.[15] Casagrande, however, in what is a latter-day return to the biographical criticism of an earlier generation, though in a more sophisticated manner, presents a more ironic view of *The Return*, with the focus on Clym rather than Eustacia. He suggests that Clym's desire to return home is symptomatic of an immature desire to go back to his childhood, which is symbolised by Egdon Heath. There are parallels between him and Johnny Nunsuch and Christian Cantle which suggest 'sexual incompleteness' and 'the failure in him of psychological and perhaps physical development'. Thomasin's ability to adjust to disappointment also contrasts with his 'confused nostalgia' and further points up his immaturity. All this is related, indirectly, to Hardy's own marital problems and his relationship with his own mother – which contrasts strikingly with Paterson's contention that 'the novel derives more from Hardy's imagination than from his observation and experience'. Yet both critics achieve valuable insight deriving from the different vantage points which their respective approaches afford them. There are no simply right or wrong ways of dealing with as complex an author as Hardy.

The consideration of conflicting interpretations of *The Mayor of Casterbridge* by previous critics leads Robert C. Schweik to the discovery of a change of posture on Hardy's part as the novel advanced – a change from presenting Henchard's career as an illustration of the dictum, 'character is fate', which implies that the universe is morally ordered, to seeing him as victim in a morally neutral world. The transition from one to the other is effectively disguised by the overall structure of the novel, consisting of successive wave-like movements of hope, anxiety and catastrophe. The reason that Schweik suggests for this modulation of the tragic concept underlying *The Mayor* – that in Hardy traditional beliefs were at variance with intellectually acquired doubt – is somewhat speculative; but the analysis is excellent in its tracing of the shifting values of the novel.

A shift in emphasis again forms the basis of other, more recent interpretations of *The Mayor of Casterbridge*. Dale Kramer, for example, in his chapter on the novel in *Thomas Hardy, the Forms of Tragedy* [16] suggests that there is a cyclic pattern determining the rise and fall of Henchard which by implication can be extended to Farfrae as well: Henchard's fall is Farfrae's rise, and Farfrae in his turn will inevitably fall, to be succeeded by some other rising star. I myself have also argued in an article in the *Critical Quarterly* that there is a change from a classically Aristotelian to a more modern, Schopenhauerian form of tragedy, though Hardy 'does not cause the one to cancel out the other, but allows the two to co-exist in a tension which is both heroic and disenchanted'. [17]

Elaine Showalter, in 'The Unmanning of the Mayor of Caster-bridge' (included in the present selection), also detects a change, but for her it is connected with the softening of Henchard's attitudes under the impact of tragedy. Initially presented as an intensely male-chauvinist figure, Henchard, paradoxically, offers convincing evidence that his creator disagreed with the prevailing Victorian ethos of male dominance and masculine assertiveness and competi-tiveness. In rejecting his wife at the beginning of the novel Henchard can be seen as seeking to disencumber himself of the feminine ties, and the feminine element in his own personality, which he regards as a drag on his career. Thus liberated he rises to the highest position in Casterbridge society by virtue of his sheer energy and aggressiveness; and it is only in his tragic decline to vulnerability and his forced change from active to more passive behaviour that he discovers the world of feeling from which he has divorced himself. In Showalter's view this 'unmanning' becomes a process by which the ultra-masculine protagonist finds, and joins himself to, the repressed feminine side of his personality, thus gaining a deeper and more complete humanity.

It is feminist criticism such as this which has had perhaps the most fruitful influence on the late-twentieth-century understanding of Hardy. He has long been recognised as in some sense a women's writer, and was at the beginning of his career actually mistaken for a woman (the serialised version of *Far from the Madding Crowd* was thought to be the work of George Eliot); that feminism should at last be making an important contribution to the understanding of his work is therefore peculiarly appropriate.

As Patricia Ingham suggests in her 'feminist reading' of Hardy,[18] the early novels tend, with some degree of uneasiness, to reflect the standard masculine ('patriarchal') prejudices built into mid-Victorian fiction. As Hardy gathers self-confidence he becomes increasingly dissatisfied with conventional ideas, especially with regard to the stereotyped 'angel-in-the-house' image of Victorian womanhood, and there is a progressive realisation of the independence and individuality of particular women, who have thoughts and desires of their own, in the sequence of heroines from Bathsheba Everdene (*Far from the Madding Crowd*) and Eustacia Vye (*The Return of the Native*) to Grace Melbury (*The Woodlanders*).[19] The full flowering of this development is to be seen in Tess Durbeyfield and Sue Bridehead, women whose tragedies are essentially to do with their departure from the imposed norms of conduct for Victorian women, and still more subtly with their own inner conflicts between convention and individuality.

Tess, according to Kristin Brady (in 'Tess and Alec: Rape or Seduction?'), 'is not, indeed, the typical betrayed maiden' of Victorian fiction 'who either forsakes normal relationships altogether in the aftermath of her social lapse or pines away hopelessly for her seducer'. She recovers from the Alec affair and the death of her illegitimate baby to fall in love with, and marry, another man. Brady's article focuses, however, on the events leading up to the deflowering of Tess, analysing them in detail to show how Hardy's Miltonically emblematic technique suggests both innocence and culpability, or complicity, on Tess's part, but with the ultimate effect of subverting any clear-cut moral judgement. What is at stake here is a sexuality which is real and complex, generating emotions which cannot be fitted into the Victorian stereotype.

The active sexuality of women is a difficult subject for a man to write about. More extreme feminists would argue that it is necessarily unknown to the male and inexpressible in a language which is both lexically and syntactically moulded to masculine experience. Rosemarie Morgan, nonetheless, argues refreshingly and vigorously, if sometimes a touch extravagantly, that Hardy has 'complete faith in the healthy, life-giving force of free, unrepressed sexual activity', and that in *Tess of the d'Urbervilles*, in particular, he gives a 'sensitive exposition of Tess in sexual ecstasy' which is marked by both 'candour and poetic truthfulness'.[20]

But perhaps the most controversial of Hardy's novels in terms of its treatment of sexuality, and more widely, is *Jude the Obscure*. There is considerable disagreement among critics as to whether this is the greatest of his novels, or his most perverse; a true 'Wessex' novel, or a curious outsider; a tragedy, or a case-history; late, but still essentially Victorian, or the novel in which Hardy finally breaks with the conventional prejudices of the Victorian reading public and allows himself to step forward as a distinctively 'modern' author. It is even a matter of dispute whether Jude or Sue is the central character. Structurally the two are in balance; or, rather, together with Phillotson and Arabella they create a quartet whose sexual relations form something like a geometrical pattern of alternating partnerships,[21] and as Hardy himself writes in his letter to Gosse, 'the book is all contrasts' (see p. 40).

For Robert Heilman Sue Bridehead is the most interesting character, 'a being whose brilliant and puzzling surface provides only partial clues to the depths in which we can sense the presence of profound and representative problems'.[22] She is a study of coquettishness, i.e. the desire to dominate men through attractiveness coupled with denial, which she indulges in for unconscious, and often self-protective, motives. Sue professes unconventional opinions, but is dangerously unaware of the extent to which she remains, at the level of emotional response, fundamentally conventional. Therefore, after her crisis, irrationally, but with a curiously relevant emotional logic, she punishes herself by returning to the most rigid extreme of conventionality. This is a profoundly typical Hardy theme, interpreted by Heilman as an instance of modern man's 'habitual rational analysis that tends to destroy the forms of feeling developed by the historical community'. As an example of close reading for a particular purpose Heilman's analysis is a model of its kind, though his conclusion that Sue's fate is more an 'illness' than a tragedy does suggest that concentration on the psychology of a single character can distort the imaginative effect of the novel as an artistic whole.

A more developed and professionally precise version of this account is to be found in Rosemary Sumner's more recent study of Hardy's psychological skill as a novelist.[23] Unlike many previous critics Sumner maintains that Hardy is not limited to the creation of stock figures in Victorian melodramatic plots, but that he is a novelist who is ahead of his time in anticipating the psychological disorders of Freud, Jung and Adler. In particular, his treatment of

Sue Bridehead shows him making 'tremendous advances on all fronts'. Her frigidity can be linked with the repression of sexuality that often goes with education, and the masochistic, self-punishing streak in her derives from 'repressed sex drives' of which she is terrified and which hence lead to apparently neurotic self-forcing. Nevertheless, Hardy does not offer a rigidly clinical analysis of Sue; and he may not be fully aware of what he is doing. He creates a puzzling, and changeable, character who is all the more effective for having a dimension that is seemingly incomprehensible since she thereby escapes the more rational patterns and 'the comparative certitude about characterisation' which is the strength, but also the limitation, of 'his nineteenth-century predecessors'.

Jude the Obscure is a novel which looks forward to later literature. As Ian Gregor remarks, with Sue Bridehead 'we find displayed the consciousness of self, the innate uncertainties, the psychic disturbance with which fiction of our own day is to make us familiar'. This points also to the modernity of *Jude* as compared with the rest of the Wessex novels. Not that the break is absolute. Gregor finds it still a nineteenth-century novel in that it bears very markedly the stamp of the authorial presence (it is recognisably the work of the 'novelist as sage'); but it is twentieth-century in its emphasis on rhythm, its orchestration of themes, and its sometimes extravagant defiance of realism. Thus the Little Time episode and the death of the children, which Gregor describes as 'the most terrible scene in Hardy's fiction, indeed it might reasonably be argued in English fiction', transcends realism and aims at 'an impersonal tragic dimension'. The novel becomes what Hardy himself in the preface to *Jude* called 'a series of seemings'. Yet the counterpointing of Sue's insulation from the feelings of others with Jude's increasing perception that his tragedy is 'inextricably involved with time, place and person' suggests not a retreat from, but a more intense engagement with, actual experience – something inevitable, and yet 'contingent on human institutions'.[24]

The old and the new meet in *Jude* in other ways as well. A new intensity of response to the actual is accompanied by a magnification of those grotesque misalliances of incident and impression so characteristic of Hardy from his earliest work. Jude's death scene is a potent example: 'By ten o'clock that night Jude was lying on the bedstead at his lodging covered with a sheet, and straight as an arrow. Through the partly opened window the joyous throb of a waltz entered from the ball-room at Cardinal.' On one level this is savage irony, on another it is representative of the curiously changeable nature of a tragedy, which is heart-rending and painful, yet, with an unpredictable shift of attitude, can easily be seen as farce. (See Hardy's own comment of 1888, reprinted below, p. 33.)

In some measure this shifting instability of mood is to be found in each of Hardy's tragic novels, but it reaches its culmination, and most consciously 'modern' expression, in *Jude*. There tragedy and comedy become close neighbours rather than opposites. In my own essay, 'Hardy's Comic Tragedy: *Jude the Obscure*', I have attempted to explore just this curiously fluctuating quality, linking it back to Fielding and the eighteenth-century mock-heroic (for which Hardy himself gives the hint) and also forward, though not too seriously, to Malcolm Bradbury's mockery of the angry young men of the 1950s. My conclusion is that *Jude* is a novel which defies traditional categories and is almost twentieth-century in its openness to contradictory responses: 'Its very modernity consists in this – that its episodes can seem both harrowing and ludicrous, and that its two main characters can seem to be both self-consciously perverse and the victims of a hypocritical, uncomprehending society.'

As a generalisation it may be said that awareness of his non-conformity is the leading feature of contemporary criticism of Hardy – taking 'non-conformity' in its widest meaning of refusal to conform with orthodox beliefs, whether religious, philosophical or political, and of awkwardly not fitting in with recognised genres and stylistic criteria or declining to follow established literary or social precedent. This is the more pertinent since Hardy often maintains an outwardly decorous, even slightly pedantic, manner; and in his work, at least prior to *Tess* and *Jude*, he can easily, as Peter Widdowson suggests, be represented, or misrepresented, as the celebrant of an old-fashioned Wessex pastoral world which suits the prejudices of conservatively sentimental and actually conformist minds.[25]

Deconstructionist critics, in particular, find ample material to work on here. George Wotton, for example, in *Thomas Hardy: Towards a Materialist Criticism*, is insistent that Hardy's work 'reflects the contradictions of its moment of production', including the class-system and assumptions about masculine superiority typical of Victorian England; but that it also develops a critical stance which exposes these contradictions, making it subversive rather than conformist in its ultimate effect. And John Goode, in

Thomas Hardy: the Offensive Truth, is equally emphatic that Hardy does not endorse, but rather questions, and even rejects, received opinion. Accordingly his chapter on *Jude the Obscure* is provocatively titled, 'Hardy's Fist', and he presents the novel as an exercise in aesthetic bathos ('It's all in the worst possible taste') intentionally 'offensive' to the respectable persons who constitute its readership and who embody the very values which it deplores.

The other major contemporary development in Hardy studies is in the field of textual scholarship, with the meticulously detailed work of editors such as Simon Gatrell, Juliet Grindle and Dale Kramer. Hardy constantly revised, adapted and re-revised his texts in ways that reveal his steady determination, notwithstanding the sometimes absurd subterfuges forced on him by Victorian publishing conditions (discussed earlier in this Introduction), to say his say as truthfully and honestly as possible. To date, the best account of this process overall is Gatrell's *Hardy the Creator*. After examining the history of Hardy's revisions Gatrell quotes Hardy's own comments on the dissatisfaction he felt with the published version of *Jude the Obscure* as compared with his original conception of it: 'You have hardly an idea how poor and feeble the book seems to me, as executed, beside the idea of it that I had formed in prospect.' And Gatrell adds the comment: 'This platonic idea might have had the power to drive Hardy to the effort of revision that accompanied each fresh setting of each of his novels – revision made not in the hope of achieving the ideal form, for he knew that to be unattainable, but in the hope of reaching the best possible human approximation to the ideal.'[26]

To this extent the study of Hardy's textual changes becomes a reflection of that unattainability of the ideal which runs, as the structuralist critic J. Hillis Miller suggests, throughout the whole of his work. A dualistic pattern of what Miller calls 'distance' and 'desire', the one implying Hardy's detachment from, the other his involvement with, the objects of his creation, can be observed as a kind of 'deep structure' or underlying control exercised almost in spite of himself by the supposedly essential Hardy, which manifests itself in the recurrent contrasts between the ideal and the real which are to be found again and again throughout his work and in all the forms in which he wrote – short stories, poems and plays, as well as novels.[27]

However, for Hardy's readers it is the way this pattern issues in particular conflicts and contradictions at the variable surface that matters; and it is this *how* of the pattern's fictional realisation rather than the presumed existence of a common source which must continue to be the focus of attention. And this is what provides the unifying concern of the essays and extracts, both early and late, which constitute the substance of this Casebook. Although they range over more than a hundred years and necessarily reflect changing, sometimes seemingly 'dated' tastes and standards of judgement, each pays tribute to the fascination which Hardy's tragic novels have exercised, and continue to exercise, over their readers, and each one seeks to explain and enhance the deep satisfaction which they offer by careful analysis of the qualities they possess as uniquely literary texts.

NOTES

1. This novel was never published in its original form, but parts of it may have been used in *Under the Greenwood Tree* and *An Indiscretion in The Life of an Heiress*. (See Carl J. Weber's edition of the latter, 1935; reissued New York, 1965.)

2. Florence Emily Hardy, *The Life of Thomas Hardy, 1840–1928* (Macmillan, 1962, reprinted 1972) p. 61. (Originally printed in two vols, *The Early Life of Thomas Hardy, 1840–1891*, 1928 and *The Later Years of Thomas Hardy, 1892–1928*, 1930.)

3. For details see John Paterson, *The Making of 'The Return of the Native'* (University of California Press, 1960); Mary Ellen Chase, *Thomas Hardy from Serial to Novel* (University of Minnesota Press, 1922; rev. edn, New York, 1964); and R. L. Purdy, *Thomas Hardy: A Bibliographical Study* (Oxford University Press, 1954). The following discussion of Hardy's publication difficulties is indebted to the above sources and the *Life*.

4. Paterson, *The Making of 'The Return of the Native'*, p. 30.

5. See *Thomas Hardy from Serial to Novel*, pp. 198–201.

6. *Life*, p. 279. The review appeared in the New York *World* (8 December 1895). The critic responsible for this outburst was Jeanette Gilder, who later sought a journalistic interview with Hardy 'to get your side of the argument'. Hardy replied, 'Those readers who, like yourself, could not see that *Jude* (though a book quite without a "purpose" as it is called) makes for morality more than any other book I have written, are not likely to be made to do so by a newspaper article, even from your attractive pen.' (*Life*, p. 280.)

7. 1912 Preface to *Tess*. In Purdy's Bibliography there is a photograph

(opposite p. 71) of the MS draft of the title-page bearing the words, 'To supersede copy previously sent'.

8. Havelock Ellis, 'Thomas Hardy's Novels', *Westminster Review* (April 1883), and 'Concerning *Jude the Obscure*', *Savoy Magazine* (October 1896); R. H. Hutton, review of *The Mayor of Casterbridge*, *Spectator* (5 June 1886); William Watson, review of *Tess*, *Academy* (6 February 1892); Edmund Gosse, review of *Jude*, *Cosmopolis* (January 1896). (See R. G. Cox (ed.), *Thomas Hardy, the Critical Heritage*, Routledge & Kegan Paul, London, 1970.)

9. For further discussion of Hardy's style see David Lodge's 'Tess, Nature and the Voices of Hardy' included in this selection. Most critics comment on Hardy's so-called pessimism, but see, in particular, Roy Morrell, *Thomas Hardy, the Will and the Way* (University of Malaya Press, 1965). Morrell argues that Hardy is not a pessimist, but simply anxious that people shall not deceive themselves with easy hopes: '. . . no Being, or Force, is going to change the course of things for us . . . we must do something ourselves' (pp. 37–8).

10. *Thomas Hardy's Personal Writings*, ed. Harold Orel (Macmillan, 1967), p. 46.

11. See Brown's *Thomas Hardy* (Longman, London, 1954) and *Hardy 'The Mayor of Casterbridge'* (Edward Arnold, London, 1962).

12. In *Imagined Worlds*, ed. Ian Gregor and Maynard Mack (London, Faber & Faber, 1968), pp. 225–33. Reprinted in the earlier version of this Casebook.

13. *Personal Writings*, p. 18.

14. *Thomas Hardy*, p. 91. (See extract printed in the earlier version of this Casebook.)

15. See ibid, p. 13 and footnote 3. Paterson's conclusions are summarised in his Preface to Harper & Row's 1966 edition of *The Return of the Native*, which also contains his considered critical judgements on the novel and is, therefore, the piece chosen for reprinting here.

16. *Thomas Hardy, the Forms of Tragedy* (Macmillan, London and Basingstoke, 1975), pp. 69–91.

17. *Critical Quarterly*, 25, 1 (Spring 1983), 57–70.

18. Patricia Ingham, *Thomas Hardy*, Feminist Readings Series (Harvester Wheatsheaf, Hemel Hempstead, 1989).

19. Interrupting this sequence in a deliberately comico-satiric vein which is alien to the tragic novels – until, that is, the last one, *Jude the Obscure* – is the strikingly unconventional Ethelberta Chickerel, of *The Hand of Ethelberta*, who earns her own living by giving public performances as a story-teller and who upsets all the usual sentimental assumptions about love and marriage by taking a rich old roué for her husband.

20. Rosemarie Morgan, *Women and Sexuality in the Novels of Thomas Hardy* (Routledge, London, 1988), pp. x and 88.

21. A detailed analysis of this structure is given by the French critic Fernand Lagarde in 'A propos de la construction de *Jude the Obscure*', *Caliban* (January 1966). Though brilliant, this analysis is carried out with such thoroughgoing efficiency as to make the novel seem more of an artificial *tour de force* than a moving human document.

22. Robert B. Heilman, 'Hardy's Sue Bridehead', *Nineteenth Century Fiction*, 20 (March 1966), 307–23. Reprinted in the earlier version of this Casebook, pp. 209–26.

23. Rosemary Sumner, *Thomas Hardy: Psychological Novelist* (Macmillan, London, 1981).

24. Ian Gregor, *The Great Web: The Form of Hardy's Major Fiction* (Faber & Faber, London, 1984), pp. 208–28; reprinted in the earlier version of this Casebook, pp. 227–47.

25. See Peter Widdowson, *Hardy in History: A Study in Literary Sociology* (Routledge, London, 1989).

26. *Hardy the Creator* (Clarendon Press, Oxford, 1988), p. 224.

27. See J. Hillis Miller, *Thomas Hardy: Distance and Desire* (Harvard University Press, Cambridge, Mass., 1970).

PART ONE

Comments by Hardy

1. EXTRACTS FROM *THE LIFE OF THOMAS HARDY*

GENERAL COMMENTS

April 1878. Note. A Plot, or Tragedy, should arise from the gradual closing in of a situation that comes of ordinary human passions, prejudices, and ambitions, by reason of the characters taking no trouble to ward off the disastrous events produced by the said passions, prejudices, and ambitions. (p. 120)

19 April 1885. [Hardy had just finished *The Mayor of Casterbridge* two days before.] The business of the poet and novelist is to show the sorriness underlying the grandest things, and the grandeur underlying the sorriest things. (p. 171)

21–2 November 1885. ... Tragedy. It may be put thus in brief: a tragedy exhibits a state of things in the life of an individual which unavoidably causes some natural aim or desire of his to end in a catastrophe when carried out. (p. 176)

21 December 1885. The Hypocrisy of things. Nature is an archdissembler. A child is deceived completely; the older members of society more or less according to their penetration; though even they seldom get to realize that *nothing* is as it appears. (p. 176)

15–21 October 1888. ... If you look beneath the surface of any farce you see a tragedy; and, on the contrary, if you blind yourself to the deeper issues of a tragedy you see a farce. (p. 215)

5 May 1889. ... That which, socially, is a great tragedy, may be in Nature no alarming circumstance. (p. 218)

5 August 1890. Reflections on Art. Art is a changing of the actual proportions and order of things, so as to bring out more forcibly than might otherwise be done that feature in them which appeals most strongly to the idiosyncrasy of the artist. The changing, or

distortion, may be of two kinds: (1) The kind which increases the sense of vraisemblance: (2) That which diminishes it. (1) is high art: (2) is low art.

High art may choose to depict evil as well as good, without losing its quality. Its choice of evil, however, must be limited by the sense of worthiness.

Art is a disproportioning – (i.e. distorting, throwing out of proportion) – of realities, to show more clearly the features that matter in those realities, which, if merely copied or reported inventorially, might possibly be observed, but would more probably be overlooked. Hence 'realism' is not Art. [Last paragraph added a little later than the rest.] (pp. 228–9)

24 October 1892. The best tragedy – highest tragedy in short – is that of the WORTHY encompassed by the INEVITABLE. The tragedies of immoral and worthless people are not of the best. (p. 251)

1895? [The outcome of some reviews of *Jude the Obscure*.] Tragedy may be created by an opposing environment either of things inherent in the universe, or of human institutions. If the former be the means exhibited and deplored, the writer is regarded as impious; if the latter, as subversive and dangerous; when all the while he may never have questioned the necessity or urged the non-necessity of either.... (p. 274)

ON 'THE RETURN OF THE NATIVE'

22 April 1878. The method of Boldini, the painter of 'The Morning Walk' in the French Gallery two or three years ago (a young lady beside an ugly blank wall on an ugly highway) – of Hobbema, in his view of a road with formal lopped trees and flat tame scenery – is that of infusing emotion into the baldest external objects either by the presence of a human figure among them, or by mark of some human connection with them.

This accords with my feeling about, say, Heidelberg and Baden *versus* Scheveningen – as I wrote at the beginning of *The Return of the Native* – that the beauty of association is entirely superior to the beauty of aspect, and a beloved relative's old battered tankard to the finest Greek vase. Paradoxically put, it is to see the beauty in ugliness. (pp. 120–1)

September 1878. [Hardy writes to his publishers.] I enclose a sketch-map of the supposed scene in which *The Return of the Native* is laid, copied from the one I used in writing the story; and my suggestion is that we place an engraving of it as frontispiece to the first volume. Unity of place is so seldom preserved in novels that a map of the scene of action is as a rule quite impracticable. But since the present story affords an opportunity of doing so I am of opinion that it would be a desirable novelty. (p. 122)

[In a letter of 1923? Hardy wrote about his play, *The Queen of Cornwall*, that it 'strictly preserved' the unities, and added: 'I, myself, am old-fashioned enough to think there *is* a virtue in it, if it can be done without artificiality. The only other case I remember attempting it in was *The Return of the Native*' (p. 422).]

ON 'THE MAYOR OF CASTERBRIDGE'

1886 – 2 January, *The Mayor of Casterbridge* begins to-day in the *Graphic* newspaper and *Harper's Weekly*. – I fear it will not be so good as I meant, but after all, it is not improbabilities of incident but improbabilities of character that matter. (p. 176)

The Mayor of Casterbridge was issued complete about the end of May [1886]. It was a story which Hardy fancied he had damaged more recklessly as an artistic whole, in the interest of the newspaper in which it appeared serially, than perhaps any other of his novels, his aiming to get an incident into almost every week's part causing him in his own judgment to add events to the narrative somewhat too freely. However, as at this time he called his novel-writing 'mere journeywork' he cared little about it as art, though it must be said in favour of the plot, as he admitted later, that it was quite coherent and organic, in spite of its complication. (p. 179)

ON 'TESS OF THE D'URBERVILLES'

And it was about this date [1853–4] that he [Hardy] formed one of a trio of youths (the vicar's sons being the other two) who taught in the Sunday School of the parish, where as a pupil in his class he had a dairymaid four years older than himself, who afterwards appeared in *Tess of the d'Urbervilles* as Marian – one of the few portraits from life in his works. This pink and plump damsel had a marvellous power of memorizing whole chapters in the Bible, and would repeat to him by heart in class, to his boredom, the long gospels before Easter without missing a word, and with evident delight in her facility; though she was by no means a model of virtue in her love-affairs. (p. 25)

... the business immediately in hand [ca October 1889] was the new story *Tess of the d'Urbervilles*, for the serial use of which Hardy had three requests, if not more, on his list; and in October as much of it as was written was offered to the first who had asked for it, the editor of *Murray's Magazine*. It was declined and returned to him in the middle of November virtually on the score of its improper explicit-ness. It was at once sent on to the second, the editor of *Macmillan's Magazine*, and on the 25th was declined by him for practically the same reason. Hardy would now have much preferred to finish the story and bring it out in volume form only, but there were reasons why he could not afford to do this; and he adopted a plan till then, it is believed, unprecedented in the annals of fiction. This was not to offer the novel intact to the third editor on his list (his experience with the first two editors having taught him that it would be useless to send it to the third as it stood), but to send it up with some chapters or parts of chapters cut out, and instead of destroying these to publish them, or much of them, elsewhere, if practicable, as episodic adventures of anonymous personages (which in fact was done, with the omission of a few paragraphs); till they could be put back in their places at the printing of the whole in volume form. In addition several passages were modified. Hardy carried out this unceremonious concession to conventionality with cynical amuse-ment, knowing the novel was moral enough and to spare. But the work was sheer drudgery, the modified passages having to be written in coloured ink, that the originals might be easily restored, and he frequently asserted that it would have been almost easier for him to write a new story altogether. Hence the labour brought no profit. He resolved to get away from the supply of family fiction to magazines as soon as he conveniently could do so. (pp. 221–2)

As the year [1891] drew to a close an incident that took place during the publication of *Tess of the d'Ubervilles* as a serial in the *Graphic* might have prepared him for certain events that were to follow. The editor objected to the description of Angel Clare carrying in his arms, across a flooded lane, Tess and her three dairymaid companions. He suggested that it would be more decorous and suitable for the pages of a periodical intended for family reading if the damsels were wheeled across the lane in a wheel-barrow. This was accordingly done. (p. 240)

1892. [Hardy on 'The President of the Immortals had finished his sport with Tess', in reply to a critic who wrote that 'Hardy postulates an all-powerful being endowed with the baser human passions...'] As I need hardly inform any thinking reader, I do not hold, and never have held, the ludicrous opinions here assumed to be mine – which are really, or approximately, those of the primitive believer in his man-shaped tribal god. And in seeking to ascertain how any exponent of English literature could have supposed that I held them I find that the writer of the estimate has harked back to a passage in a novel of mine, printed many years ago, in which the forces opposed to the heroine were allegorized as a personality (a method not unusual in imaginative prose or poetry) by the use of a well-known trope, explained in that venerable work, Campbell's *Philosophy of Rhetoric*, as 'one in which life, perception, activity, design, passion, or any property of sentient beings, is attributed to things inanimate'.

Under this species of criticism if an author were to say 'Aeolus maliciously tugged at her garments, and tore her hair in his wrath', the sapient critic would no doubt announce that author's evil creed to be that the wind is 'a powerful being endowed with the baser human passions', etc., etc.

However, I must put up with it, and say as Parrhasius of Ephesus said about his pictures: There is nothing that men will not find fault with. (p. 244)

15 April 1982. *Good Friday*. Read review of *Tess* in *The Quarterly*. A smart and amusing article; but it is easy to be smart and amusing if a man will forgo veracity and sincerity. ... How strange that one may write a book without knowing what one puts into it – or rather, the reader reads into it. Well, if this sort of thing continues no more novel-writing for me. A man must be a fool to deliberately stand up to be shot at. (p. 246)

ON 'JUDE THE OBSCURE'

28 April 1888. A short story of a young man – 'who could not go to
Oxford' – His struggles and ultimate failure. Suicide. [Probably the
germ of *Jude the Obscure*.] There is something [in this] the world
ought to be shown, and I am the one to show it to them – though I
was not altogether hindered going, at least to Cambridge, and could
have gone up easily at five-and-twenty. (pp. 207–8; the square
brackets here are in *The Life*)

20 September 1926. [Concerning 'a proposed dramatisation of *Jude
the Obscure*':] Would not Arabella be the villain of the piece? – or
Jude's personal constitution? – so far as there is any villain more
than blind Chance. Christminster is of course the tragic influence of
Jude's drama in one sense, but innocently so, and merely as crass
obstruction. By the way it is not meant to be exclusively Oxford, but
any old-fashioned University about the date of the story, 1860–1870,
before there were such chances for poor men as there are now. I have
somewhere printed that I had no feeling against Oxford in particular. (p. 433)

THREE LETTERS TO EDMUND GOSSE (1895–6)

I. 10 November 1895

.... Your review (of *Jude the Obscure*) is the most discriminating that
has yet appeared. It required an artist to see that the plot is almost
geometrically constructed – I ought not to say *constructed*, for,
beyond a certain point, the characters necessitated it, and I simply
let it come. As for the story itself, it is really sent out to those into
whose souls the iron has entered, and has entered deeply at some
time of their lives. But one cannot choose one's readers.

It is curious that some of the papers should look upon the novel as
a manifesto on 'the marriage question' (although, of course, it
involves it), seeing that it is concerned first with the labours of a
poor student to get a University degree, and secondly with the tragic
issues of two bad marriages, owing in the main to a doom or curse of
hereditary temperament peculiar to the family of the parties. The
only remarks which can be said to bear on the *general* marriage
question occur in dialogue, and comprise no more than half a dozen

pages in a book of five hundred. And of these remarks I state that my own views are not expressed therein. I suppose the attitude of these critics is to be accounted for by the accident that, during the serial publication of my story, a sheaf of 'purpose' novels on the matter appeared.

You have hardly an idea of how poor and feeble the book seems to me, as executed, beside the idea of it that I had formed in prospect.

I have received some interesting letters about it already – yours not the least so. Swinburne writes, too enthusiastically for me to quote with modesty....

P.S. One thing I did not answer. The 'grimy' features of the story go to show the contrast between the ideal life a man wished to lead, and the squalid real life he was fated to lead. The throwing of the pizzle, at the supreme moment of his young dream, is to sharply initiate this contrast. But I must have lamentably failed, as I feel I have, if this requires explanation and is not self-evident. The idea was meant to run all through the novel. It is, in fact, to be discovered in *everybody's* life, though it lies less on the surface perhaps than it does in my poor puppet's. (pp. 271–2)

II. 20 November 1895

I am keen about the new magazine. How interesting that you should be writing this review for it! I wish the book were more worthy of such notice and place.

You are quite right; there is nothing perverted or depraved in Sue's nature. The abnormalism consists in disproportion, not in inversion, her sexual instinct being healthy as far as it goes, but unusually weak and fastidious. Her sensibilities remain painfully alert notwithstanding, as they do in nature with such women. One point illustrating this I could not dwell upon: that, though she has children, her intimacies with Jude have never been more than occasional, even when they were living together (I mention that they occupy separate rooms, except towards the end), and one of her reasons for fearing the marriage ceremony is that she fears it would be breaking faith with Jude to withhold herself at pleasure, or altogether, after it; though while uncontracted she feels at liberty to yield herself as seldom as she chooses. This has tended to keep his passion as hot at the end as at the beginning, and helps to break his heart. He has never really possessed her as freely as he desired.

Sue is a type of woman which has always had an attraction for me, but the difficulty of drawing the type has kept me from attempting it till now.

Of course the book is all contrasts – or was meant to be in its original conception. Alas, what a miserable accomplishment it is, when I compare it with what I meant to make it! – e.g. Sue and her heathen gods set against Jude's reading the Greek testament; Christminster academical, Christminster in the slums; Jude the saint, Jude the sinner; Sue the Pagan, Sue the saint; marriage, no marriage; &c., &c.

As to the 'coarse' scenes with Arabella, the battle in the school-room, etc., the newspaper critics might, I thought, have sneered at them for their Fieldingism rather than for their Zolaism. But your everyday critic knows nothing of Fielding. I am read in Zola very little, but have felt akin locally to Fielding, so many of his scenes having been laid down this way, and his home near.

Did I tell you I feared I should seem too High-Churchy at the end of the book where Sue recants? You can imagine my surprise at some of the reviews.... (pp. 272–3)

III. 4 January 1896

For the last three days I have been tantalized by a difficulty in getting *Cosmopolis*, and had only just read your review when I received your note. My sincere thanks for the generous view you take of the book, which to me is a mass of imperfections. We have both been amused – or rather delighted – by the sub-humour (is there such a word?) of your writing. I think it a rare quality in living essayists, and that you ought to make more of it – I mean write more in that vein than you do.

But this is apart from the review itself, of which I will talk to you when we meet. The rectangular lines of the story were not premeditated, but came by chance: except, of course, that the involutions of four lives must necessarily be a sort of quadrille. The only point in the novel on which I feel sure is that it makes for morality; and that delicacy or indelicacy in a writer is according to his object. If I say to a lady 'I met a naked woman', it is indelicate. But if I go on to say 'I found she was mad with sorrow', it ceases to be indelicate. And in writing Jude my mind was fixed on the ending.... (p. 273)

December 1895. When they [Hardy and his wife] got back to Dorchester during December Hardy had plenty of time to read the reviews of *Jude* that continued to pour out. Some paragraphists knowingly assured the public that the book was an honest autobiography, and Hardy did not take the trouble to deny it till more than twenty years later, when he wrote to an inquirer with whom the superstition still lingered that no book he had ever written contained less of his own life, which of course had been known to his friends from the beginning. Some of the incidents were real in so far as that he had heard of them, or come in contact with them when they were occurring to people he knew; but no more. It is interesting to mention that on his way to school he did once meet with a youth like Jude who drove the bread-cart of a widow, a baker, like Mrs. Fawley, and carried on his studies at the same time, to the serious risk of other drivers in the lanes; which youth asked him to lend him his Latin grammar. But Hardy lost sight of this fearful student, and never knew if he profited by his plan. (p. 274)

SOURCE: Florence Emily Hardy, *The Life of Thomas Hardy* (1962).

2. FROM 'THE DORSETSHIRE LABOURER' (1883)

It seldom happens that a nickname which affects to portray a class is honestly indicative of the individuals composing that class. The few features distinguishing them from other bodies of men have been seized on and exaggerated, while the incomparably more numerous features common to all humanity have been ignored. In the great world this wild colouring of so-called typical portraits is clearly enough recognised. Nationalities, the aristocracy, the plutocracy, the citizen class, and many others have their allegorical representatives, which are received with due allowance for flights of imagination in the direction of burlesque.

But when the class lies somewhat out of the ken of ordinary society the caricature begins to be taken as truth. Moreover, the original is held to be an actual unit of the multitude signified. He ceases to be an abstract figure and becomes a sample. Thus when we arrive at the farm-labouring community we find it to be seriously personified by the pitiable picture known as Hodge; not only so, but the community is assumed to be a uniform collection of concrete Hodges.

This supposed real but highly conventional Hodge is a degraded being of uncouth manner and aspect, stolid understanding, and snail-like movement. His speech is such a chaotic corruption of regular language that few persons of progressive aims consider it worth while to enquire what views, if any, of life, of nature, or of society are conveyed in these utterances. Hodge hangs his head or looks sheepish when spoken to, and thinks Lunnon a place paved with gold. Misery and fever lurk in his cottage, while, to paraphrase the words of a recent writer on the labouring classes, in his future there are only the workhouse and the grave. He hardly dares to think at all. He has few thoughts of joy, and little hope of rest. His life slopes into a darkness not 'quieted by hope'.

If one of the many thoughtful persons who hold this view were to go by rail to Dorset, where Hodge in his most unmitigated form is supposed to reside, and seek out a retired district, he might by and by certainly meet a man who, at first contact with an intelligence fresh from the contrasting world of London, would seem to exhibit some of the above-mentioned qualities. The latter items in the list, the mental miseries, the visitor might hardly look for in their fulness, since it would have become perceptible to him as an explorer, and to any but the chamber theorist, that no uneducated community, rich or poor, bond or free, possessing average health and personal liberty, could exist in an unchangeable slough of despond, or that it would for many months if it could. Its members, like the accursed swine, would rush down a steep place and be choked in the waters. He would have learnt that wherever a mode of supporting life is neither noxious nor absolutely inadequate, there springs up happiness, and will spring up happiness, of some sort or other. Indeed, it is among such communities as these that happiness will find her last refuge on earth, since it is among them that a perfect insight into the conditions of existence will be longest postponed.

That in their future there are only the workhouse and the grave is no more and no less true than that in the future of the average well-to-do householder there are only the invalid chair and the brick vault.

Waiving these points, however, the investigator would insist that the man he had encountered exhibited a suspicious blankness of gaze, a great uncouthness and inactivity; and he might truly approach the unintelligible if addressed by a stranger on any but the commonest subject. But suppose that, by some accident, the visitor were obliged to go home with this man, take pot-luck with him and his, as one of the family. For the nonce the very sitting down would seem an undignified performance, and at first, the ideas, the modes, and the surroundings generally, would be puzzling – even impenetrable; or if in a measure penetrable, would seem to have but little meaning. But living on there for a few days the sojourner would become conscious of a new aspect in the life around him. He would find that, without any objective change whatever, variety had taken the place of monotony; that the man who had brought him home – the typical Hodge, as he conjectured – was somehow not typical of anyone but himself. His host's brothers, uncles, and neighbours, as they became personally known, would appear as different from his host himself as one member of a club, or inhabitant of a city street, from another. As, to the eye of a diver, contrasting colours shine out by degrees from what has originally painted itself of an unrelieved earthy hue, so would shine out the characters, capacities, and interests of these people to him. He would, for one thing, find that the language, instead of being a vile corruption of cultivated speech, was a tongue with grammatical inflection rarely disregarded by his entertainer, though his entertainer's children would occasionally make a sad hash of their talk. Having attended the National School they would mix the printed tongue as taught therein with the unwritten, dying, Wessex English that they had learnt of their parents, the result of this transitional state of theirs being a composite language without rule or harmony.

Six months pass, and our gentleman leaves the cottage, bidding his friends good-bye with genuine regret. The great change in his perception is that Hodge, the dull, unvarying, joyless one, has ceased to exist for him. He has become disintegrated into a number of dissimilar fellow-creatures, men of many minds, infinite in difference; some happy, many serene, a few depressed; some clever, even to genius, some stupid, some wanton, some austere; some mutely Miltonic, some Cromwellian; into men who have private views of each other, as he has of his friends; who applaud or condemn each other; amuse or sadden themselves by the contemplation of each other's foibles or vices; and each of whom walks in his own way the road to dusty death....

To see the Dorset labourer at his worst and saddest time, he should be viewed when attending a wet hiring-fair at Candlemas, in search of a new master. His natural cheerfulness bravely struggles against the weather and the incertitude; but as the day passes on, and his clothes get wet through, and he is still unhired, there does appear a factitiousness in the smile which, with a self-repressing mannerliness hardly to be found among any other class, he yet has ready when he encounters and talks with friends who have been more fortunate. In youth and manhood, this disappointment occurs but seldom; but at threescore and over, it is frequently the lot of those who have no sons and daughters to fall back upon, or whose children are ingrates, or far away.

Here, at the corner of the street, in this aforesaid wet hiring-fair, stands an old shepherd. He is evidently a lonely man. The battle of life has always been a sharp one with him, for, to begin with, he is a man of small frame. He is now so bowed by hard work and years, that, approaching from behind, you can scarcely see his head. He has planted the stem of his crook in the gutter, and rests upon the bow, which is polished to silver brightness by the long friction of his hands. He has quite forgotten where he is and what he has come for, his eyes being bent on the ground. 'There's work in en,' says one farmer to another, as they look dubiously across; 'there's work left in en still; but not so much as I want for my acreage.' 'You'd get en cheap,' says the other. The shepherd does not hear them, and there seems to be passing through his mind pleasant visions of the hiring successes of his prime – when his skill in ovine surgery laid open any farm to him for the asking, and his employer would say uneasily in the early days of February, 'You don't mean to leave us this year?'

But the hale and the strong have not to wait thus, and having secured places in the morning, the day passes merrily enough with them....

Of all the days in the year, people who love the rural poor of the south-west should pray for a fine day then [i.e. Lady Day, the day when workers move to new employment]. Dwellers near the highways of the country are reminded of the anniversary surely enough. They are conscious of a disturbance of their night's rest by noises beginning in the small hours of darkness, and intermittently continuing till daylight – noises as certain to recur on that particular night of the month as the voice of the cuckoo on the third or fourth week of the same. The day of fulfilment has come, and the labourers are on the point of being fetched from the old farm by the carters of the new. For it is always by the waggon and horses of the farmer who requires his services that the hired man is conveyed to his destination; and that this may be accomplished within the day is the reason that the noises begin so soon after midnight. Suppose the distance to be an ordinary one of a dozen or fifteen miles. The carter at the prospective place rises 'when Charles's Wain is over the new chimney', harnesses his team of three horses by lantern light, and proceeds to the present home of his coming comrade. It is the passing of these empty waggons in all directions that is heard breaking the stillness of the hours before dawn. The aim is usually to be at the door of the removing household by six o'clock, when the loading of goods at once begins; and at nine or ten the start to the new home is made. From this hour till one or two in the day, when the other family arrives at the old house, the cottage is empty, and it is only in that short interval that the interior can be in a way cleaned and limewhitened for the new comers, however dirty it may have become, or whatever sickness may have prevailed among members of the departed family.

Should the migrant himself be a carter there is a slight modification in the arrangement, for carters do not fetch carters, as they fetch shepherds and general hands. In this case the man has to transfer himself. He relinquishes charge of the horses of the old farm in the afternoon of 5 April, and starts on foot the same afternoon for the new place. There he makes the acquaintance of the horses which are to be under his care for the ensuing year, and passes the night sometimes on a bundle of clean straw in the stable, for he is as yet a stranger here, and too indifferent to the comforts of a bed on this particular evening to take much trouble to secure one. From this couch he uncurls himself about two o'clock, a.m. (for the distance we have assumed), and, harnessing his new charges, moves off with them to his old home, where, on his arrival, the packing is already advanced by the wife, and loading goes on as before mentioned.

The goods are built up on the waggon to a well-nigh unvarying pattern, which is probably as peculiar to the country labourer as the hexagon to the bee. The dresser, with its finger-marks and domestic evidence thick upon it, stands importantly in front, over the backs of the shaft horses, in its erect and natural position, like some Ark of the Covenant, which must not be handled slightingly or overturned. The hive of bees is slung up to the axle of the waggon, and alongside it the cooking pot or crock, within which are stowed the roots of garden flowers. Barrels are largely used for crockery, and budding gooseberry bushes are suspended by the roots; while on the top of the furniture a circular nest is made of the bed and bedding for the matron and children, who sit there through the journey. If there is no infant in arms, the woman holds the head of the clock, which at any exceptional lurch of the waggon strikes one, in thin tones. The other object of solicitude is the looking-glass, usually held in the lap of the eldest girl. It is emphatically spoken of as *the* looking-glass, there being but one in the house, except possibly a small shaving-glass for the husband. But labouring men are not much dependent upon mirrors for a clean chin. I have seen many men shaving in the chimney corner, looking into the fire; or, in the summer, in the garden, with their eyes fixed upon a gooseberry-bush, gazing as steadfastly as if there were a perfect reflection of their image – from which it would seem that the concentrated look of shavers in general was originally demanded rather by the mind than by the eye. On the other hand, I knew a man who used to walk about the room all the time he was engaged in the operation, and how he escaped cutting himself was a marvel. Certain luxurious dandies of the furrow, who could not do without a reflected image of themselves when using the razor, obtained it till quite recently by placing the crown of an old hat outside the window-pane, then confronting it inside the room and falling to – a contrivance which formed a very clear reflection of a face in high light.

The day of removal, if fine, wears an aspect of jollity, and the whole proceeding is a blithe one. A bundle of provisions for the journey is usually hung up at the side of the vehicle, together with a three-pint stone jar of extra strong ale; for it is as impossible to move house without beer as without horses. Roadside inns, too, are patronized, where, during the halt, a mug is seen ascending and descending through the air to and from the feminine portion of the household at the top of the waggon. The drinking at these times is, however, moderate, the beer supplied to travelling labourers being of a preternaturally small brew; as was illustrated by a dialogue which took place on such an occasion quite recently. The liquor was not quite to the taste of the male travellers, and they complained. But the landlady upheld its merits. ''Tis our own brewing, and there is nothing in it but malt and hops', she said, with rectitude. 'Yes, there is', said the traveller. 'There's water.' 'Oh, I forgot the water', the landlady replied. 'I'm d——d if you did, mis'ess', replied the man; 'for there's hardly anything else in the cup.'

Ten or a dozen of these families, with their goods, may be seen halting simultaneously at an out-of-the-way inn, and it is not possible to walk a mile on any of the high roads this day without meeting several. This annual migration from farm to farm is much in excess of what it was formerly. For example, on a particular farm where, a generation ago, not more than one cottage on an average changed occupants yearly, and where the majority remained all their lifetime, the whole number of tenants were changed at Lady Day just past, and this though nearly all of them had been new arrivals on the previous Lady Day. Dorset labourers now look upon an annual removal as the most natural thing in the world, and it becomes with the younger families a pleasant excitement. Change is also a certain sort of education. Many advantages accrue to the labourers from the varied experience it brings, apart from the discovery of the best market for their abilities. They have become shrewder and sharper men of the world, and have learnt how to hold their own with firmness and judgment. Whenever the habitually-removing man comes into contact with one of the old-fashioned stationary sort, who are still to be found, it is impossible not to perceive that the former is much more wide awake than his fellow-worker, astonishing him with stories of the wide world comprised in a twenty-mile radius from their homes.

They are also losing their peculiarities as a class; hence the humorous simplicity which formerly characterised the men and the unsophisticated modesty of the women are rapidly disappearing or lessening, under the constant attrition of lives mildly approximating to those of workers in a manufacturing town. It is the common remark of villagers above the labouring class, who know the latter well as personal acquaintances, that 'there are no nice homely workfolk now as there used to be'. There may be, and is, some exaggeration in this, but it is only natural that, now different districts of them are shaken together once a year and redistributed, like a shuffled pack of cards, they have ceased to be so local in feeling or manner as formerly, and have entered on the condition of inter-social citizens, 'whose city stretches the whole country over'. Their brains are less frequently than they once were 'as dry as the remainder biscuit after a voyage', and they vent less often the result of their own observations than what they have heard to be the current ideas of smart chaps in towns. The women have, in many districts, acquired the rollicking air of factory hands. The seclusion and immutability, which was so bad for their pockets, was an unrivalled fosterer of their personal charm in the eyes of those whose experiences had been less limited. But the artistic merit of their old condition is scarcely a reason why they should have continued in it when other communities were marching on so vigorously towards uniformity and mental equality. It is only the old story that progress and picturesqueness do not harmonise. They are losing their individuality, but they are widening the range of their ideas, and gaining in freedom. It is too much to expect them to remain stagnant and old-fashioned for the pleasure of romantic spectators. . . .

Women's labour, too, is highly in request, for a woman who, like a boy, fills the place of a man at half the wages, can be better depended on for steadiness. Thus where a boy is useful in driving a cart or a plough, a woman is invaluable in work which, though somewhat lighter, demands thought. In winter and spring a farm-woman's occupation is often 'turnip-hacking' – that is, picking out from the land the stumps of turnips which have been eaten off by the sheep – or feeding the threshing-machine, clearing away straw from the same, and standing on the rick to hand forward the sheaves. In mid-spring and early summer her services are required for weeding wheat and barley (cutting up thistles and other noxious plants with a spud), and clearing weeds from pasture-land in like manner. In late summer her time is entirely engrossed by haymaking – quite a science, though it appears the easiest thing in the world to toss hay about in the sun. The length to which a skilful raker will work and retain command over her rake without moving her feet is dependent largely upon practice, and quite astonishing to the uninitiated.

Haymaking is no sooner over than the women are hurried off to the harvest-field. This is a lively time. The bonus in wages during these few weeks, the cleanliness of the occupation, the heat, the cider and ale, influence to facetiousness and vocal strains. Quite the reverse do these lively women feel in the occupation which may be said to stand, emotionally, at the opposite pole to gathering in corn: that is, threshing it. Not a woman in the county but hates the threshing machine. The dust, the din, the sustained exertion demanded to keep up with the steam tyrant, are distasteful to all women but the coarsest. I am not sure whether, at the present time, women are employed to feed the machine, but some years ago a woman had frequently to stand just above the whizzing wire drum, and feed from morning to night – a performance for which she was quite unfitted, and many were the manœuvres to escape that responsible position. A thin saucer-eyed woman of fifty-five, who had been feeding the machine all day, declared on one occasion that in crossing a field on her way home in the fog after dusk, she was so dizzy from the work as to be unable to find the opposite gate, and there she walked round and round the field, bewildered and terrified, till three o'clock in the morning, before she could get out. The farmer said that the ale had got into her head, but she maintained that it was the spinning of the machine. The point was never clearly settled between them; and the poor woman is now dead and buried.

To be just, however, to the farmers, they do not enforce the letter of the Candlemas agreement in relation to the woman, if she makes any reasonable excuse for breaking it; and indeed, many a nervous farmer is put to flight by a matron who has a tongue with a tang, and who chooses to assert, without giving any reason whatever, that, though she had made fifty agreements, 'be cust if she will come out unless she is minded' – possibly terrifying him with accusations of brutality at asking her, when he knows 'how she is just now'. A farmer of the present essayist's acquaintance, who has a tendency to blush in the presence of beauty, and is in other respects a bashful man for his years, says that when the ladies of his farm are all together in the field, and he is the single one of the male sex present, he would as soon put his head into a hornet's nest as utter a word of complaint, or even a request beyond the commonest.

The changes which are so increasingly discernible in village life by no means originate entirely with the agricultural unrest. A depopulation is going on which in some quarters is truly alarming. Villages used to contain, in addition to the agricultural inhabitants, an interesting and better-informed class, ranking distinctly above those – the blacksmith, the carpenter, the shoe-maker, the small higgler, the shopkeeper (whose stock-in-trade consisted of a couple of loaves, a pound of candles, a bottle of brandy-balls and lumps of delight, three or four scrubbing-brushes, and a frying-pan), together with nondescript-workers other than farm-labourers, who had remained in the houses where they were born for no especial reason beyond an instinct of association with the spot. Many of these families had been life-holders, who built at their own expense the cottages they occupied, and as the lives dropped, and the property fell in they would have been glad to remain as weekly or monthly tenants of the owner. But the policy of all but some few philanthropic landowners is to disapprove of these petty tenants who are not in the estate's employ, and to pull down each cottage as it falls in, leaving standing a sufficient number for the use of the farmer's men and no more. The occupants who formed the backbone of the village life have to seek refuge in the boroughs. This process, which is designated by statisticians as 'the tendency of the rural population towards the large towns', is really the tendency of water to flow uphill when forced. The poignant regret of those who are thus obliged to forsake the old nest can only be realised by people who have witnessed it – concealed as it often is under a mask of indifference. It is anomalous that landowners who are showing unprecedented activity in the erection of comfortable cottages for their farm labourers, should see no reason for benefiting in the same way these unattached natives of the village who are nobody's care. They might often expostulate in the words addressed to King Henry the Fourth by his fallen subject: –

> Our house, my sovereign liege, little deserves
> The scourge of greatness to be used on it;
> And that same greatness, too, which our own hands
> Have holp to make so portly.

The system is much to be deplored, for every one of these banished people imbibes a sworn enmity to the existing order of things, and not a few of them, far from becoming merely honest Radicals, degenerate into Anarchists, waiters on chance, to whom danger to the State, the town – nay, the street they live in, is a welcomed opportunity.

A reason frequently advanced for dismissing these families from the villages where they have lived for centuries is that it is done in the interests of morality; and it is quite true that some of the 'liviers' (as these half-independent villagers used to be called) were not always shining examples of churchgoing, temperance, and quiet walking. But a natural tendency to evil, which develops to unlawful action when excited by contact with others like-minded, would often have remained latent amid the simple isolated experiences of a village life. The cause of morality cannot be served by compelling a population hitherto evenly distributed over the country to concentrate in a few towns, with the inevitable results of overcrowding and want of regular employment. But the question of the Dorset cottager here merges in that of all the houseless and landless poor, and the vast topic of the Rights of Man, to consider which is beyond the scope of a merely descriptive article.

SOURCE: *Longman's Magazine* (July 1883); reprinted in *Thomas Hardy's Personal Writings*, ed. Harold Orel (1967), pp. 168–89.

3. FROM 'CANDOUR IN ENGLISH FICTION' (1890)

... By a sincere school of Fiction we may understand a Fiction that expresses truly the views of life prevalent in its time, by means of a selected chain of action best suited for their exhibition. What are the prevalent views of life just now is a question upon which it is not necessary to enter further than to suggest that the most natural method of presenting them, the method most in accordance with the views themselves, seems to be by a procedure mainly impassive in its tone and tragic in its developments.

Things move in cycles; dormant principles renew themselves, and exhausted principles are thrust by. There is a revival of the artistic instincts towards great dramatic motives – setting forth that 'collision between the individual and the general' – formerly worked out with such force by the Periclean and Elizabethan dramatists, to name no other. More than this, the periodicity which marks the course of taste in civilised countries does not take the form of a true cycle of repetition, but what Comte, in speaking of general progress, happily characterises as 'a looped orbit': not a movement of revolution but – to use the current word – evolution. Hence, in perceiving that taste is arriving anew at the point of high tragedy, writers are conscious that its revived presentation demands enrichment by further truths – in other words, original treatment: treatment which seeks to show Nature's unconsciousness not of essential laws, but of those laws framed merely as social expedients by humanity, without a basis in the heart of things; treatment which expresses the triumph of the crowd over the hero, of the commonplace majority over the exceptional few.

But originality makes scores of failures for one final success, precisely because its essence is to acknowledge no immediate precursor or guide. It is probably to these inevitable conditions of further acquisition that may be attributed some developments of naturalism in French novelists of the present day, and certain crude results from meritorious attempts in the same direction by intellectual adventurers here and there among our own authors.

Anyhow, conscientious fiction alone it is which can excite a reflective and abiding interest in the minds of thoughtful readers of mature age, who are weary of puerile inventions and famishing for accuracy; who consider that, in representations of the world, the passions ought to be proportioned as in the world itself. This is the interest which was excited in the minds of the Athenians by their immortal tragedies, and in the minds of Londoners at the first performance of the finer plays of three hundred years ago. They reflected life, revealed life, criticised life. Life being a physiological fact, its honest portrayal must be largely concerned with, for one thing, the relations of the sexes, and the substitution for such catastrophes as favour the false colouring best expressed by the regulation finish that 'they married and were happy ever after', of catastrophes based upon sexual relations as it is. To this expansion English society opposes a well-nigh insuperable bar.

The popular vehicles for the introduction of a novel to the public have grown to be, from one cause and another, the magazine and the circulating library; and the object of the magazine and circulating library is not upward advance but lateral advance; to suit themselves to what is called household reading, which means, or is made to mean, the reading either of the majority in a household or of the household collectively. The number of adults, even in a large household, being normally two, and these being the members which, as a rule, have least time on their hands to bestow on current literature, the taste of the majority can hardly be, and seldom is, tempered by the ripe judgment which desires fidelity. However, the immature members of a household often keep an open mind, and they might, and no doubt would, take sincere fiction with the rest but for another condition, almost generally co-existent: which is that adults who would desire true views for their own reading insist, for a plausible but questionable reason, upon false views for the reading of their young people.

As a consequence, the magazine in particular and the circulating library in general do not foster the growth of the novel which reflects and reveals life. They directly tend to exterminate it by monopolising all literary space. Cause and effect were never more clearly conjoined, though commentators upon the result, both French and English, seem seldom if ever to trace their connection. A sincere and comprehensive sequence of the ruling passions, however moral in its ultimate bearings, must not be put on paper as the foundation of imaginative works, which have to claim notice through the above-named channels, though it is extensively welcomed in the form of newspaper reports. That the magazine and library have arrogated to themselves the dispensation of fiction is not the fault of the authors, but of circumstances over which they, as representatives of Grub Street, have no control.

What this practically amounts to is that the patrons of literature – no longer Peers with a taste – acting under the censorship of prudery, rigorously exclude from the pages they regulate subjects that have been made, by general approval of the best judges, the bases of the finest imaginative compositions since literature rose to the dignity of an art. The crash of broken commandments is as necessary an accompaniment to the catastrophe of a tragedy as the noise of drum and cymbals to a triumphal march. But the crash of broken commandments shall not be heard; or, if at all, but gently, like the roaring of Bottom – gently as any sucking dove, or as 'twere any nightingale, lest we should fright the ladies out of their wits. More precisely, an arbitrary proclamation has gone forth that certain picked commandments of the ten shall be preserved intact – to wit, the first, third, and seventh; that the ninth shall be infringed but gingerly; the sixth only as much as necessary; and the remainder alone as much as you please, in a genteel manner.

SOURCE: *New Review* (January 1890); reprinted in *Thomas Hardy's Personal Writings*, ed. Orel (1967), pp. 126–9.

4. FROM THE GENERAL PREFACE TO THE NOVELS AND POEMS

... It has sometimes been conceived of novels that evolve their action on a circumscribed scene – as do many (though not all) of these – that they cannot be so inclusive in their exhibition of human nature as novels wherein the scenes cover large extents of country, in which events figure amid towns and cities, even wander over the four quarters of the globe. I am not concerned to argue this point further than to suggest that the conception is an untrue one in respect of the elementary passions. But I would state that the geographical limits of the stage here trodden were not absolutely forced upon the writer by circumstances; he forced them upon himself from judgment. I considered that our magnificent heritage from the Greeks in dramatic literature found sufficient room for a large proportion of its action in an extent of their country not much larger than the half-dozen counties here reunited under the old name of Wessex, that the domestic emotions have throbbed in Wessex nooks with as much intensity as in the palaces of Europe, and that, anyhow, there was quite enough human nature in Wessex for one man's literary purpose. So far was I possessed by this idea that I kept within the frontiers when it would have been easier to overleap them and give more cosmopolitan features to the narrative.

Thus, though the people in most of the novels (and in much of the shorter verse) are dwellers in a province bounded on the north by the Thames, on the south by the English Channel, on the east by a line running from Hayling Island to Windsor Forest, and on the west by the Cornish coast, they were meant to be typically and essentially those of any and every place where

> Thought's the slave of life, and life time's fool,

– beings in whose hearts and minds that which is apparently local should be really universal.

But whatever the success of this intention, and the value of these novels as delineations of humanity, they have at least a humble supplementary quality of which I may be justified in reminding the reader, though it is one that was quite unintentional and unforeseen. At the dates represented in the various narrations things were like that in Wessex: the inhabitants lived in certain ways, engaged in certain occupations, kept alive certain customs, just as they are shown doing in these pages. And in particularizing such I have often been reminded of Boswell's remarks on the trouble to which he was put and the pilgrimages he was obliged to make to authenticate some detail, though the labour was one which would bring him no praise. Unlike his achievement, however, on which an error would as he says have brought discredit, if these country customs and vocations, obsolete and obsolescent, had been detailed wrongly, nobody would have discovered such errors to the end of Time. Yet I have instituted inquiries to correct tricks of memory, and striven against temptations to exaggerate, in order to preserve for my own satisfaction a fairly true record of a vanishing life.

SOURCE: Volume I of the 'Wessex Edition' of Hardy's Works (1912); reprinted in *Thomas Hardy's Personal Writings*, ed. Orel (1967).

PART TWO

Early and More Recent Comments

Lionel Johnson The Characteristics of Hardy's Art (1894)

Throughout the preceding essays, I have laid stress upon the strength and the stability of character, which Mr. Hardy loves to present; upon his souls of a somewhat pagan severity, grand in the endurance of dooms; upon their simplicity, resoluteness, and power: yet I have also spoken of Mr. Hardy, as a novelist typical of modern literature in this, that he loves the complexity of things, the clash of principles and of motives, the encounter of subtile emotions. Both criticisms, as I dare think, are true: and in these two characteristics, brought together, contrasted, made to illustrate each other, lies the power of Mr. Hardy's art. For he chooses to present the play of life, tragic and comic, first of all, in a definite tract or province of England; in the Kingdom of Wessex: whither new influences penetrate but slowly. Secondly, he takes for his chief characters, men of powerful natures, men of the country, men of little acquired virtue in mind and soul: but men disciplined by the facts and by the necessities of life, as a primitive experience manifests them. Thirdly, he surrounds them with men of the same origin and class, but men of less strongly marked a power, of less finely touched a spirit: the rank and file of country labour. Fourthly, he brings his few men of that stronger and finer nature, his rustic heroes, into contact and into contrast with a few men, commonly their superiors in education, and sometimes in position, but their inferiors in strength and fineness of nature: men, whom more modern experiences have redeemed from being clowns, at the risk of becoming curs. Fifthly, he makes this contact and this contrast most effective, through the passion of love: to which end, he brings upon the scene women of various natures; less plainly marked in character than the men; for the most part, nearer to the flashy prigs and pretty fellows in outward sentiment, fashion, and culture; but nearer to the stronger and finer men, in the depths of their souls. Sixthly, the narratives are conducted slowly at the first, and great pains are given to make clear the spirit of the country, with its works and ways: when that has been made clear, the play quickens into passion, the actors come into conflict, there is strong attraction and strong repulsion, 'spirits are finely touched': then, there is a period of waiting, a breathing space, an ominous stillness and a pause; till, at the last, with increased force and motion, the play goes forward to its 'fine issues'; all the inherent necessities of things cause their effects, tragic or comic, triumphs of the right or of the wrong; and the end of all is told with a soft solemnity, a sense of pity striving against a sense of fate.

I do not say that any one novel presents those features, in precisely that way: it is but an attempt to construct a mechanical type, to which all Mr. Hardy's novels tend to conform. At the least, it is true of them all, that they present, either the resolution of a discord into a harmony, or the breaking of a harmony by a discord: always the contrast, and the various issue, according to the worth of the performers with that strange organ, the human mind. Tess was changing from peasant ignorance and convention, when she met Clare, changing from the conventional culture and belief of a higher station; the woman struggling up from superstition, the man struggling free from prejudice: the two natures, breaking with the past, came together, she straining towards his level of thought, he stooping to her level of life: the result was a tragic discord. It might be interpreted in many ways. Perhaps the superstitious faith of the Durbeyfield household, and the Calvinist faith of the Clare household, were more nearly in accord with the essential verities of life, than the new aims and impulses of their offspring: perhaps Tess and Clare carried right theories into wrong practice: perhaps one alone did so: certainly, we have in this story a singular presentation of the struggle between old and new, in various ranks of life and ranges of thought; of the contact of the new in one rank and range with the new in another; of the curious reversion, in each case, of the new to the old. Tess acts, on several occasions, from impulses and in ways, which derive, so her maker hints, from her knightly ancestors: Clare, at the crisis of her life and of his own, falls back in cruel cowardice to the conventional standards of that society, which he so greatly scorns. Tess, again, having learned by ear and heart Clare's arguments against Christian theology, repeats them to her old betrayer, Alec d'Urberville, then a fanatical convert to the Calvinism of Clare's father: and she enables him thereby to become a second time her betrayer. Finally, this tangled play of new things upon old comes to its wretched end at Stonehenge, the most ancient of religious monuments in England, and at Winchester, the ancient capital of England: religion, however stern, society, however cruel, are vindicated in the presence of their august memorials. The old, we are meant to feel, was wrong, and the new was right: but the inhuman irony of fate turned all to misunderstanding and to despair: the new devil quoted the new scriptures in the ears of the new believers; and they went to the old destruction.

But the human comedy of Tess must be elsewhere discussed in detail: now it merely serves to illustrate a characteristic common to almost all Mr. Hardy's books. Norris of Bemerton, 'the English Malebranche', has this saying in his third *Contemplation*: ''Twas a Celebrated Problem among the Ancient Mythologists, What was the *strongest* thing, what the *wisest*, and what the *greatest*? Concerning which 'twas thus determin'd, that the *strongest* Thing was *Necessity*, the *wisest* was *Time*; and the *greatest* was the *Heart* of Man.' That would seem to be the determination of Mr. Hardy also, at his best and deepest: almost over conscious of the fatal strength, ever delighted with the growing wisdom, strongly moved by the unsatisfied greatness, he sends out his characters to that forlorn hope, life: forlorn, but not lost, and promising at least the noblest of defeats. I remember but few of Mr. Hardy's general sentiments, about the meaning of the unconscious universe, or of conscious mankind, with which I do not disagree: his tone of thought about human progress, about the province and the testimony of physical science, about the sanctions of natural and social ethics, neither charms, nor compels, me to acquiescence: but it is because I am thus averse from the attitude of a disciple, that I admire Mr. Hardy's art so confidently.

SOURCE: *The Art of Thomas Hardy* (1894), pp. 406–10.

F. Manning 'Novels of Character and Environment' (1912)

In the preface to the new edition of his works Mr. Hardy has the following passage:

Positive views on the whence and wherefore of things have never been advanced by this pen as a consistent philosophy. Nor is it likely, indeed, that imaginative writings extending over more than forty years would exhibit a coherent scientific theory of the universe, even if it had been attempted – of that universe concerning which Spencer owns to the 'paralysing thought' that possibly there exists no comprehension of it anywhere. But such objectless consistency never has been attempted, and the sentiments in the following pages have been stated truly to be mere impressions of the moment, and not convictions or arguments. That these impressions have been condemned as 'pessimistic' – as if that were a very wicked adjective – shows a curious muddle-mindedness. It must be obvious that there is a higher characteristic of philosophy than pessimism, or than meliorism, or even than the optimisim of these critics – which is truth.

There is in this last sentence, and perhaps we may be forgiven if we draw attention to it, a touch of *naïveté*. Mr. Hardy probably was not blind to it himself, since he continues:

Differing natures find their tongue in the presence of differing spectacles. Some natures become vocal at tragedy, some are made vocal by comedy, and it seems to me that to whichever of these aspects of life a writer's instinct for expression the more readily responds, to that he should allow it to respond. That before a contrasting side of things he remains undemonstrative need not be assumed to mean that he remains unperceiving.

We have every sympathy with these remarks in so far as they represent a protest gainst the habit of classifying all writers under convenient heads, even though we recognize that such a scheme of classification upon proper occasions may be extremely useful. Great art is representative of life, not critical of it. The great artist has a delicacy and mobility of mind by which he is able to capture and reflect the most various and fluid moods, to seize upon the contrasting aspects of life and present each with a perfect impartiality. Such a mind is delicate in the way it realizes with an exquisite tact the essential character of every object; and mobile in its range, in the comprehensive nature of its sympathy. In our own conscious life the sensations of pain or of pleasure, emotions of hatred or of love, moods of joy or of sorrow, have no definite and objective existence for us, though we may connect them in our minds with the realities about us which have this definite existence. They flow through us; but, though they may leave some traces of their passage, they do not remain with us. To the normal mind, life, not being a solid block, but a continuous flux, is neither to be viewed from an entirely pessimistic nor from an entirely optimistic standpoint; it is an affair of compensations. Some natures, as Mr. Hardy observes, may be more responsive to the tragedy of life, and yet perceive another side, for our consciousness is always dissolving, and the aspects of life continually changing under it. On the other hand, a nature which only becomes vocal at tragedy, and which perceives another aspect of life without responding to it, is a nature in which the will has inclined the balance upon one side; and to view life almost entirely in its tragic significance is to view it incompletely. Great art, the art of Sophocles or of Shakespeare, does not leave our minds impressed by a pessimistic conception of existence. It represents the flux of all things, the cessation of pain and grief as well as of joy and pleasure. It has its compensating values. The effect of tragedy upon the mind is ultimately one of relief at the cessation of pain. We consider the quality or characteristic from which the tragic development proceeds less as an essential than as an accidental feature, a flaw in the material; and the solution of a tragic situation brings with it a sense of relief at the eradication of this flaw, the restoration to some extent of ideal conditions, and thus the recovery of balance. The significance of tragedy is not merely tragic. It leaves upon our mind the idea of compensation and readjustment; and when literature ceases to have this effect upon us it ceases to be great literature; it is no longer representative, but didactic. This, we think, is an objection which may be urged in all fairness against the art of Mr. Hardy. His nature is one which responds instinctively to tragedy, and this responsiveness to one particular aspect of life has been cultivated to the neglect of another kind of responsiveness. Truth, that higher characteristic of philosophy, to some extent, however slightly still appreciably, suffers and diminishes in proportion as a habit of thought is formed. Not only his critics, but his admirers and disciples, are apt to find in Mr. Hardy's work a didactic tendency. Well, in so far as that tendency is present in his work it is present as a flaw.

Moreover, that kind of tragedy which is based upon the idea of an ultimate compensation, and which presents life to us as a perpetual collision and readjustment of opposed forces, the effects of which are being dissolved, and from which new forces are being generated continually and in infinite variety, implies naturally a certain activity and freedom of will. Whether the notion of ourselves which we have gained from experience in practical affairs be true or false, it is at least sufficiently true to say that we regard ourselves as active agents to whom is allowed a certain freedom of choice, and upon whom ultimately falls the sole responsibility for the choice. Possibly this notion of ourselves may be an illusion, but it is an illusion which life compels us to accept. We are not concerned here with a philosophic but with an artistic conception of truth. We do not wish to be involved in the damnation of those who have attributed a consistent philosophy to Mr. Hardy. To us Mr. Hardy's nature is not a rational but an emotional nature. It is in the depth and richness of his emotional nature that he is great, and it is in *Tess of the d'Urbervilles* and *Jude the Obscure* that his nature has found its most complete expression. At the same time we do not think that, considered purely as works of art, these are Mr. Hardy's best novels. In *Tess of the d'Urbervilles* the whole of the reader's attention is focused upon a single aspect of life, and that aspect is reflected in a single person. Considered apart from Tess, Alec d'Urberville and Angel Clare are purely superficial characters. It is only in their relation to her, only when we see them bathed in the light of her own consciousness, only in so far as she turns from one to the other of them, that they interest us. On the other hand, Tess herself is an almost entirely passive character. She interests us, not by what she does or says, but entirely by what she feels, entirely by her capacity for suffering. To understand such a nature *il faut s'abêtir*, as Pascal said; it is spontaneous, instinctive, moody; it lacks both the control of will and the control of reason. It is one of the simplest organisms, in which the nerve-centres are not localized, but spread over the whole surface of the body, and in which thought is practically identical with sensation. It is essentially feminine. The passivity of her character is so firmly insisted upon by her author, in his eagerness to retain our sympathy, as in some measure to defeat his end, for in order that our sympathy with her should be complete we must realize her own responsibility. 'Why was it that upon this beautiful feminine tissue, sensitive as gossamer, and practically blank as snow as yet, there should have been traced such a coarse pattern as it was doomed to receive; why so often the coarse appropriates the finer thus, the wrong man the woman, the wrong woman the man, many thousand years of analytical philosophy have failed to explain to our sense of order. One may, indeed, admit the possibility of a retribution lurking in the present catastrophe. ... As Tess's own people down in those retreats are never tired of saying among each other in their fatalistic way: "It was to be." There lay the pity of it.' This is partly ironical, no doubt; practically all Mr. Hardy's references to justice and retribution are ironical; the conflict for him resolves itself mainly into a conflict between natural instincts and social regulations. But thus to shift the responsibility for the catastrophe to God, or Nature, or Fate, or Chance, is a fault in art. The passage may be admirable as a criticism of life, or as an expression of feeling; but it destroys the illusions of an individual will and of individual activity. Sympathy is not regulated by any considerations of justice, of which it is quite independent; but we do require that the person or character with whom we are asked to sympathize should be a responsible agent. Shakespeare's Cleopatra, Euripides' Phædra, Thackeray's Becky Sharp, are all severally and in their different ways loaded with will. With the first two the question we put to ourselves is not whether their will is directed towards a proper object, but whether it is sufficiently intense. When a character is willing to sacrifice everything else in order to attain the object desired we no longer measure it by ordinary standards. The sacrifice purges the offence; and even if the object be not attained the catastrophe is the consummation of desire, the final effort of the will. Any return would be fatal to our sympathy; the will, finally immolating itself for the sake of its object, achieves some measure of triumph. It is a fault in art to substitute for this individual will the blind, impersonal forces of nature.

If, however, the tendency of Mr. Hardy's mind has been towards the expression of one particular aspect of life, the tendency is only discernible when we view the novels in their chronological order, and that is not a proper way to criticize his work. *Tess* is a great work of subjectivity, a masterpiece of its kind, but of a very special kind. No other writer, we think, of the Victorian age has shown such emotional power or so intuitive a vision. Considered, however, from another point of view, we prefer *The Return of the Native*. *Tess*, perhaps, is more complete as an expression of the peculiar qualities of Mr. Hardy's genius, but *The Return of the Native* is more complete as a representation of life. Life in it is more fluid and more various, the contrasting aspects are more impartially presented, the blind forces of nature and the tragic grandeur of humanity pitted against them are there, but implied rather by the wild expanse of Egdon Heath than expressed in any particular action. Every incident is perfectly realized: the bonfires on the heath, the stones thrown into the pond as a signal to Eustacia, the mummers, the sympathetic magic, the game of dice played by Wildeve and the reddleman by the light of glowworms, the drowning. An unreal glamour plays over the whole, and yet it is full of a human warmth; full, too, of that almost Shakespearean humour with which Mr. Hardy has endowed his clowns, a humour occasionally suffused with tears, as in that scene from *The Mayor of Casterbridge* when the village gossips talk over Mrs. Henchard's death. It is by this intuitive sympathy with humanity in all its moods that Mr. Hardy is great. His pessimism, after all, is only a habit of thought, a weariness with life that comes upon all of us sometimes, if it does not remain with us always; and that, too, springs from his sympathy with mankind, from the depth and richness of his emotional nature.

SOURCE: *Spectator* (7 September 1912).

D. H. Lawrence   The Real Tragedy   (1914)

It is urged against Thomas Hardy's characters that they do unreasonable things – quite, quite unreasonable things. They are always going off unexpectedly and doing something that nobody would do. That is quite true, and the charge is amusing. These people of Wessex are always bursting suddenly out of bud and taking a wild flight into flower, always shooting suddenly out of a tight convention, a tight, hide-bound cabbage state into something quite madly personal. It would be amusing to count the number of special marriage licenses taken out in Hardy's books. Nowhere, except perhaps in Jude, is there the slightest development of personal action in the characters: it is all explosive. Jude, however, does see more or less what he is doing, and acts from choice. He is more consecutive. The rest explode out of the convention. They are people each with a real, vital, potential self, even the apparently wishy-washy heroines of the earlier books, and this self suddenly bursts the shell of manner and convention and commonplace opinion, and acts independently, absurdly, without mental knowledge or acquiescence.

   And from such an outburst the tragedy usually develops. For there does exist, after all, the great self-preservation scheme, and in it we must all live. Now to live in it after bursting out of it was the problem these Wessex people found themselves faced with. And they never solved the problem, none of them except the comically, insufficiently treated Ethelberta.

This because they must subscribe to the system in themselves. From the more immediate claims of self-preservation they could free themselves: from money, from ambition for social success. None of the heroes or heroines of Hardy cared much for these things. But there is the greater idea of self-preservation, which is formulated in the State, in the whole modelling of the community. And from this idea, the heroes and heroines of Wessex, like the heroes and heroines of almost anywhere else, could not free themselves. In the long run, the State, the Community, the established form of life remained, remained intact and impregnable, the individual, trying to break forth from it, died of fear, of exhaustion, or of exposure to attacks from all sides, like men who have left the walled city to live outside in the precarious open.

This is the tragedy of Hardy, always the same: the tragedy of those who, more or less pioneers, have died in the wilderness, whither they had escaped for free action, after having left the walled security, and the comparative imprisonment, of the established convention. This is the theme of novel after novel: remain quite within the convention, and you are good, safe, and happy in the long run, though you never have the vivid pang of sympathy on your side: or, on the other hand, be passionate, individual, wilful, you will find the security of the convention a walled prison, you will escape, and you will die, either of your own lack of strength to bear the isolation and the exposure, or by direct revenge from the community, or from both. This is the tragedy, and only this: it is nothing more metaphysical than the division of a man against himself in such a way: first, that he is a member of the community, and must, upon his honour, in no way move to disintegrate the community, either in its moral or its practical form; second, that the convention of the community is a prison to his natural, individual desire, a desire that compels him, whether he feels justified or not, to break the bounds of the community, lands him outside the pale, there to stand alone, and say: 'I was right, my desire was real and inevitable; if I was to be myself I must fulfil it, convention or no convention', or else, there to stand alone, doubting, and saying: 'Was I right, was I wrong? If I was wrong, oh, let me die!' – in which case he courts death.

The growth and the development of this tragedy, the deeper and deeper realization of this division and this problem, the coming towards some conclusion, is the one theme of the Wessex novels. . . .

The real sense of tragedy [in *The Return of the Native*] is got from the setting. What is the great, tragic power in the book? It is Egdon Heath. And who are the real spirits of the Heath? First, Eustacia, then Clym's mother, then Wildeve. The natives have little or nothing in common with the place.

What is the real stuff of tragedy in the book? It is the Heath. It is the primitive, primal earth, where the instinctive life heaves up. There, in the deep, rude stirring of the instincts, there was the reality that worked the tragedy. Close to the body of things, there can be heard the stir that makes us and destroys us. The heath heaved with raw instinct. Egdon, whose dark soil was strong and crude and organic as the body of a beast. Out of the body of this crude earth are born Eustacia, Wildeve, Mistress Yeobright, Clym, and all the others. They are one year's accidental crop. What matters if some are drowned or dead, and others preaching or married: what matter, any more than the withering heath, the reddening berries, the seedy furze, and the dead fern of one autumn of Egdon? The Heath persists. Its body is strong and fecund, it will bear many more crops beside this. Here is the sombre, latent power that will go on producing, no matter what happens to the product. Here is the deep, black source from whence all these little contents of lives are drawn. And the contents of the small lives are spilled and wasted. There is savage satisfaction in it: for so much more remains to come, such a black, powerful fecundity is working there that what does it matter?

Three people die and are taken back into the Heath: they mingle their strong earth again with its powerful soil, having been broken off at their stem. It is very good. Not Egdon is futile, sending forth life on the powerful heave of passion. It cannot be futile, for it is eternal. What is futile is the purpose of man.

Man has a purpose which he has divorced from the passionate purpose that issued him out of the earth into being. The Heath threw forth its shaggy heather and furze and fern, clean into being. It threw forth Eustacia and Wildeve and Mistress Yeobright and Clym, but to what purpose? Eustacia thought she wanted the hats and bonnets of Paris. Perhaps she was right. The heavy, strong soil of Egdon, breeding original native beings, is under Paris as well as under Wessex, and Eustacia sought herself in the gay city. She thought life there, in Paris, would be tropical, and all her energy and passion out of Egdon would there come into handsome flower. And if Paris real had been Paris as she imagined it, no doubt she was right, and her instinct was soundly expressed. But Paris real was not Eustacia's imagined Paris. Where was her imagined Paris, the place where her powerful nature could come to blossom? Beside some strong-passioned, unconfined man, her mate.

Which mate Clym might have been. He was born out of passionate Egdon to live as a passionate being whose strong feelings moved him ever further into being. But quite early his life became narrowed down to a small purpose: he must of necessity go into business, and submit his whole being, body and soul as well as mind, to the business and to the greater system it represented. His feelings, that should have produced the man, were suppressed and contained, he worked according to a system imposed from without. The dark struggle of Egdon, a struggle into being as the furze struggles into flower, went on in him, but could not burst the enclosure of the idea, the system which contained him. Impotent to *be*, he must transform himself, and live in an abstraction, in a generalization, he must identify himself with the system. He must live as Man or Humanity, or as the Community, or as Society, or as Civilization. 'An inner strenuousness was preying on his outer symmetry, and they rated his look as singular. . . . His countenance was overlaid with legible meanings. Without being thought-worn, he yet had certain marks derived from a perception of his surroundings, such as are not infrequently found on man at the end of four or five years of endeavour which follow the close of placid pupilage. He already showed that thought is a disease of the flesh, and indirectly bore evidence that ideal physical beauty is incompatible with emotional development and a full recognition of the coil of things. Mental luminousness must be fed with the oil of life, even if there is already a physical seed for it; and the pitiful sight of two demands on one supply was just showing itself here.'

But did the face of Clym show that thought is a disease of flesh, or merely that in his case a dis-ease, an un-ease, of flesh produced thought? One does not catch thought like a fever: one produces it. If it be in any way a disease of flesh, it is rather the rash that indicates the disease than the disease itself. The 'inner strenuousness' of Clym's nature was not fighting against his physical symmetry, but against the limits imposed on his physical movement. By

nature, as a passionate, violent product of Egdon he should have
loved and suffered in flesh and in soul from love, long before this age.
He should have lived and moved and had his being, whereas he had
only his business, and afterwards his inactivity. His years of
pupilage were past, 'he was one of whom something original was
expected', yet he continued in pupilage. For he produced nothing
original in being or in act, and certainly no original thought. None of
his ideas were original. Even he himself was not original. He was
over-taught, and had become an echo. His life had been arrested,
and this activity turned into repetition. Far from being emotionally
developed, he was emotionally undeveloped, almost entirely. Only
his mental faculties were developed. And, hid, his emotions were
obliged to work according to the label he put upon them: a ready-
made label.

Yet he remained for all that an original, the force of life was in
him, however much he frustrated and suppressed its natural movement. 'As is usual with bright natures, the deity that lies ignomi-
niously chained within an ephemeral human carcass shone out of
him like a ray.' But was the deity chained within his ephemeral
human carcass, or within his limited human consciousness? Was it
his blood, which rose dark and potent out of Egdon, which hampered and confined the deity, or was it his mind, that house built of
extraneous knowledge and guarded by his will, which formed the
prison?

He came back to Egdon – what for? To re-unite himself with the
strong, free flow of life that rose out of Egdon as from a source? No –
'to preach to the Egdon eremites that they might rise to a serene
comprehensiveness without going through the process of enriching
themselves'. As if the Egdon eremites had not already far more
serene comprehensiveness than ever he had himself, rooted as they
were in the soil of all things, and living from the root! What did it
matter how they enriched themselves, so long as they kept this
strong, deep root in the primal soil, so long as their instincts moved
out to action and to expression? The system was big enough for
them, and had no power over their instincts. They should have
taught him rather than he them.

And Egdon made him marry Eustacia. Here was action and life,
here was a move into being on his part. But as soon as he got her, she
became an idea to him, she had to fit in his system of ideas.
According to his way of living, he knew her already, she was labelled

and classed and fixed down. He had got into this way of living, and he could not get out of it. He had identified himself with the system, and he could not extricate himself. He did not know that Eustacia had her being beyond his. He did not know that she existed untouched by his system and his mind, where no system had sway and where no consciousness had risen to the surface. He did not know that she was Egdon, the powerful, eternal origin seething with production. He thought he knew. Egdon to him was the tract of common land, producing familiar rough herbage, and having some few unenlightened inhabitants. So he skated over heaven and hell, and having made a map of the surface, thought he knew all. But underneath and among his mapped world, the eternal powerful fecundity worked on heedless of him and his arrogance. His preaching, his superficiality made no difference. What did it matter if he had calculated a moral chart from the surface of life? Could that affect life, any more than a chart of the heavens affects the stars, affects the whole stellar universe which exists beyond our knowledge? Could the sound of his words affect the working of the body of Egdon, where in the unfathomable womb was begot and conceived all that would ever come forth? Did not his own heart beat far removed and immune from his thinking and talking? Had he been able to put even his own heart's mysterious resonance upon his map, from which he charted the course of lives in his moral system? And how much more completely, then, had he left out, in utter ignorance, the dark, powerful source whence all things rise into being, whence they will always continue to rise, to struggle forward to further being? A little of the static surface he could see, and map out. Then he thought his map was the thing itself. How blind he was, how utterly blind to the tremendous movement carrying and producing the surface. He did not know that the greater part of every life is underground, like roots in the dark in contact with the beyond. He preached, thinking lives could be moved like hen-houses from here to there. His blindness indeed brought on the calamity. But what matter if Eustacia or Wildeve or Mrs. Yeobright died: what matter if he himself became a mere rattle of repetitive words – what did it matter? It was regrettable; no more. Egdon, the primal impulsive body, would go on producing all that was to be produced, eternally, though the will of man should destroy the blossom yet in bud, over and over again. At last he must learn what it is to be at one, in his mind and will, with the primal impulses that rise in him. Till then, let him perish or preach. The great reality on which the little tragedies enact themselves cannot be detracted from. The will and words which militate against it are the only vanity.

This is a constant revelation in Hardy's novels: that there exists a great background, vital and vivid, which matters more than the people who move upon it. Against the background of dark, passionate Egdon, of the leafy, sappy passion and sentiment of the woodlands, of the unfathomed stars, is drawn the lesser scheme of lives: *The Return of the Native*, *The Woodlanders*, or *Two on a Tower*. Upon the vast, incomprehensible pattern of some primal morality greater than ever the human mind can grasp, is drawn the little, pathetic pattern of man's moral life and struggle, pathetic, almost ridiculous. The little fold of law and order, the little walled city within which man has to defend himself from the waste enormity of nature, becomes always too small, and the pioneers venturing out with the code of the walled city upon them, die in the bonds of that code, free and yet unfree, preaching the walled city and looking to the waste.

This is the wonder of Hardy's novels, and gives them their beauty. The vast, unexplored morality of life itself, what we call the immorality of nature, surrounds us in its eternal incomprehensibility, and in its midst goes on the little human morality play, with its queer frame of morality and its mechanized movement; seriously, portentously, till some one of the protagonists chances to look out of the charmed circle, weary of the stage, to look into the wilderness raging round. Then he is lost, his little drama falls to pieces, or becomes mere repetition, but the stupendous theatre outside goes on enacting its own incomprehensible drama, untouched. There is this quality in almost all Hardy's work, and this is the magnificent irony it all contains, the challenge, the contempt. Not the deliberate ironies, little tales of widows or widowers, contain the irony of human life as we live it in our self-aggrandized gravity, but the big novels, *The Return of the Native*, and the others.

And this is the quality Hardy shares with the great writers, Shakespeare or Sophocles or Tolstoi, this setting behind the small action of his protagonists the terrific action of unfathomed nature; setting a smaller system of morality, the one grasped and formulated by the human consciousness within the vast, uncomprehended and incomprehensible morality of nature or of life itself, surpassing human consciousness. The difference is, that whereas in Shakespeare or Sophocles the greater, uncomprehended morality, or fate, is actively transgressed and gives active punishment, in Hardy and Tolstoi the lesser, human morality, the mechanical system is actively transgressed, and holds, and punishes the protagonist, whilst the greater morality is only passively, negatively transgressed, it is represented merely as being present in background, in scenery, not taking any active part, having no direct connexion with the protagonist. Œdipus, Hamlet, Macbeth set themselves up against, or find themselves set up against, the unfathomed moral forces of nature, and out of this unfathomed force comes their death. Whereas Anna Karenina, Eustacia, Tess, Sue, and Jude find themselves up against the established system of human government and morality, they cannot detach themselves, and are brought down. Their real tragedy is that they are unfaithful to the greater unwritten morality, which would have bidden Anna Karenina be patient and wait until she, by virtue of greater right, could take what she needed from society; would have bidden Vronsky detach himself from the system, become an individual, creating a new colony of morality with Anna; would have bidden Eustacia fight Clym for his own soul, and Tess take and claim her Angel, since she had the greater light; would have bidden Jude and Sue endure for very honour's sake, since one must bide by the best that one has known, and not succumb to the lesser good.

Had Œdipus, Hamlet, Macbeth been weaker, less full of real, potent life, they would have made no tragedy; they would have comprehended and contrived some arrangement of their affairs, sheltering in the human morality from the great stress and attack of the unknown morality. But being, as they are, men to the fullest capacity, when they find themselves, daggers drawn, with the very forces of life itself, they can only fight till they themselves are killed, since the morality of life, the greater morality, is eternally unalterable and invincible. It can be dodged for some time, but not opposed. On the other hand, Anna, Eustacia, Tess or Sue – what was there in their position that was necessarily tragic? Necessarily painful it was, but they were not at war with God, only with Society. Yet they were all cowed by the mere judgment of man upon them, and all the while by their own souls they were right. And the judgment of men killed them, not the judgment of their own souls or the judgment of Eternal God.

Which is the weakness of modern tragedy, where transgression against the social code is made to bring destruction, as though the social code worked our irrevocable fate. Like Clym, the map appears to us more real than the land. Shortsighted almost to blindness, we pore over the chart, map out journeys, and confirm them: and we cannot see life itself giving us the lie the whole time.

SOURCE: *Study of Thomas Hardy* (1914), reprinted in *Phoenix* (1936).

Virginia Woolf The Novels of Thomas Hardy (1928)

In every book three or four figures predominate, and stand up like lightning conductors to attract the force of the elements. Oak and Troy and Bathsheba; Eustacia, Wildeve, and Venn; Henchard, Lucetta, and Farfrae; Jude, Sue Bridehead, and Phillotson. There is even a certain likeness between the different groups. They live as individuals and they differ as individuals; but they also live as types and have a likeness as types. Bathsheba is Bathsheba, but she is woman and sister to Eustacia and Lucetta and Sue; Gabriel Oak is Gabriel Oak, but he is man and brother to Henchard, Venn, and Jude. However lovable and charming Bathsheba may be, still she is weak; however stubborn and ill-guided Henchard may be, still he is strong. This is a fundamental part of Hardy's vision; the staple of many of his books. The woman is the weaker and the fleshlier, and she clings to the stronger and obscures his vision. How freely, nevertheless, in his greater books life is poured over the unalterable framework! When Bathsheba sits in the wagon among her plants, smiling at her own loveliness in the little looking-glass, we may know, and it is proof of Hardy's power that we do know, how severely she will suffer and cause others to suffer before the end. But the moment has all the bloom and beauty of life. And so it is, time and time again. His characters, both men and women, were creatures to him of an infinite attraction. For the women he shows a more tender solicitude than for the men, and in them, perhaps, he takes a keener interest. Vain might their beauty be and terrible their fate, but while the glow of life is in them their step is free, their laughter sweet, and theirs is the power to sink into the breast of Nature and become part of her silence and solemnity, or to rise and put on them the movement of the clouds and the wildness of the flowering woodlands. The men who suffer, not like the women through dependence upon other human beings, but through conflict with fate, enlist our sterner sympathies. For such a man as Gabriel Oak we need have no passing fears. Honour him we must, though it is not granted us to love him quite so freely. He is firmly set upon his feet and can give as shrewd a blow, to men at least, as any he is likely to receive. He has a prevision of what is to be expected that springs from character rather than from education. He is stable in his temperament, steadfast in his affections, and capable of open-eyed endurance without flinching. But he, too, is no puppet. He is a homely, humdrum fellow on ordinary occasions. He can walk the street without making people turn to stare at him. In short, nobody can deny Hardy's power – the true novelist's power – to make us believe that his characters are fellow-beings driven by their own passions and idiosyncrasies, while they have – and this is the poet's gift – something symbolical about them which is common to us all.

And it is when we are considering Hardy's power of creating men and women that we become most conscious of the profound differences that distinguish him from his peers. We look back at a number of these characters and ask ourselves what it is that we remember them for. We recall their passions. We remember how deeply they have loved each other and often with what tragic results. We remember the faithful love of Oak for Bathsheba; the tumultuous but fleeting passions of men like Wildeve, Troy, and Fitzpiers; we remember the filial love of Clym for his mother, the jealous paternal passion of Henchard for Elizabeth Jane. But we do not remember how they have loved. We do not remember how they talked and changed and got to know each other, finely, gradually, from step to step and from stage to stage. Their relationship is not composed of those intellectual apprehensions and subtleties of perception which seem so slight yet are so profound. In all the books love is one of the great facts that mould human life. But it is a catastrophe; it happens suddenly and overwhelmingly, and there is little to be said about it. The talk between the lovers when it is not passionate is practical or philosophic, as though the discharge of their daily duties left them with more desire to question life and its

purpose than to investigate each other's sensibilities. Even if it were
in their power to analyse their emotions, life is too stirring to give
them time. They need all their strength to deal with the downright
blows, the freakish ingenuity, the gradually increasing malignity of
fate. They have none to spend upon the subtleties and delicacies of
the human comedy.

Thus there comes a time when we can say with certainty that we
shall not find in Hardy some of the qualities that have given us most
delight in the works of other novelists. He has not the perfection of
Jane Austen, or the wit of Meredith; or the range of Thackeray, or
Tolstoy's amazing intellectual power. There is in the work of the
great classical writers a finality of effect which places certain of their
scenes, apart from the story, beyond the reach of change. We do not
ask what bearing they have upon the narrative, nor do we make use
of them to interpret problems which lie on the outskirts of the scene.
A laugh, a blush, half a dozen words of dialogue, and it is enough;
the source of our delight is perennial. But Hardy has none of this
concentration and completeness. His light does not fall directly upon
the human heart. It passes over it and out on to the darkness of the
heath and upon the trees swaying in the storm. When we look back
into the room the group by the fireside is dispersed. Each man or
woman is battling with the storm, alone, revealing himself most
when he is least under the observation of other human beings. We
do not know them as we know Pierre or Natasha or Becky Sharp.
We do not know them in and out and all round as they are revealed
to the casual caller, to the Government official, to the great lady, to
the general on the battlefield. We do not know the complication and
involvement and turmoil of their thoughts. Geographically, too, they
remain fixed to the same stretch of the English country-side. It is
seldom, and always with unhappy results, that Hardy leaves the
yeoman or farmer to describe the class above theirs in the social
scale. In the drawing-room and club-room and ballroom, where
people of leisure and education come together, where comedy is bred
and shades of character revealed, he is awkward and ill at ease. But
the opposite is equally true. If we do not know his men and women
in their relations to each other, we know them in their relations to
time, death, and fate. If we do not see them in quick agitation
against the lights and crowds of cities, we see them against the earth,
the storm, and the seasons. We know their attitude towards some of
the most tremendous problems that can confront mankind. They

take on a more than mortal size in memory. We see them, not in detail but enlarged and dignified. We see Tess reading the baptismal service in her nightgown 'with an impress of dignity that was almost regal'. We see Marty South, 'like a being who had rejected with indifference the attribute of sex for the loftier quality of abstract humanism', laying the flowers on Winterborne's grave. Their speech has a Biblical dignity and poetry. They have a force in them which cannot be defined, a force of love or of hate, a force which in the men is the cause of rebellion against life, and in the women implies an illimitable capacity for suffering, and it is this which dominates the character and makes it unnecessary that we should see the finer features that lie hid. This is the tragic power; and, if we are to place Hardy among his fellows, we must call him the greatest tragic writer among English novelists.

But let us, as we approach the danger-zone of Hardy's philosophy, be on our guard. Nothing is more necessary, in reading an imaginative writer, than to keep at the right distance above his page. Nothing is easier, especially with a writer of marked idiosyncrasy, than to fasten on opinions, convict him of a creed, tether him to a consistent point of view. Nor was Hardy any exception to the rule that the mind which is most capable of receiving impressions is very often the least capable of drawing conclusions. It is for the reader, steeped in the impression, to supply the comment. It is his part to know when to put aside the writer's conscious intention in favour of some deeper intention of which perhaps he may be unconscious. Hardy himself was aware of this. A novel 'is an impression, not an argument', he has warned us, and, again: 'Unadjusted impressions have their value, and the road to a true philosophy of life seems to lie in humbly recording diverse readings of its phenomena as they are forced upon us by chance and change'.

Certainly it is true to say of him, at his greatest, he gives us impressions; at his weakest, arguments. In *The Woodlanders, The Return of the Native, Far From the Madding Crowd*, and, above all, in *The Mayor of Casterbridge*, we have Hardy's impression of life as it came to him without conscious ordering. Let him once begin to tamper with his direct intuitions and his power is gone. 'Did you say the stars were worlds, Tess?' asks little Abraham as they drive to market with their beehives. Tess replies that they are like 'the apples on our stubbard-tree, most of them splendid and sound – a few blighted'. 'Which do we live on – a splendid or a blighted one?' 'A blighted one', she replies, or rather the mournful thinker who has assumed her mask speaks for her. The words protrude, cold and raw, like the springs of a machine where we had seen only flesh and blood. We are crudely jolted out of that mood of sympathy which is renewed a moment later when the little cart is run down and we have a concrete instance of the ironical methods which rule our planet.

That is the reason why *Jude the Obscure* is the most painful of all Hardy's books, and the only one against which we can fairly bring the charge of pessimism. In *Jude the Obscure* argument is allowed to dominate impression, with the result that though the misery of the book is overwhelming it is not tragic. As calamity succeeds calamity we feel that the case against society is not being argued fairly or with profound understanding of the facts. Here is nothing of that width and force and knowledge of mankind which, when Tolstoy criticises society, makes his indictment formidable. Here we have revealed to us the petty cruelty of men, not the large injustice of the gods. It is only necessary to compare *Jude the Obscure* with *The Mayor of Casterbridge* to see where Hardy's true power lay. Jude carries on his miserable contest against the deans of colleges and the conventions of sophisticated society. Henchard is pitted, not against another man, but against something outside himself which is opposed to men of his ambition and power. No human being wishes him ill. Even Farfrae and Newson and Elizabeth Jane whom he has wronged all come to pity him, and even to admire his strength of character. He is standing up to fate, and in backing the old Mayor whose ruin has been largely his own fault, Hardy makes us feel that we are backing human nature in an unequal contest. There is no pessimism here. Throughout the book we are aware of the sublimity of the issue, and yet it is presented to us in the most concrete form. From the opening scene in which Henchard sells his wife to the sailor at the fair to his death on Egdon Heath the vigour of the story is superb, its humour rich and racy, its movement large-limbed and free. The skimmity ride, the fight between Farfrae and Henchard in the loft, Mrs. Cuxsom's speech upon the death of Mrs Henchard, the talk of the ruffians at Peter's Finger with Nature present in the background or mysteriously dominating the foreground, are among the glories of English fiction. Brief and scanty, it may be, is the measure of happiness allowed to each, but so long as the struggle is, as Henchard's was, with the decrees of fate and not with the laws of man, so long as it is in the open air and calls for activity of the body rather than of the brain, there is greatness in the contest, there is pride and pleasure in it, and the death of the broken corn merchant in his cottage on Egdon Heath is comparable to the death of Ajax, lord of Salamis. The true tragic emotion is ours.

Before such power as this we are made to feel that the ordinary tests which we apply to fiction are futile enough. Do we insist that a great novelist shall be a master of melodious prose? Hardy was no such thing. He feels his way by dint of sagacity and uncompromising sincerity to the phrase he wants, and it is often of unforgettable pungency. Failing it, he will make do with any homely or clumsy or old-fashioned turn of speech, now of the utmost angularity, now of a bookish elaboration. No style in literature, save Scott's, is so difficult to analyse; it is on the face of it so bad, yet it achieves its aim so unmistakably. As well might one attempt to rationalise the charm of a muddy country road, or of a plain field of roots in winter. And then, like Dorsetshire itself, out of these very elements of stiffness and angularity his prose will put on greatness; will roll with a Latin sonority; will shape itself in a massive and monumental symmetry like that of his own bare downs. Then again, do we require that a novelist shall observe the probabilities, and keep close to reality? To find anything approaching the violence and convolution of Hardy's plots one must go back to the Elizabethan drama. Yet we accept his story completely as we read it; more than that, it becomes obvious that his violence and his melodrama, when they are not due to a curious peasant-like love of the monstrous for its own sake, are part of that wild spirit of poetry which saw with intense irony and grimness that no reading of life can possibly outdo the strangeness of life itself, no symbol of caprice and unreason be too extreme to represent the astonishing circumstances of our existence.

But as we consider the great structure of the Wessex novels it seems irrelevant to fasten on little points – this character, that scene, this phrase of deep and poetic beauty. It is something larger that Hardy has bequeathed to us. The Wessex Novels are not one book, but many. They cover an immense stretch; inevitably they are full of imperfections – some are failures, and others exhibit only the wrong side of their maker's genius. But undoubtedly, when we have submitted ourselves fully to them, when we come to take stock of our impressions of the whole, the effect is commanding and satisfactory. We have been freed from the cramp and pettiness imposed by life.

Our imaginations have been stretched and heightened; our humour has been made to laugh out; we have drunk deep of the beauty of the earth. Also we have been made to enter the shade of a sorrowful and brooding spirit which, even in its saddest mood, bore itself with a grave uprightness and never, even when most moved to anger, lost its deep compassion for the sufferings of men and women. Thus it is no mere transcript of life at a certain time and place that Hardy has given us. It is a vision of the world and of man's lot as they revealed themselves to a powerful imagination, a profound and poetic genius, a gentle and humane soul.

SOURCE: *The Common Reader: Second Series* (1932; written in 1928), pp. 250–7.

Jean Brooks The Poetic Structure (1971)

The poet's gift has not gone unremarked, but what it means to Hardy's art has not been explored in great detail in the light of modern poetic structure. One could, without much profit, compare some of Hardy's poems with their prosed counterparts to discover the link between poet and poetic novelist. Different kinds of poetry – philosophical, lyrical, elegiac, narrative/dramatic – isolate microscopically various ingredients which unite in the novels to produce the true Hardeian flavour. They crystallize a certain mood or moment of vision which are emotional arias in the novels. 'Beyond the Last Lamp', 'Tess's Lament', 'Proud Songsters', and 'A Light Snow-fall after Frost' (*Tess of the d'Urbervilles*); 'The Pine Planters' and 'In a Wood' (*The Woodlanders*); 'Childhood among the Ferns' and 'Midnight on the Great Western' (*Jude the Obscure*) are fine poems in their own right, because Hardy has added or subtracted features which re-create them in terms of lyric. Usually, however, the prosed poems are more successful in the novels, where they are an organic part of narrative structure and emotional accumulation of detail. To compare 'The Puzzled Game-Birds' with the end of Chapter XLI of *Tess* proves the futility of computer exercises.

The poetic strain is more complex. It is a way of looking at and ordering experience. It includes the ballad qualities of Hardy's narrative, poetic presentation of event and character, his poetic sense of place and history in the re-creation of Wessex, his imaginative blending of new Victorian science and old folk superstition, and the Gothic strangeness of his vision and style. It includes a sensuous apprehension of daily life that embraces the contemplative and metaphysical. Virginia Woolf reminds us ('Impassioned Prose', *T.L.S.* (1926), reprinted in *Granite and Rainbow*, Hogarth Press, 1958) that the novelist has his hands full of the facts of daily living, so 'how can we ask [him] . . . to modulate beautifully off into rhapsodies about Time and Death . . .?' Hardy's achievement of this difficult transition vindicates him as a poetic novelist.

The poetic impulse, expressing the basic but multiple faces of experience, defines the Hardeian quality. He thought of himself as 'an English poet who had written some stories in prose', and in prose tried to preserve the poetry. 'He had mostly aimed at keeping his narratives close to natural life and as near to poetry in their subject as the conditions would allow, and had often regretted that those conditions would not let him keep them nearer still.' (*The Life of Thomas Hardy*, Macmillan, 1930, p. 291.) It reconciles all the seeming contradictions of Hardy's subject, style, and philosophy by giving them equal weight but no synthesis. Hardy anticipates the modern anguish of unresolved tensions in the stylized forms which contain the undirected chaos of life; the traditional character types who reveal Freudian subtleties of psychology; grand gestures punctured by absurd and vulgar intrusions; the dichotomies of common and uncommon, simple and complex, protest and acquiescence. Yeats's definition of the double face of poetry is appropriate to the powerful tensions that constitute the Hardy vision: 'The passion . . . comes from the fact that the speakers are holding down violence or madness – "down Hysterica passio". All depends on the completeness of the holding down, on the stirring of the beast underneath. . . . Without this conflict we have no passion only sentiment and thought.' (Letter to Dorothy Wellesley, 5 August 1936.)

The multiple perspective of poetry is more often a strength than a weakness. It gives simultaneously the personal and formal vision; the subjective feel of experience falling on 'all that side of the mind which is exposed in solitude' (Virginia Woolf, 'Impassioned Prose') and the bold epic relief of those characters who 'stand up like lightning conductors to attract the force of the elements' ('The Novels of Thomas Hardy', *The Common Reader*) in their mythopoeic relation to time, death, and fate, both enhanced and diminished by the time-marked Wessex scene that rings their actions. It is the source of Hardy's distinctive ironic tone and structure, his tragi-comedy, his blend of fatalism and belief in the power of chance, and his profound sense of tragedy.

Hardy's ironic mode is the reverse face of his compassion. The pattern of what is runs in tension with the pattern of what ought to be according to human values. Mismatings, mistimings and un-desired substitutions for an intended effect point to the 'if only' structure of Hardeian irony. If only Newson had entered the tent a few minutes earlier or later; if only Angel had danced with Tess on the green; if only Tess had not been 'doomed to be seen and coveted that day by the wrong man' instead of by the 'missing counterpart' who 'wandered independently about the earth waiting in crass obtuseness till the late time came'. Hardy's notorious use of coincidence to demonstrate cosmic absurdity is shadowed by its traditional function as an agent of cosmic design. As Barbara Hardy points out in *The Appropriate Form* (Athlone Press, 1964), the use of coincidence in *Jane Eyre* is directed by Charlotte Brontë's belief in Providence; in *Jude the Obscure* by Hardy's belief in the absence of Providence. In Victorian melodrama the 'heroine' of *Tess of the d'Urbervilles* would have been rescued providentially by the 'hero' from the 'villain'. Hardy has neither hero, villain, nor Providence, and the alternative reasons he suggests for Tess's seduction point to the impenetrable mystery of the cosmic scheme.

When passionate personal emotion counterpoints the control of a traditional form, the ironic double vision thus obtained questions the unthinking acceptance of cosmic and social arrangements im-plied by the patterns Hardy took over from popular narrative and drama. Received morality is shaken and measured by the morality of compassion; poetic and Divine justice by the honesty that allows Arabella and Fitzpiers to flourish while Jude and Winterborne suffer unjustly and die, in a world where personal worth does not decide the issue. The internal tensions between the betrayed-maid arche-type of balladry and the fallen woman of Victorian moral literature, set against the intense subjective world of Tess, provoke a complex reaction to her story. The psychological study of a frustrated woman strains against the breathless action of the sensation novel in

Desperate Remedies. The Golden-Age pastoral exposes the cosmic dissonances of *Far From the Madding Crowd* and *The Woodlanders*. The expected end of the story in marriage or death takes on a bitter irony in *Jude the Obscure*, where the marriage of Sue is more tragic than the death of Jude. The hymn metres behind some of Hardy's poetic questionings of the First Cause; the ballad of revenge behind his ballads of generous action; the popular conception of romantic love behind the cruel, blind, sexual force that sweeps his characters to ecstasy, madness, suffering, and death, make the ironic mode of double vision inseparable from style. The puzzled game-birds in the poem of that name sing their bewilderment at man's inconsistent cruelty in a graceful triolet. 'The Voice' sets Hardy's grief for his wife's death to the gay tune of a remembered dance. The harsh physical facts of death deflate the pattern of the consolation poem in which 'Transformations' is written. Marsden points out that the beautiful patterns made on the page by 'The Pedigree' bring out the subtle variations and irregularities of structure which enact personal defiance of the realization of heredity to which the poem moves – 'I am merest mimicker and counterfeit! – ' (K. Marsden, *The Poems of Thomas Hardy*, Athlone Press, 1969, p. 120.)

Hardy's multiple vision of experience brings him close to the modern-Absurdist form of tragi-comedy or comi-tragedy. 'If you look beneath the surface of any farce you see a tragedy; and, on the contrary, if you blind yourself to the deeper issues of a tragedy you see a farce' (*Life*). The comic court-room scene of *The Mayor of Casterbridge* in which the furmity hag works Henchard's downfall, the comic constables who take the foreground while Lucetta lies dying from the shock of the skimmity ride their incompetence has been unable to prevent; the rustics who discuss, at length, folklore remedies as Mrs Yeobright lies mortally wounded from snakebite; the two lovers who quarrel about their precedence in Elfride's affections when they have travelled unknowingly with her dead body; the farcical conjunctions of Ethelberta's three lovers; the love-sick de Stancy's undignified eavesdropping on Paula's gymnastic exercises in pink flannel; the Kafka-like distortions of figure or scene, stress the ironic deflation of romance, heroism, and tragedy by the objective incursions of absurdity; without, however, denigrating the value of romance, heroism, and suffering. 'All tragedy is grotesque – if you allow yourself to see it as such' (*Life*).

In all his work Hardy's personal voice, with its humane values, its

Gothic irregularities, its human contradictions and rough edges, its commonness and uncommonness, strains against the rigidities of traditional patterns and expectations. The first two paragraphs of *The Mayor of Casterbridge*, for example, can provide the mixture to be found in all the other novels, *The Dynasts*, and most of the poems – the amalgam of homely simplicity, awkward periphrasis, triteness, and sharp sensuous vision that invests an ordinary scene with the significance of myth and Sophoclean grandeur. The dissonance of the multiple vision dramatically enacts Hardy's metaphysic of man's predicament as a striving, sensitive, imperfect individual in a rigid, non-sentient, absurd cosmos, which rewards him only with eternal death.

The predicament is tragic. A poetic ambiguity of perspective is inherent in the nature of tragedy. It is part of the texture of human hope. 'The end of tragedy . . . is to show the dignity of man for all his helpless littleness in face of the universe, for all his nullity under the blotting hand of time' (Bonamy Dobrée, *The Lamp and the Lute*, Clarendon Press, 1929). In Hardy's tragedy one finds the tragic protagonist, defined for his role by a tragic greatness (not in high estate, as in Sophocles and Shakespeare, but in character alone) that intensifies the sense of life, and flawed by a tragic vulnerability that unfits him for the particular tragic situation he has to face. Jude's sexual and self-degrading impulses are disastrous in view of the obstacles to higher education for working men. Henchard's rash and inflexible temper cannot ride the agricultural changes that overtake Casterbridge. In the tragic universe human errors become tragic errors which co-operate with Fate (those circumstances within and without, which man did not make and cannot unmake, incarnated as natural forces, the clockwork laws of cause and effect, the workings of chance, coincidence, and time, irrational impulses, man-made conventions, and the search for happiness) to bring evil out of his goodness and good intentions, and to bring down on him, and innocent people connected with him, tragic suffering and catastrophe out of all proportion to its cause. The irresponsible sending of a valentine, the concealment of a seduction until the day of the wedding to another man, the careless sealing of love letters and choice of an untrustworthy messenger, release forces of death and destruction which inspire tragic terror at the contemplation of the painful mystery of the workings of inexorable law. Tragic pity is aroused, as Dobrée points out, 'not because someone suffers, but because something fine is bruised and broken' – something too sensitively organized for an insentient world of defect.

But the sense of tragic waste is tempered by tragic joy, because in the tragic confrontation with futility and absurdity Hardy affirms some of the highest values men and women can achieve.

The great writer of tragedy manages to convey that though this be the truth, it is well that men should behave thus and thus; that in spite of all the seeming cruelty and futility of existence, one way of life is better than another; that Orestes is right and Clytemnestra wrong, that Othello is fairer than Iago. Not that fault is to be imputed to the wrongdoer; he also is a pebble of fate, destined to play his part in the eternal drama of good and evil. (Dobrée, *The Lamp and the Lute*)

These values remain unchanged when the people who embodied them are destroyed, and whether the gods are alive or dead. Giles Winterborne's death may contain a criticism of his former back-wardness and of Victorian sexual hypocrisy, but in its essence it celebrates the selfless love that can see further than temporary satisfaction of physical desire to the preservation of Grace's image untarnished to posterity. Modern permissiveness cannot change his nobility or the value of his suffering. Giles, Clym, Henchard, Tess, Jude, and Sue are not fulfilled in the eyes of the world. But their tragedy asserts the values for which they suffered (even Eustacia, whose selfishness limits our sympathy, asserts the value of self-assertion), stripped of all recommendations of success.

Hardy's tragic figures, rooted in an unconscious life-process more deterministic than their own, try to mould their lives according to human values, personal will, feeling, and aspiration. Though their self-assertion is overcome by the impersonality of the cosmos, including those instinctive drives they share with the natural world, their endeavour to stamp a humane personal design on cosmic indifference makes them nobler than what destroys them. Hardy had no time for Nietzsche. 'To model our conduct on Nature's apparent conduct, as Nietzsche would have taught, can only bring disaster to humanity' (*Life*). His characters' close and conscious relationship to unconscious nature defines the hope that is contained in the tragic suffering. Hardy's greatest novels are tragic actions which demonstrate the incomplete evolutionary state of man, a throb of the universal pulse, suffering as the pioneer of a more compassionate cosmic awareness – the hope towards which the whole of *The Dynasts* moves. His poems are the cries of tragic love, tragic error, tragic injustice, tragic waste, and tragic awareness with which tragic poets and dramatists from Aeschylus to Beckett have defined the sense of life.

> HAMM: What's he doing? . . .
> CLOV: He's crying. . . .
> HAMM: Then he's living. (Samuel Beckett: *Endgame*)

That Hardy's voice still has the authentic tragic note defines his importance to the modern world. Recent assertions (as in George Steiner's *The Death of Tragedy*) that tragedy died with the gods and an ordered system of Hellenic or Christian values shared by artist and audience, which gave reasons for the suffering and struggle, can hardly stand against the tragic experience of Hardy's work. Hardeian man, sustained only by his own qualities as a human being, defies the chaotic void as Hellenic and Shakespearean man, placed in reference to cosmic myth, defied powers which were, if cruel and unknowable, at least *there* to be defied.

> Then would I bear it, clench myself, and die,
> Steeled by the sense of ire unmerited;
> Half-eased in that a Powerfuller than I
> Had willed and meted me the tears I shed. ('Hap')

A strong plot, 'exceptional enough to justify its telling', explicit in the novels and implicit in many poems, was Hardy's formal correlative for the tragic vision of man confronting his destiny. As Bonamy Dobrée points out, plot ('this is how things happen') is a more important symbol for tragedy than character ('this is what people are like'), 'since the tragic writer is concerned with the littleness of man (even though his greatness in his littleness) in the face of unescapable odds'. The hammer strokes of a clockwork universe on human sensitivity are enacted in a pattern as rigid as scientific law, likened by Lascelles Abercrombie to a process of chemistry, in which the elements 'are irresistibly moved to work towards one another by strong affinity; and the human molecules in which they are ingredients are dragged along with them, until the elemental affinity is satisfied, in a sudden flashing moment of disintegration and re-compounding' (*Thomas Hardy*, Martin Secker,

1912). There is no inconsistency between Hardy's determinism and the important role in his works of chance and coincidence. Chance is direction which we cannot see; but it is the direction of a blind, groping force, unrelated to anything we can conceive as conscious purpose. Once more the double perspective of chaos and determinism conjures up a richly complex poetic response to the fate of living creatures subject to inhuman cause and effect.

The symmetry and intensity of Hardy's plots, with every link in the chain of cause and effect made clear, join with his poetic vision of natural rhythms, and traditional devices of dramatic development, in a disproportioning of reality to bring out the pattern of the larger forces driving the cosmos and its creatures. Sensational events, disastrous coincidences, untimely reappearances, overheard or revealed secrets, present a universe where every action is a hostage to a predetermined and hidden fate. The supernatural detail, the rural superstition and folk belief, stand in for the missing Providential direction. Without Providence, everything contributes to the longing for significance. Besides giving the poetic *frisson* at inexplicable mysteries, Hardy's use of superstition is integral to the characters' relation to fate. The tragedy of *The Woodlanders* is touched off by old John South's anthropological involvement with a tree. The primitive emotion conjured up by the events at the Midsummer Eve 'larries' lays the foundation of Grace's marriage, her separation, and Mrs Charmond's death. As J. O. Bailey demonstrates in 'Hardy's Visions of the Self' (*Studies in Philology*, LVI, 1959) the Hardeian 'ghost' (a walking vision, a dream, a real sight suggesting guilt, or a mental image presented to the reader) plays the part of a directing Nemesis in revealing to the character his own inner nature, causing him to accept responsibility for disasters he had blamed on circumstances, and to take the action that brings the novel to a conclusion.

The characters too have a simple epic and tragic strength. They are types, though not without individuality. All the subtleties of psychology and sociology that might obscure the pattern of their ritual interaction with Fate are stripped away. Life is reduced to its basic elements: birth, mating, death, the weather, man's pain and helplessness in an indifferent universe; the passions and conflicts that spring from an enclosed rural community with its roots in an ancient past and an ancient countryside, its pagan fatalism and ballad values and personal loyalties, being gradually invaded by modern urban restlessness and alienation. The catastrophic passions of the main characters are set off by a peasant chorus quietly enduring the realistic slow trivialities of daily living, which shape human fate by steady accumulation. They are as slow to change as the natural rhythms they are part of. Hardy creates a fundamental persistence from the tension between the two kinds of stability; the eternal recurrence of the natural cycle and the recurrent finiteness of men.

They compose a pool of common wisdom, of common humour, a fund of perpetual life. They comment upon the actions of the hero and heroine, but while Troy or Oak or Fanny or Bathsheba come in and out and pass away, Jan Coggan and Henry [sic] Fray and Joseph Poorgrass remain. They drink by night and they plough the fields by day. They are eternal. We meet them over and over again in the novels, and they always have something typical about them, more of the character that marks a race than of the features which belong to an individual. The peasants are the great sanctuary of sanity, the country the last stronghold of happiness. When they disappear, there is no hope for the race (Virginia Woolf, 'The Novels of Thomas Hardy').

They are equivalent to Camus's nostalgia for a lost paradisal homeland of harmony with things as they are.

The human emotional force of the characters counterpoints the regularity of plot and scientific process; a process which they both obey and defy. Hardy's double vision of man's greatness in values and littleness in the cosmic scheme keeps the tragic balance between fate – the impersonal nature of things – and personal responsibility. When Henchard disregards his wife's last wishes and reads the letter in which she discloses that Elizabeth-Jane is not his child, 'he could not help thinking that the concatenation of events this evening had produced was the scheme of some sinister intelligence bent on punishing him. Yet they had developed naturally. If he had not revealed his past history to Elizabeth he would not have searched the drawer for papers, and so on.' The doubt reflects the painful ambiguity and inscrutability of things; a poetic asset. While it is true that Hardy's poetic pattern stresses the action of fate, it does so to stress too the human responsibility to deflect fate from its path before it is too late. Misery, which teaches Henchard 'nothing more than a defiant endurance of it', teaches Clym to limit his ambitions and Oak to keep one step ahead of an infuriated universe. The adaptive resourcefulness of Farfrae, the loving-kindness of Viviette which triumphs over her sexual passion for Swithin, the determination of Paula to follow her lover through Europe regardless of etiquette, modify a fate that seemed predetermined. Their conscious purpose redefines the concept of fate as what must be *only if no resistance is made*.

In the complexity of things resistance itself has a double edge. The greatest value ephemeral man can find to stand against the threat of meaninglessness is love. It promises to satisfy the thirst for happiness and harmony with cosmic purposes. Hardy's definition of love is unfashionably wide. It includes, as well as the physiological fact and frank relationship between the sexes which he wanted to show his Victorian readers, Viviette's sublimated maternal love for her young lover Swithin, Mr Melbury's for his daughter and Mrs Yeobright's for her son, Henchard's for Farfrae and the girl who is not his daughter. Charley's idealized love for his mistress Eustacia, Clym's for suffering mankind, and the life-loyalties of the interrelated Hintock community. But because its roots are in the impersonal sexual impulses that drive the natural world, love contributes to the tragedy of human consciousness. Respect for the real being of the beloved is lost in illusory wish-projections which cause suffering when they clash with reality. Angel's image of Tess as an inhumanly pure woman, Clym's vision of Eustacia as a school matron and Eustacia's of Clym as a gay Parisian escort, Bathsheba's defence of Troy as a regular churchgoer, Jude's intermittent treatment of Sue as the 'average' woman, are nature's devices, working on the human tendency to idealization, to accomplish the mating process. The projection causes pain when it moves from lover to lover; love rarely ceases for both at the same moment. But though agony is the inevitable corollary of ecstasy, the pain affirms the life-enhancing quality of love. The caprice it inspires in women – a type of the cosmic caprice of fate – is also a measure of their vitality and truth to life. The will to enjoy, inseparably bound up with the opposing will to suffer (part of 'the circumstantial will against enjoyment'); the instinctive zest for existence modified by the modern view of life as a thing to be put up with, can bring maturity and even happiness. Bathsheba attains maturity and a realistic appraisal of Oak's controlled fidelity. Even Tess is only robbed of the purely human Paradise promised in Talbothays by the inhumanity of man.

Virginia Woolf accepts the great emotional crises as part of Hardy's poetic pattern. 'In all the books love is one of the great facts that mould human life. But it is a catastrophe; it happens suddenly and overwhelmingly, and there is little to be said about it' ('The Novels of Thomas Hardy').

T. S. Eliot, on the other hand, attacks the 'emotional paroxysms' which seem to him a 'symptom of decadence' expressing 'a powerful personality uncurbed by any institutional attachment or by submission to any objective beliefs. . . . He seems to me to have written as nearly for the sake of "self-expression" as a man well can; and the self which he had to express does not strike me as a particularly wholesome or edifying matter of communication . . .' (*After Strange Gods*, Harcourt Brace & Co., 1934). His criticism suggests the distrust of someone who feels the meaning of orthodox allegiances threatened by the affirmation of a life without God or ultimate purpose. But in a world where Eliot's own poetry has revealed the dehumanization of hollow men living in an emotionless waste land, the intense emotion of Hardy's characters and Hardy's personal voice affirm the response of living passion to the human predicament. 'The function of the artist is to justify life by feeling it intensely' (J. E. Barton, 'The Poetry of Thomas Hardy'). Far from robbing the characters of their human individuality, as Eliot claims, heightened emotion stresses both their basic humanness and the resistance of the unique personality to the habit of despair which Camus found worse than despair itself ('None of us was capable any longer of an exalted emotion; all had trite, monotonous feelings' – *The Plague*), and which Matthew Arnold had defined in a letter to Clough (14 December 1852) as 'the modern situation in its true *blankness* and *barrenness*, and *unpoetrylessness*'.

Hardy's poetic persona is untouched by the modern taboo on tenderness and top notes, though the understatement of deep feeling also forms part of his vision. His emotional scenes are operatic rather than melodramatic; arias which reveal the inner quality of life, with all its dissonant primary passions reconciled in the musico-poetic form, while the outer action is suspended. The effect of Boldwood's final gesture, with its poignant return of his old courtesy, 'Then he broke from Samway, crossed the room to Bathsheba, and kissed her hand', in the context of his murder of Troy, can only be compared with the return of the love leitmotif at the end of Verdi's *Otello*. (The *Life* proves that Verdi was a composer with whom Hardy felt some affinity.) As the emotional persuasiveness of music suspends disbelief in what would be absurd in spoken drama,

Hardy's poetic heightening carries him through operatic implausibilities of action and clumsinesses of style. The unrealistic 'libretto' of the quarrel between Clym and Eustacia, reminiscent of the quarrel of Brachiano and Vittoria in *The White Devil*, directs attention away from the technicalities of expression to the white-hot emotion underneath that compels the jerky speech rhythms, the trembling of Eustacia's hands, and the agony of a man still in love with the wife he is rejecting on principle, who while he ties her bonnet strings for her, 'turned his eyes aside, that he might not be tempted to softness'.

It is the emotion of Hardy's work which one remembers. It expresses the whole of his many-sided personality, spilling over the barriers of artistic form to make his work an experience which is musical and artistic as well as literary. Virginia Woolf's definition of the special quality of Hardy's characters – 'We recall their passions. We remember how deeply they have loved each other and often with what tragic results. . . . But we do not remember how they have loved. We do not remember how they talked and changed and got to know each other, finely, gradually, from step to step and from stage to stage. . . .' ('The Novels of Thomas Hardy') – places his work with those sister arts (in which Hardy was a competent practitioner) which create a universal image of the essence of things to transcend the personal and local details that gave it birth. As W. H. Auden remarked about his experience of writing opera libretti (the T. S. Eliot Memorial lectures given at the University of Kent at Canterbury, 1967): 'Music can, I believe, express the equivalent of *I love*, but it is incapable of saying whom or what I love, you, God, or the decimal system.' In the extraordinary states of violent emotion that distinguish the operatic mode, all differences in social standing, sex, and age are abolished, so that even in a foreign language one can tell the emotion that is being expressed.

Hardy's equivalent for the operatic state often takes a form that is both musical and pictorial. Dance and song are linked with ritual survivals of fertility rites that are an 'irresistible attack upon . . . social order', as in the village gipsying on Egdon and the dance that inspires the change of marriage partners in 'The History of the Hardcomes'. The folk or church music that was part of Hardy's heritage often moves a sexual or compassionate emotion that precipitates a definite step in the story. The step is not always disastrous. The sound of children's voices singing 'Lead kindly Light' re-establishes Bathsheba's relationship with Oak after her

tragedy; Farfrae's song stops Henchard from killing him in the loft.
Boldwood feels encouraged to consider himself as good as engaged
to Bathsheba after their exhibition of harmony at the shearing
supper. Wildeve feels there is nothing else to do but marry Tamsin
after they have been celebrated by Grandfer's crew as a married
couple. Farfrae's modest dance with Elizabeth-Jane at his entertain-
ment precipitates a half-declaration of love. Tess's interest in
Angel's music rivets his attention on this unusual milkmaid, whose
'fluty' tones had interrupted his meditations on a music score. The
hymn tune of the Wessex composer, which made Sue and Jude clasp
hands by an 'unpremeditated instinct', gives rise to her confession of
an 'incomplete' marriage with Phillotson, and points to her search
for spiritual harmony with Jude. Even Melbury's irritation at
Cawtree's low ballad, which contributes to his rejection of Giles as a
suitable mate for his daughter, is a refusal to recognize the primitive
side of Grace's nature which is in harmony with the sentiments of
the song and the simple woodland company who sang it. The effect
of ritual music becomes a correlative for the operations of the
Immanent Will, moving people through their emotions to obey its
own inscrutable purposes.

Ritual itself is, in modern terms, total theatre. The ritual character of Hardy's operatic scenes – the village gipsying, the skimmity
ride, the Egdon bonfires, the arrest at Stonehenge – is stressed by his
balletic groupings and his description of scene and characters in
terms of the strong contrast of light and shade. This pictorial
treatment abstracts personality from the actors and leaves their
faces mask-like, with no 'permanent moral expression'. The
silhouette, employed most frequently in descriptions of the rustic
chorus, expresses a communal emotion rather than individual
idiosyncrasy. The figure defined in sharp relief against a dun background, like Clym against the settle or Mrs Yeobright against the
heath, or suddenly illuminated, Rembrandt-fashion, in a long shaft
of light (Marty at the window, Eustacia in the light from Susan
Nunsuch's cottage), suddenly fixes the moving characters through
the distancing of pictorial art as eternal tableaux of the littleness of
conscious human experience in the surrounding darkness. (Alastair
Smart, 'Pictorial Imagery in the Novels of Thomas Hardy', *Review
of English Studies*, XII, 1961.) As Cytherea's father falls to his death
from the tower, shafts of light falling across the room become for her
an objective correlative of tragedy. The essential nature of Arabella

and her opposite Sue Bridehead is caught in the framed picture of Delilah and the comparison of Sue to a Parthenon frieze. When the heart and inner meaning has thus been established in a frozen image, it dissolves once more into the drama of people in motion acting out that reality, leaving the reader with a new perspective of their place in the cosmic scheme. . . .

SOURCE: *Thomas Hardy: The Poetic Structure* (1971), pp. 10–23.

Raymond Williams 'The Educated Observer and the Passionate Participant' (1970)

The Hardy country is of course Wessex: that is to say mainly Dorset and its neighbouring counties. But the real Hardy country, I feel more and more, is that border country so many of us have been living in: between custom and education, between work and ideas, between love of place and an experience of change. This has a special importance to a particular generation, who have gone to the university from ordinary families and have to discover, through a life, what that experience means. But it has also a much more general importance; for in Britain generally this is what has been happening: a moving out from old ways and places and ideas and feelings; a discovery in the new of certain unlooked-for problems, unexpected and very sharp crises, conflicts of desire and possibility.

In this characteristic world, rooted and mobile, familiar yet newly conscious and self-conscious, the figure of Hardy stands like a landmark. It is not from an old rural world or from a remote region that Hardy now speaks to us; but from the heart of a still active experience, of the familiar and the changing, which we can know as an idea but which is important finally in what seem the personal pressures – the making and failing of relationships, the crises of physical and mental personality – which Hardy as a novelist at once describes and enacts.

But of course we miss all this, or finding it we do not know how to speak of it and value it, if we have picked up, here and there, the tone of belittling Hardy.

I want to bring this into the open. Imagine if you will the appearance and the character of the man who wrote this: 'When the ladies retired to the drawing-room I found myself sitting next to Thomas Hardy. I remember a little man with an earthy face. In his evening clothes, with his boiled shirt and high collar, he had still a strange look of the soil.' Not the appearance and the character of Thomas Hardy; but of the man who could write that about him, that confidently, that sure of his readers, in just those words.

It is of course Somerset Maugham, with one of his characteristic tales after dinner. It is a world, one may think, Hardy should never have got near; never have let himself be exposed to. But it is characteristic and important, all the way from that dinner-table and that drawing-room to the 'look of the soil', in that rural distance. All the way to the land, the work, that comes up in silver as vegetables, or to the labour that enters that company – that customary civilised company – with what is seen as an earthy face.

In fact I remember Maugham, remember his tone, when I read Henry James on 'the good little Thomas Hardy', or F. R. Leavis saying that *Jude the Obscure* is impressive 'in its clumsy way'. For in several ways, some of them unexpected, we have arrived at that place where custom and education, one way of life and another, are in the most direct and interesting and I'd say necessary conflict.

The tone of social patronage, that is to say, supported by crude and direct suppositions about origin, connects interestingly with a tone of literary patronage and in ways meant to be damaging with a strong and directing supposition about the substance of Hardy's fiction. If he was a countryman, a peasant, a man with the look of the soil, then this is the point of view, the essential literary standpoint, of the novels. That is to say the fiction is not only about Wessex peasants, it is by one of them, who of course had managed to get a little (though hardly enough) education. Some discriminations of tone and fact have then to be made.

First, we had better drop 'peasant' altogether. Where Hardy lived and worked, as in most other parts of England, there were virtually no peasants, although 'peasantry' as a generic word for country people was still used by writers. The actual country people were landowners, tenant farmers, dealers, craftsmen and labourers, and that social structure – the actual material, in a social sense, of the novels – is radically different, in its variety, its shading, and many of its basic human attitudes from the structure of a peasantry. Secondly, Hardy is none of these people. Outside his writing he was one of the many professional men who worked within this structure, often with uncertainty about where they really belonged in it. A slow gradation of classes is characteristic of capitalism anywhere, and of rural capitalism very clearly. Hardy's father was a builder who employed six or seven workmen. Hardy did not like to hear their house referred to as a cottage, because he was aware of this employing situation. The house is indeed quite small but there is a little window at the back through which the men were paid, and the cottages down the lane are certainly smaller. At the same time, on his walk to school, he would see the mansion of Kingston Maurward (now happily an agricultural college) on which his father did some of the estate work, and this showed a sudden difference of degree which made the other distinction comparatively small though still not unimportant. In becoming an architect and a friend of the family of a vicar (the kind of family, also, from which his wife came) Hardy moved to a different point in the social structure, with connections to the educated but not the owning class, and yet also with connections through his family to that shifting body of small employers, dealers, craftsmen and cottagers who were themselves never wholly distinct, in family, from the labourers. Within his writing his position is similar. He is neither owner nor tenant, dealer nor labourer, but an observer and chronicler, often again with uncertainty about his actual relation. Moreover he was not writing for them, but about them, to a mainly metropolitan and unconnected literary public. The effect of these two points is to return attention to where it properly belongs, which is Hardy's attempt to describe and value a way of life with which he was closely yet uncertainly connected, and the literary methods which follow from the nature of this attempt. And so often when the current social stereotypes are removed the critical problem becomes clear in a new way.

It is the critical problem of so much of English fiction, since the actual yet incomplete and ambiguous social mobility of the nineteenth century. And it is a question of substance as much as of method. It is common to reduce Hardy's fiction to the impact of an urban alien on the 'timeless pattern' of English rural life. Yet though this is sometimes there the more common pattern is the relation between the changing nature of country living, determined as much

by its own pressures as by pressures from 'outside', and one or more
characters who have become in some degree separated from it yet
who remain by some tie of family inescapably involved. It is here
that the social values are dramatised in a very complex way and it is
here that most of the problems of Hardy's actual writing seem to arise.

   One small and one larger point may illustrate this argument, in a
preliminary way. Nearly everyone seems to treat Tess as simply the
passionate peasant girl seduced from outside, and it is then surprising to read quite early in the novel one of the clearest statements
of what has become a classical experience of mobility: 'Mrs.
Durbeyfield habitually spoke the dialect; her daughter, who had
passed the Sixth Standard in the National School under a London-
trained mistress, spoke two languages: the dialect at home, more or
less; ordinary English abroad and to persons of quality.' Grace in
The Woodlanders, Clym in *The Return of the Native* represent this
experience more completely, but it is in any case a continuing
theme, at a level much more important than the trivialities of accent.
And when we see this we need not be tempted, as so often and so
significantly in recent criticism, to detach *Jude the Obscure* as a quite
separate kind of novel.

   A more remarkable example of what this kind of separation means
and involves is a description of Clym in *The Return of the Native*
which belongs in a quite central way to the argument I traced in
Culture and Society: 'Yeobright loved his kind. He had a conviction
that the want of most men was knowledge of a sort which brings
wisdom rather than affluence. He wished to raise the class at the
expense of individuals rather than individuals at the expense of the
class. What was more, he was ready at once to be the first unit
sacrificed.' The idea of sacrifice relates in the whole action to the
familiar theme of a vocation thwarted or damaged by a mistaken
marriage, and we shall have to look again at this characteristic Hardy
deadlock. But it relates also to the general action of change which is
a persistent social theme. As in all major realist fiction the quality
and destiny of persons and the quality and destiny of a whole way of
life are seen in the same dimension and not as separable issues. It is
Hardy the observer who sets this context for personal failure:

In passing from the bucolic to the intellectual life the intermediate stages are
usually two at least, frequently many more; and one of these stages is sure to
be worldly advance. We can hardly imagine bucolic placidity quickening to

intellectual aims without imagining social aims as the transitional phase. Yeobright's local peculiarity was that in striving at high thinking he still cleaved to plain living – nay, wild and meagre living in many respects, and brotherliness with clowns. He was a John the Baptist who took ennoblement rather than repentance for his text. Mentally he was in a provincial future, that is, he was in many points abreast with the central town thinkers of his date. ... In consequence of this relatively advanced position, Yeobright might have been called unfortunate. The rural world was not ripe for him. A man should be only partially before his time; to be completely to the vanward in aspirations is fatal to fame. ... A man who advocates aesthetic effort and deprecates social effort is only likely to be understood by a class to which social effort has become a stale matter. To argue upon the possibility of culture before luxury to the bucolic world may be to argue truly, but it is an attempt to disturb a sequence to which humanity has been long accustomed.

The subtlety and intelligence of this argument from the late 1870s come from a mind accustomed to relative and historical thinking, not merely in the abstract but in the process of observing a personal experience of mobility. This is not country against town, or even in any simple way custom against conscious intelligence. It is the more complicated and more urgent historical process in which education is tied to social advancement within a class society, so that it is difficult, except by a bizarre personal demonstration, to hold both to education and to social solidarity ('he wished to raise the class'). It is the process also in which culture and affluence come to be recognised as alternative aims, at whatever cost to both, and the wry recognition that the latter will always be the first choice, in any real history (as Morris also observed and indeed welcomed).

The relation between the migrant and his former group is then exceptionally complicated. His loyalty drives him to actions which the group can see no sense in, its overt values supporting the association of education with personal advancement which his new group has already made but which for that very reason he cannot accept.

'I am astonished, Clym. How can you want to do better than you've been doing?'

'But I hate that business of mine. ... I want to do some worthy things before I die.'

'After all the trouble that has been taken to give you a start, and when there is nothing to do but keep straight on towards affluence, you say you ...

it disturbs me, Clym, to find you have come home with such thoughts. . . . I
hadn't the least idea you meant to go backward in the world by your own
free choice. . . .'

'I cannot help it,' said Clym, in a troubled tone.

'Why can't you do . . . as well as others?'

'I don't know, except that there are many things other people care for
which I don't. . . .'

'And yet you might have been a wealthy man if you had only persevered.
. . . I suppose you will be like your father. Like him, you are getting weary of
doing well.'

'Mother, what is doing well?'

The question is familiar but still after all these years no question is
more relevant or more radical. Within these complex pressures the
return of the native has a certain inevitable nullity, and his only
possible overt actions can come to seem merely perverse. Thus
the need for social identification with the labourers produces Clym's
characteristic negative identification with them; becoming a labourer
himself and making his original enterprise that much more difficult:
'the monotony of his occupation soothed him, and was in itself a
pleasure'.

All this is understood and controlled by Hardy but the pressure
has further and less conscious effects. Levin's choice of physical
labour, in *Anna Karenina*, includes some of the same motives but in
the end is a choosing of people rather than a choosing of an abstract
Nature – a choice of men to work with rather than a natural force in
which to get lost. This crucial point is obscured by the ordinary
discussion of Hardy's attachment to country life, which would run
together the 'timeless' heaths or woods and the men working
together on them. The original humanist impulse – 'he loved his
kind' – can indeed become anti-human: men can be seen as
creatures crawling on this timeless expanse, as the imagery of the
heath and Clym's work on it so powerfully suggests. It is a very
common transition in the literature of that period but Hardy is never
very comfortable with it, and the original impulse, as in *Jude the
Obscure*, keeps coming back and making more precise identifica-
tions.

At the same time the separation of the returned native is not only
a separation from the standards of the educated and affluent world
'outside'. It is also to some degree inevitably from the people who
have not made his journey; or more often a separation which can

mask itself as a romantic attachment to a way of life in which the people are merely instrumental: figures in a landscape or when the literary tone fails in a ballad. It is then easy, in an apparently warm-hearted way, to observe for the benefit of others the crudity and limitations but also the picturesqueness, the rough humour, the smocked innocence of 'the bucolic'. The complexity of Hardy's fiction shows in nothing more than this: that he runs the whole gamut from an external observation of customs and quaintnesses, modulated by a distinctly patronising affection (as in *Under the Greenwood Tree*), through a very positive identification of intuitions of nature and the values of shared work with human depth and fidelity (as in *The Woodlanders*), to the much more impressive but also much more difficult humane perception of limitations, which cannot be resolved by nostalgia or charm or an approach to mysticism, but which are lived through by all the characters, in the real life to which all belong, the limitations of the educated and the affluent bearing an organic relation to the limitations of the ignorant and the poor (as in parts of *Return of the Native* and in *Tess* and *Jude*). But to make these distinctions and to see the variations of response with the necessary clarity we have to get beyond the stereotypes of the autodidact and the countryman and see Hardy in his real identity: both the educated observer and the passionate participant, in a period of general and radical change....

*   *   *

The complication is that this is a very difficult and exposed position for Hardy to maintain. Without the insights of consciously learned history and of the educated understanding of nature and behaviour he cannot really observe at all, at a level of extended human respect. Even the sense of what is now called the 'timeless' – in fact the sense of history, of the barrows, the Roman remains, the rise and fall of families, the tablets and monuments in the churches – is a function of education. That real perception of tradition is available only to the man who has read about it, though what he then sees through it is his native country, to which he is already deeply bound by memory and experience of another kind: a family and a childhood; an intense association of people and places, which has been his own history. To see tradition in both ways is indeed Hardy's special gift: the native place and experience but also the education, the conscious inquiry. Yet then to see living people, within this complicated sense of past and present, is another problem again. He sees as a participant who is also an observer; this is the source of the strain. For the process which allows him to observe is very clearly in Hardy's time one which includes, in its attachment to class feelings and class separations, a decisive alienation.

If these two noticed Angel's growing social ineptness, he noticed their growing mental limitations. Felix seemed to him all Church; Cuthbert all College. His Diocesan Synod and Visitations were the mainsprings of the world to the one; Cambridge to the other. Each brother candidly recognized that there were a few unimportant scores of millions of outsiders in civilized society, persons who were neither University men nor Churchmen; but they were to be tolerated rather than reckoned with and respected.

This is what is sometimes called Hardy's bitterness, but in fact it is only sober and just observation. What Hardy sees and feels about the educated world of his day, locked in its deep social prejudices and in its consequent human alienation, is so clearly true that the only surprise is why critics now should still feel sufficiently identified with that world – the world which coarsely and coldly dismissed Jude and millions of other men – to be willing to perform the literary equivalent of that stalest of political tactics: the transfer of bitterness, of a merely class way of thinking, from those who exclude to those who protest. We did not after all have to wait for Lawrence to be shown the human nullity of that apparently articulate world. Hardy shows it convincingly again and again. But the isolation which then follows, while the observer holds to educated procedures but is unable to feel with the existing educated class, is severe. It is not the countryman awkward in his town clothes but the more significant tension – of course with its awkwardness and its spurts of bitterness and nostalgia – of the man caught by his personal history in the general structure and crisis of the relations between education and class, relations which in practice are between intelligence and fellow-feeling. Hardy could not take the James way out, telling his story in a 'spirit of intellectual superiority' to the 'elementary passions'. As he observes again of the Clare brothers: 'Perhaps, as with many men, their opportunities of observation were not so good as their opportunities of expression.' That after all is the nullity, in a time in which education is used to train members of a class and to divide them from other men as surely as from their own passions (for the two processes are deeply connected). And yet there could be no simple going back.

They had planted together, and together they had felled; together they had, with the run of the years, mentally collected those remoter signs and symbols which seen in few are of runic obscurity, but all together made an alphabet. From the light lashing of the twigs upon their faces when brushing through them in the dark, they could pronounce upon the species of tree whence they stretched; from the quality of the wind's murmur through a bough, they could in like manner name its sort afar off.

This is the language of the immediate apprehension of 'nature', for in that form, always, Hardy could retain a directness of communication. But it is also more specifically the language of shared work, in 'the run of the years', and while it is available as a memory, the world which made it possible is, for Hardy, at a distance which is already enough to detach him: a closeness, paradoxically, that he is still involved with but must also observe and 'pronounce upon'. It is in this sense finally that we must consider Hardy's fundamental attitudes to the country world he was writing about. The tension is not between rural and urban, in the ordinary senses, nor between an abstracted intuition and an abstracted intelligence. The tension, rather, is in his own position, his own lived history, within a general process of change which could come clear and alive in him because it was not only general but in every detail of his feeling observation and writing immediate and particular.

Every attempt has of course been made to reduce the social crisis in which Hardy lived to the more negotiable and detachable forms of the disturbance of a 'timeless order'. But there was nothing timeless about nineteenth-century rural England. It was changing constantly in Hardy's lifetime and before it. It is not only that the next village to Puddletown is Tolpuddle, where you can look from the Martyrs' Tree back to what we know through Hardy as Egdon Heath. It is also that in the 1860s and 1870s, when Hardy was starting to write, it was what he himself described as 'a modern Wessex of railways, the penny post, mowing and reaping machines, union workhouses, lucifer matches, labourers who could read and write, and National school children'. Virtually every feature of this modernity preceded Hardy's own life (the railway came to Dorchester when he was a child of seven). The effects of the changes of course continued. The country was not timeless but it was not static either; indeed, it is because the change was long (and Hardy knew it was long) that the crisis took its particular forms.

We then miss most of what Hardy has to show us if we impose on the actual relationships he describes a pastoral convention of the countryman as an age-old figure, or a vision of a prospering countryside being disintegrated by Corn Law repeal or the railways or agricultural machinery. It is not only that Corn Law repeal and the cheap imports of grain made less difference to Dorset: a county mainly of grazing and mixed farming in which the coming of the railway gave a direct commercial advantage in the supply of milk to London: the economic process described with Hardy's characteristic accuracy in *Tess*:

> They reached the feeble light, which came from the smoky lamp of a little railway station; a poor enough terrestrial star, yet in one sense of more importance to Talbothays Dairy and mankind than the celestial ones to which it stood in such humiliating contrast. The cans of new milk were unladen in the rain, Tess getting a little shelter from a neighbouring holly tree....
> ... 'Londoners will drink it at their breakfasts tomorrow, won't they?' she asked. 'Strange people that we have never seen ... who don't know anything of us, and where it comes from; or think how we two drove miles across the moor tonight in the rain that it might reach 'em in time?'

It is also that the social forces within his fiction are deeply based in the rural economy itself: in a system of rent and trade; in the hazards of ownership and tenancy; in the differing conditions of labour on good and bad land and in socially different villages (as in the contrast between Talbothays and Flintcomb Ash); in what happens to people and to families in the interaction between general forces and personal histories – that complex area of ruin or survival, exposure or continuity. This is his actual society, and we cannot suppress it in favour of an external view of a seamless abstracted country 'way of life'.

It is true that there are continuities beyond a dominant social situation in the lives of a particular community (though two or three generations, in a still partly oral culture, can often sustain an illusion of timelessness). It is also obvious that in most rural landscapes there are very old and often unaltered physical features, which sustain a quite different time-scale. Hardy gives great importance to these, and this is not really surprising when we consider his whole structure of feeling. But all these elements are over-ridden, as for a novelist they must be, by the immediate and actual relationships between people, which occur within existing contemporary pressures and are at most modulated and interpreted by the available continuities.

The pressures to which Hardy's characters are subjected are then pressures from within the system of living, not from outside it. It is not urbanism but the hazard of small-capital farming that changes Gabriel Oak from an independent farmer to a hired labourer and then a bailiff. Henchard is not destroyed by a new and alien kind of dealing but by a development of his own trade which he has himself invited. It is Henchard in Casterbridge who speculates in grain as he had speculated in people; who is in every sense, within an observed way of life, a dealer and a destructive one; his strength compromised by that. Grace Melbury is not a country girl 'lured' by the fashionable world but the daughter of a successful timber merchant whose own social expectations, at this point of his success, include a fashionable education for his daughter. Tess is not a peasant girl seduced by the squire; she is the daughter of a lifeholder and small dealer who is seduced by the son of a retired manufacturer. The latter buys his way into a country house and an old name. Tess's father and, under pressure, Tess herself, are damaged by a similar process, in which an old name and pride are one side of the coin and the exposure of those subject to them the other. That one family fell and one rose is the common and damaging history of what had been happening, for centuries, to ownership and to its consequences in those subject to it. The Lady Day migrations, the hiring fairs, the intellectually arrogant parson, the casual gentleman farmer, the landowner spending her substance elsewhere: all these are as much parts of the country 'way of life' as the dedicated craftsman, the group of labourers and the dances on the green. It is not only that Hardy sees the realities of labouring work, as in Marty South's hands on the spars and Tess in the swede field. It is also that he sees the harshness of economic processes, in inheritance, capital, rent and trade, within the continuity of the natural processes and persistently cutting across them. The social process created in this interaction is one of class and separation, as well as of chronic insecurity, as this capitalist farming and dealing takes its course. The profound disturbances that Hardy records cannot then be seen in the sentimental terms of a pastoral: the contrast between country and town. The exposed and separated individuals, whom Hardy puts at the centre of his fiction, are only the most developed cases of a general exposure and separation. Yet they are never merely

illustrations of this change in a way of life. Each has a dominant
personal history, which in psychological terms bears a direct
relation to the social character of the change.

SOURCE: *The English Novel from Dickens to Lawrence* (1970) pp. 98–
   106, 109–15.

THE RETURN OF THE NATIVE

John Paterson An Attempt at Grand Tragedy (1966)

The Return of the Native has been ranked by some indulgent readers with *The Mayor of Casterbridge* and *Tess of the d'Urbervilles* and *Jude the Obscure*; but, for all its superficial impressiveness, it doesn't really belong in their distinguished company. Too studied and self-conscious an imitation of classical tragedy, it doesn't have their immediate reality, their powerful authenticity. In the ceremonial chapters of Egdon Heath and Eustacia Vye, in the set speeches and soliloquies of the heroine, in the novel's conscientious observation of the unities of time and space, in its organization (as originally planned) in terms of the five parts or 'acts' of traditional tragedy, *The Return of the Native* was meant to recall the immensities of Sophocles and Shakespeare. But the facts of its fiction simply do not justify the application of so grand, so grandiose, a machinery. Its men and women are seldom equal after all to the sublime world they are asked to occupy. In the Vyes and the Yeobrights, Hardy evidently intended a little aristocracy fit to bear the solemn burdens of tragedy. But they remain a species of stuffy local gentility and as such incapable of heroic transformations. Eustacia may justify the formidable frame of reference in which she is set, but to associate Clym, the translated shopkeeper, with the likes of Oedipus and Aeneas is to emphasize how far short of them he really falls. Mrs. Yeobright's identification with Lear – in her final agony she is equipped with a heath, a hovel and a fool – is perhaps more deserved, but it shows too visibly and seems only slightly less wilful than Clym's identification with heroes of classical fame. In the unfolding of her fate, money, her collection of precious guineas, surely plays a more crucial part than should consist with an action of Sophoclean or Shakespearean size. Even the death of the splendid Eustacia is in part determined by a shortage of funds.

The plot of the novel, then, lacks the terrific and terrifying logic of cause and effect that marks the plots of the greatest exercises in this line. That it operates the way it does is more accidental than necessary. If Diggory had known that half the guineas belonged to Clym, if Mrs. Yeobright's arrival at her son's house had not coincided with Wildeve's, if Eustacia had not mistakenly thought her husband awake, if she had received his letter or had had a few more pence in her purse, then the tragic disaster would not have taken place at all. The presence of the fateful and the inevitable is felt as little in the 'action' of the characters as in the action of the plot. Their motives for doing what they do, for contriving their own undoing, are often only specious and arbitrary and seem determined by the needs of a tyrannical plot. Diggory's sentimental motive for haunting the heath speaks well for his heart but may impress the reader as odd and even gratuitous. Eustacia's reasons for not at once opening the door to Mrs. Yeobright seem strained and dubious and even her reasons for doing herself in at the end are not wholly convincing. Hardy does manage on the whole to bring these things off, but not without arousing in the reader the uneasy sensation that he has had the narrowest of escapes, that all the time he has been skating on the thinnest of ice. The inexorability of its tragic development has seemed too often to express, in short, not the natural needs or necessities of the novel but the applied will or wilfulness of the author....

But *The Return of the Native* is better than its defects; it breathes a reality that its very manifest weaknesses are powerless to explain away. The sources of this reality are not easily identifiable. That they don't exist in Hardy's conceptions that are usually trite or clumsy or obvious is clear enough. That they don't exist in the raw materials he worked with, in that traditional stockpile of ruined maids, mysterious strangers, dashing soldiers and sailors, lovers faithful or faithless, dark-dyed villains, etc., is equally clear. Few readers briefed in advance on the plots and characters of *Far From the Madding Crowd, The Woodlanders, Tess of the d'Urbervilles, The Return of the Native*, would think them worth the trouble of a further exploration. Their matter would seem too thin or too poor or too simple-minded for artistic conversion. It is just here, though, that the sources of Hardy's power to chasten and subdue disclose themselves. It was in the life and imagination he brought with so much simple faith and fervour to his large but crude conceptions, to his rude but primitive images, that his power to persuade resides. In spite of the many excellent and obvious reasons for not believing in the experience of the novel, we do in the end believe in it because Hardy himself did. He wins our consent because what he records has been both closely observed and deeply felt....

In the end, however, the novel derives more from Hardy's imagination than from his observation and experience, so that the detail that provides its intensest and most vivid pages is better described as poetic than as realistic. Like Wordsworth, Hardy worked to transfigure the trivial and the commonplace, to make the ordinary extraordinary. The business of the artist was, he said, to make Nature's defects 'the basis of a hitherto unperceived beauty, by irradiating them with "the light that never was"...'. As the creatures of a tragic or symbolic or conceptual machinery, Hardy's people may sometimes fail at the purely realistic level, but because they are made to move as often as they are in an ambience of poetic beauty and wonder, these intermittent failures are not decisive. Images like Thomasin gathering holly boughs 'amid the glistening green and scarlet masses of the tree' or Eustacia unclosing her lips in a laugh 'so that the sun shone into her mouth as into a tulip and lent it a similar scarlet fire' exercise a chemical influence out of all proportion to their mass or quantity and have the effect of compensating for the novel's many flat and sandy moments. Even a character as tenuous and abstract as Clym can be quickened into vital life on occasion by the magic of Hardy's incandescent imagination as when 'the eclipsed moonlight shines upon [his] face with a strange foreign colour, and shows its shape as if it were cut out of gold'. The same transfiguring force enters the novel's individual scenes and episodes. Eustacia's voyage across the moonlit heath with the mummers, the weird nocturnal game of dice between Wildeve and the reddleman, the unearthly trancelike dance on the green at East Egdon – such radiant scenes as these have the power to cancel out the occasional lapses in the novel's plotting or causation. It was this power to change the ordinary stuff of reality into something rich and strange, this power to discover beneath the surface of ordinary life and being rare and mysterious states of life and being, that led D. H. Lawrence to discover in Hardy a brother under the skin.[1]

The same powerful imagination everywhere informs and transforms the novel. *The Return of the Native* can survive the defects of its plot because the plot as such all but disappears in the greater and more inclusive music of theme and imagery. Though its action scarcely qualifies as a tragic action, the novel does evoke, in its accumulating allusions to the geography, history and literature of classical antiquity, the heroic world out of which tragedy came and to this extent places the otherwise purely local or domestic action in a context that enlarges and enrichens. Variously described as the home of the Titans, as Dante's Limbo, as 'Homer's Cimmerian land', Egdon Heath can suggest the lightless underworld of the ancients. Representing the diminished consciousness of modern times, Clym's is explicitly contrasted with the heroic consciousness of Hardy's prelapsarian Greeks. Persistently identified with the legend and literature of antiquity, Eustacia, on the other hand, suggests the anachronistic and hence foredoomed revival of that consciousness. Her profile compares with Sappho's; she 'can utter oracles of Delphian ambiguity'; her dream has 'as many ramifications as the Cretan labyrinth'. In the most dazzling of her Mediterranean associations, she is established as the lineal descendant of Homeric kings, as the last of the house of Phaeacia's princely Alcinous.

What most energetically enters and irradiates the matter of *The Return of the Native*, however, is its Promethean theme and imagery. Clym and his Egdon Heath are specifically affiliated with the banished Titan, with the fallen benefactor of mankind; but it is the novel's fire imagery, by inference Promethean, that most fully asserts this primary motif. The darkness of the heath is thus disturbed, early in the novel, by fires that mark the anniversary of the Gunpowder Plot. Wildeve makes his presence known by releasing at Eustacia's window a moth that perishes in the flames of her candle. On the day Mrs. Yeobright dies, the universe of Egdon is imagined as almost literally in flames and her death is a symbolic death-by-fire: 'The sun ... stood directly in her face, like some merciless incendiary, brand in hand, waiting to consume her.' Eustacia herself will perish in the same fatal flames: burned in effigy by Susan Nunsuch and acting out the parable of Wildeve's moth-signal, she will hurl herself into 'the boiling caldron' of the weir. This theme affects not only the major imagery of action and setting but also the minor imagery of word and phrase. In Eustacia's presence, 'the revived embers of an old passion glowed clearly in Wildeve', who fancies himself victimized by 'the curse of inflammability'. 'A blaze of love, and extinction' Eustacia herself refers characteristically to 'a lantern glimmer of the same'. After first meeting Clym she is 'warmed with an inner fire' and she will later denounce Mrs. Yeobright 'with a smothered fire of feeling' and with 'scalding tears' trickling from her eyes.

At the very last, however, the source of the novel's 'felt' life or power is much more elusive, less accessible, than the chemistry of its language and imagery. That ultimate source can only approximately be identified as what Francis Fergusson would call its 'action', the sensitive inner movement or motion of its feeling. It may be difficult to accept, to believe in, the novel's rickety and arbitrarily directed plot; but it is not at all difficult to accept and believe in its 'action', the curve of the emotion that animates it and is the true shape of its 'felt' life. What eventually overcomes us is the tragic rhythm of the action as it moves in the experience of the chief characters through the phases first of purpose or will or desire, then of passion or suffering as what the characters intend or desire is resisted and defeated, and finally of perception or knowledge as they recognize the limits of their world and of their power to change it. If *The Return of the Native* does not rank with the greatest novels, it is because it fails, in the imagery of character and plot, to enact with full and confident power this tragic rhythm of action. But if it remains a good or nearly great novel, it is because it does enact, however imperfectly, this powerful and profoundly felt rhythm. . . .

The novel as Hardy initially conceived it was a very different novel from the one we now have. Now Mrs. Yeobright's niece and Clym's cousin, Thomasin was originally conceived as Mrs. Yeobright's daughter and Clym's sister. Now a witch in only the metaphorical sense, Eustacia was at first imagined as a witch in the more literal sense and, as such, was more malevolently the persecutor of a helpless Thomasin Yeobright than she now is. In the novel's present form, Thomasin leaves one morning with Wildeve to be married but returns that evening alone, hysterical and unmarried because the license produced by her husband-to-be has proved invalid. According to the original or provisional terms of the novel, however, Thomasin was to have lived with Wildeve for a week before discovering that the marriage ceremony, perhaps by her paramour's wilful and malicious design, had been illegal. Hardy's decision to abandon the original program of the novel was doubtless determined by editorial pressure, a pressure emanating probably from the offices of the *Cornhill Magazine* to whose editor, Leslie

Stephen, it was first shown. Responsible for the serial publication of
Far From the Madding Crowd and *The Hand of Ethelberta*, Stephen
had had already in the past to restrain Hardy's difficult and
dangerous imagination. 'I may be over particular,' he wrote in
connection with *The Hand of Ethelberta*, 'but I don't like the
suggestion of the very close embrace in the London churchyard.'
Now presented with *The Return of the Native* in an evidently
embryonic form, the editor felt called upon again to correct and
control his client. 'Though he liked the opening,' Hardy reported,
'he feared that the relations between Eustacia, Wildeve and Thomasin might develop into something "dangerous" for a family magazine, and he refused to have anything to do with it unless he could
see the whole.' Although *The Return of the Native* was eventually
serialized in *Belgravia*, not in the *Cornhill*, the anxious author was
evidently inspired by Stephen's serious misgivings to subject the
novel in its germinal form to the radical revision that resulted in the
version we now have.

The history of the novel's distortion under editorial pressure was
not to end with Hardy's separation from Stephen and the *Cornhill*.
His employers on the board of *Belgravia* could have been no more
liberal than his old employers had been. Though the opposition
between Christian and pre-Christian values is vital to the novel's
total effect, no specific denigration of the Christian religion was
permitted to enter the text. In such outlandish spots as Egdon,
Hardy planned to say, 'homage to nature, self-adoration, frantic
gaieties, fragments of Teutonic rites to divinities whose names are
forgotten, have in some way or other survived medieval Christianity'. Editorial tact prevailed, however, and the phrase 'medieval
Christianity' was subsequently neutralized to 'medieval doctrine'.
Even more damaging to the novel's free imaginative development
was the suppression of all references to lips and legs and bodies.
Though the force that brings Wildeve and Eustacia together is
manifestly other than spiritual or sentimental, no explicit indication
of its sexual character was permitted. These wicked lovers were not
to be granted even the small freedom of a kiss. 'You are a pleasant
lady to know,' Wildeve was at one time permitted to say, 'and I
daresay as sweet [to kiss] as ever – almost.' The dangerous infinitive
was rigorously removed, however, from the text of the manuscript.
Just as tyrannical was the public passion for the happy ending.
Hardy had intended, as he confessed in a footnote on page 473 of the

definitive edition of 1912, to conclude *The Return of the Native* with the fifth book: with the deaths of Wildeve and Eustacia, with the widowhood of Thomasin and the disappearance of the reddleman. He was forced by editorial policy, however, to add a sixth book: to arrange the marriage of a reconstructed reddleman and a rehabilitated widow and thus to dishonor his original intention.…

[But, Paterson says, it would be a mistake to exaggerate the effect of Hardy's "exposure to prudential editorial policy"; and he goes on to say:]

There's even a question whether the energetic moral censorship of the time really affected more than the superficies of the novel. It did make it difficult for Hardy to represent his men and women as sexual as well as social creatures. But it didn't prevent him from forcibly expressing the novel's crucial criticism of Christianity. No explicit condemnation of the religious establishment was, of course, permitted to appear at the surface of the novel. But the condemnation is not the less a condemnation because it is not explicit. Indeed, much of its power may derive from the accident that it was driven underground, that Hardy was compelled by the nature of the circumstances to dramatize indirectly, at the level of artistic suggestion, what he couldn't plainly say. Identified with a world not yet touched by the spectral hand of Christianity, Eustacia Vye reincarnated on the withered parish of Egdon Heath the larger and braver vision of the ancient Greeks. In her suffering and death she dramatizes the tragic humiliation, in a diminished world, of the heroic pre-Christian understanding of things. It doesn't surprise us, therefore, that though no longer literally the witch, that immemorial antagonist of the Christian faith, she remains that black creature in the figurative sense at least. Nor does it surprise that of all the parts in the mummers' play, she should draw precisely that of the antichrist, the Turkish Knight, who must, with ritual inexorability, suffer defeat and death at the hands of the Christian champion.

Eustacia stands in this in opposition to her husband, whose allegedly advanced views only thinly disguise the Christian champion. For if Clym consistently deceives himself and sometimes his creator, he doesn't deceive his mother, who correctly understands him as a missionary in disguise, or his wife, who associates him half-satirically with the Apostle Paul. Nor does he always deceive Hardy *either*, who sometimes exposes him to the most damaging ironies. Clym's theoretical and pious intelligence suffers, for example, when contrasted with the practical and instinctive intelligence of a still-unchristened peasant community very properly skeptical of his plans to improve it. "'Tis good-hearted of the young man', says one member of that community with a condescension that events will justify. 'But, for my part, I think he had better mind his own business.' The ironies at Clym's expense are especially trenchant at the novel's end where his denial of life in a spirit of Christian self-renunciation contrasts dramatically with the life-renewing rites both of Maypole-day and of Thomasin's marriage. Whether Hardy intended it or not – and it's hard to believe he didn't – Clym's theatrical conversion is reduced by the savage rites of spring and marriage to ludicrous terms.

As the unreconstructed reddleman, Diggory Venn was evidently meant to honor the stoic and realistic values of a pre-Christian way of life and, tacitly at least, to criticize the nicer, less permissive, values that come in with Christianity. Originally meant 'to have retained his isolated and weird character to the last, and to have disappeared mysteriously from his heath', he was to have symbolized the displacement by the Christian dispensation of that elusive and nearly demoniacal spirit of fen and forest that had found its last resting place on Egdon. Identified with Cain, with Ishmael, with Mephistopheles, he was to have stood with Eustacia Vye, and to a certain extent still stands with her, outside the pale of Christian salvation. For the novel's anti-Christian character, however, the members of the peasant community with their hearty celebration of the natural life and their instinctive distrust of the church are mainly responsible. Their performances derive, that is, from levels of thinking and feeling older than and antagonistic to the innovations of Christianity. The bonfires they build in their first appearance have their antecedents in a barbaric Druidical and Anglo-Saxon past. As mummers they reenact the old folk-play, the St. George play, whose Christian veneer scarcely conceals the pre-Christian fertility rite. As participants in the ancient ritual of Maypole-day, they celebrate a vitality older and stronger than Christianity. 'In name they were parishoners,' Hardy notes with evident satisfaction, 'but virtually they belonged to no parish at all.' Hardy's denigration of Christianity is perhaps most explicit in the ludicrous figure of Christian Cantle, the caricature of the Christian man. Dissociated from the pagan community with its profane celebration of natural joy and virtue, the pious Christian alone refrains from joining the mad, demoniacal measure about the Promethean bonfire of November 5. His physical decrepitude and sexual impotence – he's the man no woman will marry – stand out beside the life-worshipping vitality of Grandfer and Timothy and the rest of that lusty crew. And where he lives in constant terror of the sights and sounds of the savage heath, they, complete pagans that they are, feel perfectly at home in this grimmest of all possible worlds. Though the subversive, anti-Christian argument of *The Return of the Native* could not openly be asserted, it was and remains everywhere active beneath the novel's unassuming surface. Hardy may have been hampered in the exercise of his artistic will by the virulent censorship of the time, but he couldn't, it's clear, be stopped by it. If his strong and stubborn imagination couldn't have its will one way, it would have it another. . . .

SOURCE: from the Introduction to *The Return of the Native* (Harper & Row edition, 1966), reprinted here under the title 'An Attempt at Grand Tragedy'.

NOTE

1. D. H. Lawrence, 'Study of Thomas Hardy', in *Phoenix; The Posthumous Papers of D. H. Lawrence* (New York, 1936).

Peter J. Casagrande Son and Lover: The Dilemma of Clym Yeobright (1982)

. . . A novelist's responsibilities in his private relationships cannot be equated with his responsibilities as a writer without confusing the truth of life and the truth of fiction. The 'truth' that Hardy attempts to convey to us in such a novel as *The Return* has to be judged not by its historical accuracy but by its concreteness, its internal logic, and its inclusiveness as a criticism of life. The 'truth' that Hardy attempted to exhibit in *The Return* is the law of nature that he had

contended with from the beginning – that all is change and all
change decay – that, in social terms, 'You can't go home again.'
Thus homecoming and its attendant hope of personal and social
renewal must be seen as futile and destructive, even unnatural. But
what is most striking here is the way Hardy chose to shape this
second version of return. Not with the elements of pastoral romance,
as in *Under the Greenwood Tree*, not with the conventions of social
realism as in *The Hand of Ethelberta*, but in the pattern of classical
tragedy, with a natural setting both pervasive and articulate, he
traced – with probably Hamlet and Oedipus his chief analogues –
the struggle of a man much like himself to resolve conflicting
loyalties to his mother and his native place on the one hand, and to
his wife and the world beyond Egdon on the other. The wonder of
The Return when we see it emerging from such lesser predecessors as
Ethelberta and *Greenwood Tree* is the finish of its structure and the
daring of its vision. Hardy suddenly found it possible to cast private
experience in tragic form, and in doing so unleashed a devastatingly
critical self-portrait. He coolly diagnosed the cause of Clym's
nostalgia, showed the folly and destructiveness of it, then declared it
incurable. In so far as *The Return* is self-portraiture, it is unflinching
self-analysis and self-censure; at the same time, it implies acceptance of the incurable defective self and of that defective order of
things which both made it so and prevents its remedy.

On one level, Clym's return from Paris to Egdon is cultural drama
– his attempt, like Fancy's in *Greenwood Tree* and Grace Melbury's
in *The Woodlanders*, to regain his position among the people and
places of his childhood. He mingles with the heath folk, welcomes
the silences and shadows of Egdon, and even embraces the opportunity to work as a furze-cutter when partial blindness blocks his
plan to open a school for the rustics. Against his mother's, then his
wife's, strong protests he comes home to stay. He ends as the faithful
keeper of his mother's house and grave, and as a preacher of moral
homilies to uninterested rustic congregations. Though Clym returns
to stay, he cannot reinstate himself in the rural society that nurtured
him. The rustics of *The Return*, unlike the townsfolk of *Greenwood
Tree*, are narrow, rigid and unforgiving toward deserters. Fancy Day
is reassimilated (not without mutterings and bad omens); Clym is
kept apart and therefore fails in this aspect of his return. He fails as
well on a second, more potent, level of return – the psychodrama in
which he at once resubmits to and contests the power and influence

of his mother. This attempt to recover a prenatal quiescence and security – suggested perhaps in his 'death' and resurrection from the waters of the weir, and in his affection for the heath – fails disastrously; and Clym is left with what one critic has called 'a tender after-view of the oedipal conflict'. . . .

Soon after his arrival at Bloom's End on Christmas Eve, Clym begins the hopeless task of reintegration. With his mother he sponsors a Christmas party for the heath folk. A Christmas party is a feature of *Greenwood Tree* (I, chs 7, 8) and *The Woodlanders* (chs 9, 10) as well. In the former it is an occasion for comedy, as Dick and Farmer Shiner, both smitten with love for Fancy, vie for her favour. In the latter it is a tragi-comic moment, for Giles's awkward and homely preparations provoke laughter at the same time as they mark his utter alienation from Grace's refined ways. In *The Return*, the Christmas party (II, chs 4–6) is the occasion of the St George play, in which the tragic folly of Clym's return is indirectly conveyed. The St George ceremony originated in pagan ceremonies whose purpose was 'to secure the regeneration of earth, animals, and humans through sympathetic magic'; in keeping with this purpose, death and resurrection, the latter usually effected by a physician, were important themes in the play. In *The Return*, however, this traditional purpose is all but obliterated. Eustacia holds both mummers and mumming in contempt; she joins the ancient ceremony only so that she might come secretly into the presence of Clym. The mummers themselves are unenthusiastic; they play their parts with so little excitement that the reader wonders, with the narrator, 'why a thing that is done so perfunctorily, should be kept up at all' (II, ch. 4). This 'fossilized survival' is watched uncritically by Clym because it gratifies his romanticism, his love of the old for its own sake, and his nostalgia, his wish to recover an earlier, happier time in both his own life and the life of the race. Hardy's point seems to be that Clym's attempt to secure redemption through return is as foolishly atavistic as the attempt through the play to secure regeneration through sympathetic magic. Associated with Christ on the one hand and with modern reformist thought on the other, Clym may be seen in fact as analogous to the quack doctor (with 'his little bottle of alicampane') who appeared in all versions of the play. That is, Clym is the physician who cannot heal his own wounds, the reformer who neither reforms himself nor his people. The law of decay overwhelms him, just as it overwhelms all myths of regeneration.

In at least one instance, Clym's actions resemble those of the worshipper in primitive myth who tried to renew things through sympathetic magic and sacrifice. The primitive worshipper, writes Karl Young, 'fancied that by dressing himself in leaves and flowers, and by hanging such objects on trees, he could encourage the earth to re-clothe itself with verdure; or that by putting to death some representative of the principle of life and subsequently reviving him, he could bring about a repetition of this act on a comprehensive scale by the mighty forces that govern the physical world'. Clym, at the urging of nostalgia rather than religion, attempts a comparable renewal. He chooses Egdon and 'some rational occupation among the people I know best' over the idleness and vanity of the diamond trade in Paris. Later, in preparation for marriage and school-teaching he takes up residence in a lonely hut at Alderworth. When hard study partially blinds him, he puts on the rough clothes of a furze-cutter and appears, even to the discerning eye of his mother, as a denizen of the heath:

He appeared of a russet hue, not more distinguishable from the scene around than the green caterpillar from the leaf it feeds on. . . . The silent being who thus occupied himself seemed to be of no more account in life than an insect. He appeared as a mere parasite of the heath, fretting its surface in his daily labour as a moth frets a garment, entirely engrossed with its products, having no knowledge of anything in the world but fern, furze, lichens, and moss. (IV, ch. 6)

The man who as a boy had been 'so inwoven with the heath that . . . hardly anybody could look upon it without thinking of him' (III, ch. 1) returns to the heath to recover the springtime of his life by awakening some of his earliest sensations:

He was permeated with its scenes, with its substance, and with its odours. He might be said to be its product. His eyes had first opened thereon; with its appearance all the first images of his memory were mingled; his estimate of life had been coloured by it; his toys had been the flint knives and arrowheads which he found there, wondering why stones should 'grow' to such odd shapes; his flowers, the purple bells and yellow furze; his animal kingdom the snakes and croppers, his society, its human haunters. . . . He gazed upon the wide prospect as he walked, and was glad. (III, ch. 2)

The death of Mrs Yeobright as a result of the wholly unintentional collaboration of Clym, Wildeve, Christian and Diggory may suggest the primitive ritual of killing the king in order to guarantee the renewal of the community's vitality and welfare, for the resurrection of the dead king had been the most significant element of the myth and ritual pattern. But Mrs Yeobright's death no more brings renewal than Clym's return to Egdon brings reinstatement; in this hint at the dying king motif, as in the use of the St George play, the regenerative element must be discounted. Hardy cannot accommodate it to his sense of time, history and human consciousness as aspects of the deteriorative course of things. This same deteriorism governs the drama of guilt and sorrow, of thwarted restoration, that is always for Hardy an integral part of the story of return.

Books V and VI of *The Return* (excluding the reunion of Diggory and Thomasin that Hardy provided in his 1912 amendment) is a study in the irreparable at whose centre is a bewildered Clym trying to make amends to both his dead mother and his estranged wife. Clym has learned from Johnny Nunsuch that his mother died broken-hearted because she thought she had been turned away from Alderworth by Clym. He is staggered by the thought that the injury done her 'could never be rectified' (V, ch. 1). He now finds himself morally in the same blind alley in which he finds himself socially because he cannot return. He craves his mother's forgiveness; that is, he wants to be to her what he was before the incident at Alderworth and the quarrel at Bloom's End. This denied him, he cries out for an ultimate peace in death or at least for torture at the hand of God: 'If there is any justice in God let Him kill me now. He has nearly blinded me, but that is not enough. If he would only strike me with more pain I would believe in Him forever!' (V, ch. 1). When he learns that it was Eustacia who ignored Mrs Yeobright's knock at Alderworth, he turns on her in fury; but even his desire for revenge is cooled by devotion to his mother: 'Phew – I shall not kill you. . . . I did think of it; but – I shall not. That would be making a martyr of you, and sending you to where she is; and I would keep you away from her till the universe comes to an end' (V, ch. 3). He even echoes his mother's scandalous reason for rejecting Eustacia: his 'How could there be any good in a woman that everybody spoke evil of?' (V, ch. 3) echoes Mrs Yeobright's 'Good girls don't get treated as witches, even on Egdon' (III, ch. 2).

Clym simply cannot free himself from the oppressive influence of his mother and her values. Johnny Nunsuch's statement to him that his face at the moment he learns of Eustacia's 'guilt' is like Mrs

Yeobright's in her last anguish reunites Clym with his mother in a horribly ironic way: the two are fused, in the words of one critic, 'in a common expression; it is the mask of tragedy which Oedipus wore after his incestuous love of Jocasta was terminated'. In all of this Clym sacrifices his former luminousness of mind, derived from study of advanced ethical thought of his time, to his mother's jealous moralizing. He moves into her house at Bloom's End (a name itself suggestive of sterility and deterioration) to put it in order, for 'it had become a religion with him to preserve in good condition all that had lapsed from his mother's hands to his own' (V, ch. 6). His hope that Eustacia will return to him is less a loving gesture toward her than a fear that he had been too harsh with 'his mother's supplanter' (ibid.). He admits to Thomasin that a man can be 'too cruel to his mother's enemy', and he writes to Eustacia pleading unusual provocation and begging her to return to him. But chance, or honest error on the part of Captain Vye, conspires with his reluctance, and a reconciliation is thwarted. In any case, Clym's attempt to gain Eustacia's forgiveness is feeble in comparison with his desire for reinstatement with his mother. And neither Eustacia's death nor his own near-death and return to life in the weir alters this. For him there is no renewal, just the same mother-worship, conventional moralizing, and moral masochism ('My great regret is that for what I have done no man or law can punish me' – V, ch. 9). Clym's lapse into timid conventionality draws Hardy's special scorn: Clym is one of those, lacking in sternness, who hesitate 'to construct a hypothesis that shall . . . degrade a First Cause . . . and, even while they sit and weep by the waters of Babylon, invent excuses for the oppression which prompts their tears' (VI, ch. 2). He frequents his beloved heath because it is familiar, maternal, and thus the temporary solution for his frustrated yearning. He is moved toward marriage with Thomasin not by her mature and gentle loveliness but by the sight of flowers 'revived and restored by Thomasin to the state in which his mother had left them':

He recalled her [Thomasin's] conduct toward him throughout the last few weeks, when they had often been working together in the garden, just as they had formerly done when they were boy and girl under his mother's eye. (VI, ch. 1).

Years ago there had been in his mother's mind a great fancy about Thomasin and himself. It had not positively amounted to a desire, but it had always been a favourite dream. That they should be man and wife in good time, if the happiness of neither was endangered thereby, was the fancy in question. So that what course save one was there now left for any son who reverenced his mother's memory as Yeobright did? (VI, ch. 3)

Full of devotion to an idealized mother, Clym, both as a man and as a preacher, ends as a mother-obsessed son:

Yeobright sat down in one of the vacant chairs, and remained in thought a long time. His mother's old chair was opposite; it had been sat in that evening by those who had scarcely remembered it was there. But to Clym she was almost a presence there now as always. Whatever she was in other people's memories, in his she was the sublime saint whose radiance even his tenderness for Eustacia could not obscure. But his heart was heavy; that mother had *not* crowned him in the day of his espousals and in the day of the gladness of his heart. And the events had borne out the accuracy of her judgment, and proved the devotedness of her care. He should have heeded her for Eustacia's sake even more than for his own. 'It was all my fault,' he whispered. 'O, my mother, my mother! would to God that I could live my life again, and endure for you what you endured for me!' (VI, ch. 4)

His discourses to people were to be sometimes secular, and sometimes religious, but never dogmatic. . . . This afternoon the words were as follows: – 'And the king rose up to meet her, and bowed himself unto her, and sat down on his throne, and caused a seat to be set for the king's mother; and she sat on his right hand. Then she said, I desire one small petition of thee: I pray thee say me not nay. And the king said unto her, Ask on, my mother: for I will not say thee nay.' (V, ch. 4)

This might amount to little more than self-gratifying fantasy if Hardy did not make it quite clear that there is deadly error in Clym's idealized devotion, that both Mrs Yeobright's possessiveness and Clym's attachment to her are pernicious. He does this by making Mrs Yeobright the chief cause of the tragic mischief of the novel. Two years before Clym's arrival, she had opposed Venn's courtship of Thomasin on the grounds that as a farmer's son he was unworthy of her. She then offended Wildeve by publicly opposing his marriage to Thomasin, and Wildeve, a moody, sensitive man, gradually drifted into a 'revengeful intention' toward her – an intention that results in his ruthless appropriation of the Yeobright guineas from Christian. Venn's retrieval and misapplication of the same guineas leads directly to tragic misunderstanding and to Mrs

Yeobright's death. Even more important, Mrs Yeobright offends Eustacia by regarding her as a voluptuary and a witch. This angers Clym, and prepares the way for the break between Clym and Mrs Yeobright that culminates in her death, in Clym's break with Eustacia, in Eustacia's and Wildeve's deaths, and in Clym's inconsolable guilt and grief. In sum, Clym is blindly loyal to a destructively jealous mother who denies her children the freedom to grow toward independence. Though Mrs Yeobright is portrayed with some sympathy, the terrible results of her intrusiveness are not to be denied.

Hardy depicted the abnormality in Clym's attachment to his mother obliquely, through the personalities and circumstances of the other 'children' of the novel: Johnny Nunsuch, Susan Nunsuch's weirdly precocious son; and Christian Cantle, Grandfer Cantle's timid, childish son. Even the presence of Eustacia Clementine, the infant daughter of Thomasin and Wildeve, can be seen to be a comment on Clym's prolongation of childhood. Like Clym, Johnny is fatherless (at least, we hear nothing of a Mr Nunsuch) and the victim of jealous maternal attention; and, again like Clym, he comes under the direct influence of Eustacia. Susan Nunsuch, like Mrs Yeobright, believes Eustacia a witch and hates her for afflicting her son. Susan's revenge, with needle and wax effigy, is savage; Mrs Yeobright's, with slander, merely more subtle.

Hardy's purpose in likening Clym to Johnny is suggested by the nature of the two episodes in which Johnny is most prominent: the one in which he stokes the fire that Eustacia uses to signal Wildeve (I, ch. 6); the other in which he watches over Mrs Yeobright during her last moments of life (IV, ch. 6). Childhood, as represented in Johnny, is not a time of radiant, innocent joyfulness, but of fear, sadness, and even terror. In the episode with Eustacia he is the 'little slave' who feeds her signal fire: 'he seemed a mere automaton galvanized into moving and speaking by the wayward Eustacia's will'. Rewarded for his strange labours with a crooked sixpence, he traipses off across the dark heath, 'singing in an old voice a little song' to keep up his courage, only to meet the devilish-looking Venn, 'a sublimation of all the horrid dreams which had afflicted the juvenile spirit since imagination began' (I, ch. 9). Similarly, in his encounter with Mrs Yeobright we find him something other than a fearful naif. There is childlike naiveté only in his first questions to her: 'What have made you so down? Have you seen an ooser?' (IV,

ch. 6). Once aware that she is weaker than he, he becomes objective
and even censorious in a cruelly precocious way. To her reply to his
two questions – 'I have seen what's worse, a woman's face looking at
me through a window pane' – he responds,

> 'You must be a very curious woman to talk like that.'
>
> 'O no, not at all. . . . Most people who grow up and have children talk as I
> do. When you grow up your mother will talk as I do too.'
>
> [He replies] 'I hope she won't; because 'tis very bad to talk nonsense' (IV,
> ch. 6)

The boldness in Johnny's remarks seems hardly childlike. Nor does
his third question, which suggests that he takes some pleasure in her
pain:

> 'Why do you, every time you take a step, go like this?' The child in
> speaking gave to his motion the jerk and limp of an invalid.
>
> 'Because I have a burden that is more than I can bear.' . . .
>
> When she had seated herself he looked long in her face and said, 'How
> funny you draw your breath – like a lamb when you drive him till he's
> nearly done for. Do you always draw your breath like that?' (IV, ch. 6)

First a naive curiosity, then a mildly accusatory contempt, and
finally an oddly detached observation and imitation of her suffering
– but not a trace of instinctive sympathy and tenderness in this sad
boy of the heath. It is as if Johnny were acting on vengeful behalf of
all the other 'children' of the novel whom this mother has injured.
Though frightened at 'beholding misery in adult quarters hitherto
deemed impregnable', Johnny finds Mrs Yeobright's suffering somehow attractive. After bringing her a drink of water – in 'an old-
fashioned teacup . . . which she had preserved since her childhood,
and had brought with her today as a small present for Clym and
Eustacia' – he abandons her.

Why would Hardy have his reader look through the eyes of this
sad and at times unfeeling boy in his circumstances much like Clym
on these two important occasions? In other words, why is the boy
exposed to the working of Eustacia's passionate nature, then to the
anguish in death of Mrs Yeobright, the second experience making
him the bearer to Clym of Mrs Yeobright's bitter last words? There
seem to be several answers to this. Johnny is made the common
element in the encounter with Eustacia and with Mrs Yeobright

because Clym is suspended between the two women. To have the boy see and speak at these crucial moments is to convey, to some degree, the incurable boyishness in Clym, his older counterpart. In this way the reader can come to see that, just as Johnny responds to Eustacia and Mrs Yeobright, so the inextinguishable boy in Clym, that part of him that cannot grow to manhood, responds to them. Clym seems to understand Eustacia, especially the passionate Eustacia whose fire Johnny feeds in the dark of Mistover, as little as Johnny does. Johnny's fearfulness is in some ways Clym's. Johnny as representative of Clym's problematic relation to his mother is somewhat different. Johnny both censures Mrs Yeobright and ministers to her, and his ambivalence is the apt embodiment of Clym's mixed feelings about a mother who wants him to return to Paris, yet wants him to remain at home, though under her, not Eustacia's, influence. This complication of feelings is familiar to Johnny because it is *his* mother's as well. He has been well-groomed by the jealously protective Susan to play this strange part in Clym's story.

The chief function of this oblique portraiture – and it is central to what has been called the self-censuring impulse in the novel – is to point up Clym's folly in trying to regain the conditions of his boyhood at Bloom's End. Johnny's circumstances illustrate Hardy's deterioristic assumption in the novel, an assumption revealed in the remark that 'a long line of disillusive centuries' had permanently displaced the Hellenic 'zest for existence':

What the Greeks only suspected we know well; what their Aeschylus imagined our nursery children feel. The old-fashioned revelling in the general situation grows less and less possible as we uncover the defects of natural laws, and see the quandary that man is in by their operation. (III, ch. 1).

Though the contours of Clym's face bear witness to this 'new recognition', he does not see what it means for his attempt to find happiness by trying to recover the conditions of childhood. 'The old-fashioned revelling' – whether in the childhood of the race or in the childhood of the individual – is gone forever. Like Little Father Time in *Jude the Obscure*, Johnny is 'Age masquerading as Juvenility'; and, just as Father Time takes from Sue the hint of despair that leads to murder and suicide, Johnny echoes his mother's jealous hatred for Eustacia when he shatters Clym by repeating before him

Mrs Yeobright's last words: 'She said I was to say that I had seen her, and she was a broken-hearted woman and cast off by her son . . .' (IV, Ch. 8; cf. V, ch. 2).

Christian Cantle, the second of Clym's childish foils, is a mixture of timid piety, fetishism and sexual impotency. As fearful as Johnny of Diggory Venn, as bewildered as Johnny by Eustacia, Christian is in several ways as boyish as Johnny is 'aged', as bad a case of arrested development as Johnny is of premature growth. And, like Johnny, he is associated with Clym. Like Clym, Christian has lost one parent and is somewhat at odds with the other. The lusty Grandfer Cantle has as little regard for his son's fearfulness as Mrs Yeobright for Clym's loss of ambition. Christian works at Bloom's End as a factotum and seems a stepson of sorts to Mrs Yeobright, who entrusts him with the delivery to Clym and Thomasin of the family guineas, and with results as disastrous (for her) as in the case of her entrusting to Clym the future of the Yeobrights. Christian's superstitious beliefs suggest Clym's secularized faith: both are unstable mixtures of belief and impiety. Christian's childish fears of injury and of the dark, his constant concern for his own safety, suggest Clym's yearning for the security of childhood. Most striking, however, is the connection between Clym's asceticism – he reminds Eustacia of the Apostle Paul (IV, ch. 6) – and Christian's sexual impotency. Christian is 'the man no woman would marry, a faltering man, with reedy hair, no shoulders, and a great quantity of wrist and ankle beyond his clothes' (I, ch. 3). He is pathetically hopeful that he will find a mate, but women scorn him as a 'slack-twisted, slim-looking, maphrotight fool' (I, ch. 3). By his own admission, he is 'only the rames of a man, and no good for my race at all' (I, ch. 3). Biologically, he is apparently no man at all, for he is described as a 'wether', that is, as a male sheep castrated before it has reached sexual maturity. During the lively dancing of the rustics atop Rainbarrow in the novel's opening scenes, Christian – like Clym at the Christmas party and at the May Day proceedings – does not participate. Dancing – as can be seen in the description of the May dance in which Eustacia and Wildeve join at one point (IV, ch. 3) – is a highly charged event in this novel (see below). Christian refrains from dancing because he believes ''tis tempting the Wicked One' to dance (I, ch. 3). It seems more likely that he is emotionally unequal to dancing, for as a close look at the episode involving the transfer of the guineas suggests, Christian is neither a mere fool nor an expression of Hardy's anti-Christian attitudes. He is the instrument of Hardy's carefully contrived attempt to show that sexual immaturity, perhaps even sexual impotency, is an important element in Clym's character.

Christian, already identified as 'no man', as a 'maphrotight [hermaphrodite] fool', and as a 'wether', is entrusted by Mrs Yeobright with the delivery of the Yeobright family guineas to Clym and Thomasin during the wedding celebration at Mistover, which Mrs Yeobright refuses to attend. On the way to Mistover, Christian meets Fairway and the others and is persuaded to go with them to the raffling of a woman's gown-piece. Christian joins in even though, as Fairway says, he's 'got no young woman nor wife . . . to give a gown-piece to' (III, ch. 7). Christian rolls the dice and wins the gown-piece:

'Mine?' asked Christian. '. . . What shall I do wi' a woman's clothes in my bedroom!' 'Keep 'em to be sure', said Fairway. '. . . Perhaps 'twill tempt some woman that thy poor carcase had no power over when standing empty-handed.' (III, ch. 7)

Pleased with the thought of attracting a woman, Christian handles the lucky dice 'fondly', and marvels at the possible 'power that's in me of multiplying money'. He asks to be allowed to keep 'them wonderful little things that carry my luck inside 'em', and leaves the raffle with Wildeve, shaking the dice in his pocket as he walks. When he loses the Yeobright family guineas to Wildeve he cries, 'The devil will toss me into the flames of his three-pronged fork for this night's work, I know! But perhaps I shall win yet, and then I'll get a wife to sit up with me o' nights, and I won't be afeard, I won't.' Christian's excitement at winning the frock-piece, his feeling that virility can somehow be secured in the form of a pair of dice, is surely related to the earlier description of him as a wether, a creature deprived of testes and therefore of the 'power . . . of multiplying'. And the intense concern with the family guineas to be delivered to Clym at his wedding celebration may be a broadly humorous reference to the phrase the 'family jewels', slang for a man's, particularly a husband's, testes, called jewels because they have inherent value as the source of new life and the guarantee of the family's future. This possibility is not contradicted by the fact that, after Christian loses the guineas to Wildeve, it is Wildeve and Diggory who vie for the guineas, just as they vie for the hand of Thomasin. It is in them, Thomasin's husbands, that the future of the Yeobrights lies. They, not Clym, who will lose Eustacia to Wildeve, and certainly not Christian, are the active, successful males in this veiled sexual combat.

Something like Christian's deprivation — more psychic than physical, perhaps — seems to be at the root of the trouble between Clym and Eustacia. It is important to note that Clym's blindness, described as the result of hard study, occurs soon after Clym learns from Eustacia that she and his mother have quarrelled and cannot be reconciled. To that point, a loving Clym and his passionate wife had lived in something like perfect reciprocity (IV, ch. 1). But Eustacia's insistence that they must move to Paris because she can never see Mrs Yeobright again is soon followed by Clym's blindness, 'an acute inflammation induced by ... night studies'. Clym's affliction may well be taken to suggest an emotional paralysis brought on by the thought of separation from his mother and the heath, for shortly after this we find Eustacia depressed and apathetic, so hungry for gaiety that she visits a village dance, where she meets Wildeve and dances with him to 'the lusty music of the East Egdon band':

Through the length of five-and-twenty couples they threaded their giddy way, and a new vitality entered her form. . . . There is a certain degree and tone of light which tends to disturb the equilibrium of the senses, and to promote dangerously the tenderer moods . . . and this light now fell upon these two from the disc of the moon. All the dancing girls felt the symptoms, but Eustacia most of all. . . . Eustacia floated round and round on Wildeve's arm, her face rapt and statuesque. . . . Her beginning to dance had been like a change of atmosphere; outside, she had been steeped in arctic frigidity by comparison with the tropical sensations here. She had entered the dance from the troubled hours of her late life as one might enter a brilliant chamber after a night walk in a wood. (IV, ch. 3).

The language and tone of this passage can hardly be intended to convey only Eustacia's relief from her disappointment with Clym's refusal to take her to Paris. Dancing with Wildeve, in all likelihood a partner in earlier sexual liaisons, is for her a ritualized form of intercourse, just as it is for many of the other dancers (enjoying 'impassioned but temporary embraces'), and she seeks it here and with Wildeve because 'the full flush of her love for Clym' is no longer reciprocated. By flanking Clym with the immature Christian and the 'mature' Johnny and showing something of him in both, Hardy subtly and effectively conveys the sexual incompleteness of Clym, the failure in him of psychological and perhaps physical development that is in part the emotional cause of his desire to return to heath, home and mother. Clym is tragically suspended between mother and wife because he is emotionally suspended between manhood and boyhood. That this may reflect in some ways Hardy's sense of his own physical and psychological make-up can be inferred from the remark in the *Life* (p. 32) that 'a clue to much of his character and action throughout his life is afforded by his lateness of development in virility, while mentally precocious'.

The birth to Thomasin of Wildeve's child (named Eustacia Clementine) at the moment of Clym's break with Eustacia (V, ch. 3) suggests – given the stability and purposiveness that follows for Thomasin – that a child might have brought peace and harmony to Eustacia, to Clym, and even to Mrs Yeobright. Perhaps Eustacia could have found in a child some of the promise of her dreams, Clym some of the glory and gleam of his lost childhood, Mrs Yeobright a new focus for her powerful maternal instincts. Certainly a great point is made of Thomasin's intense and tender love for the infant, which is seen as a fragile, vulnerable thing to be protected and cuddled. The description of it as a precious object protected by many layers of blankets – making it appear 'as the kernel to the husks' (V, ch. 8) – suggests again Hardy's view that infancy is to maturity as life is to death. During the frenzied activity around the weir, with such deadly results for Clym, Eustacia and Wildeve, the infant Eustacia Clementine is present, but held tenderly and lovingly (aloft at one memorable point) as if she were an emblem of the promises never kept, the hopes never realized by the frantic adults who thrash about in darkness and confusion.

In Thomasin, however, in Wildeve's wife and the mother of the child, is enshrined something like normality. Hardy's first description of her – as she returns in despair from her botched marriage to Wildeve – tells all:

Captain Vye: 'You have a child there, my man?'
Diggory: 'No, sir, I have a woman.' (I, ch. 2)

Thomasin is a woman, a mature person, and not a child, because, though she returns in Venn's cart in near-disgrace, she does not, like Clym, attempt to remedy her misfortune by turning back the clock.

It should be noted that her return to Egdon and Bloom's End precedes Clym's in the novel; she too is a returning native, and her stoic acceptance of change and determination to make the best of a bad thing is a silent comment on Clym's confused nostalgia. Thomasin accepts Wildeve's grim and self-serving (but in Hardy's view sound) opinion that life in actuality is never so 'pretty and sweet' as it is hoped it will be (I, ch. 5). And most important, in a novel filled with vengeful acts, Thomasin alone works persistently to make amends – by marrying Wildeve in spite of the first embarrassing error, by urging Mrs Yeobright to settle her differences with Clym and Eustacia, and, finally, by marrying Venn. She counsels Clym against excessive remorse over his mother's death and urges him to make it up with Eustacia. She is 'a practical woman' because – like Cytherea Graye, like Gabriel Oak, and like Ethelberta Petherwin – she can set aside self-interest and regret. 'I don't believe in hearts at all', she cries when, having swallowed her offended feelings, she returns to the moody Wildeve (II, ch. 8). Because she is not governed, like Clym, by a dream of lost felicity, or, like Eustacia, by a vision of future gaiety, a purity and sweetness of spirit are somehow always visible beneath her sadness (IV, ch. 3). By acceding to the law of change-as-decay, by countering it with forgiveness, she keeps a firm hold on the fading ideal and in a way recaptures it in the form of her child, named, ironically, after two frustrated idealists. Because Thomasin accepts what she cannot alter, sad experience rubs off 'nothing of the bloom' (IV, ch. 3). She leaves the house named Bloom's End when Clym takes up residence there. The epitomy of womanhood and maturity, she is the novel's chief symbol of renewal, a living rebuke to all truncated myths of regeneration, and a clear contrast with Clym's uncertain waverings between juvenility and age. But her place is not at the novel's tragic centre; she is the heroine of the novel's comic subplot, belatedly elevated.

If *The Return* is in any way a penetrating portrait of the artist or a profound criticism of life, it is because it is, as suggested earlier, a trenchant self-criticism. Clym is the victim of Hardy's irony. In both the first and the second conclusion of the novel, he is portrayed as a failure. He has failed in his ostensible purpose for returning – to improve the Egdonites and restore himself to a simpler, more joyous life. He has failed to see in marriage to Eustacia the opportunity to rediscover and renew, in a form appropriate to a man of thirty-three, the happiness he knew as a boy. His plight is complicated, of course, by Eustacia's being as desperate a dreamer as he, a dreamer moreover (of future rather than past dreams) who looks to him to fulfil her yearning. His willingness to defy his mother for a time proves that his love for Eustacia is genuine, and even after his mother's death, when he knows that Eustacia has erred, he has it in his power to forgive her and thus to preserve in their love a higher version of his lost childhood joy. But character (his guilt and nostalgia) and chance (the misdirected letter to Eustacia, the circumstances that prevent his mother's entering at Alderworth) block forgiveness and reconciliation. This is perhaps the bitterest fact of all – that forces beyond his control *both* within and without himself prevent him from forgiving Eustacia and thus from somehow countering the mutative process that blocks his attempt to go home again. To have forgiven Eustacia would have been, in a moral sense, to have granted her the foretime, to have reinstated her and himself to a semblance of that blissful time – a time of higher innocence and re-enactment of original innocence – before the door closed against Mrs Yeobright, the time of the Alderworth idyll (IV, ch. 1). But Clym cannot forgive because he cannot temper or uproot his fierce devotion to his mother and his boyhood home. And Mrs Yeobright's quarrel with Eustacia and her sudden death only serve to convince him that his deepest devotion is to his mother. This fatal fixity is the target of the novel's second conclusion, in which all – Diggory's transformation from devilish reddleman to respectable farmer, Thomasin's girlish enthusiasm, the May festivities, the budding child, the marriage ceremony – suggests that for them at least an earlier, happier time has been recovered, even if only illusively. 'Illusively' because this is truly an image of higher innocence, in which there is no denial that things are *not* as they were. The second ending of *The Return* offers an image of restoration amidst decay, but not for or through Clym Yeobright, whose virulent nostalgia blinds him to 'the inevitable movement onward' and makes him a moral failure, a man unable to forgive.

SOURCE: Extract from *Unity in Hardy's Novels* (Macmillan, London, 1982), pp. 127–143.

Robert C. Schweik Character and Fate in *The Mayor of Casterbridge* (1966)

Perhaps the most compelling evidence of really fundamental inconsistencies in *The Mayor of Casterbridge* is to be found, not in those analyses intended to show that the novel is seriously flawed,[1] but in the startlingly divergent interpretations proposed by critics who have attempted to discover some underlying consistency in Hardy's treatment of the relationship of Henchard's character to his fate. Two recent discussions of *The Mayor of Casterbridge* exemplify the almost polar extremes to which this divergence can tend: as John Paterson has interpreted the novel, Henchard is a man guilty of having violated a moral order in the world and thus brings upon himself a retribution for his crime; but, on the other hand, as *The Mayor of Casterbridge* has been explicated by Frederick Karl, Henchard is an essentially good man who is destroyed by the chance forces of a morally indifferent world upon which he has obsessively attempted to impose his will.[2] The fact is that *The Mayor of Casterbridge* is capable of supporting a variety of such conflicting assessments both of Henchard's character and of the world he inhabits, and further discussion of the novel must proceed, I think, by giving this fact more serious attention. Hardy strenuously insisted that both as novelist and as poet he dealt with 'impressions' and made no attempt at complete consistency;[3] what is worth considering is whether or not Hardy put his inconsistency to any use and what, if any, advantage he may have gained by doing so.

The sacrifice of simple consistency in fiction can yield some important compensations, particularly in the freedom it allows a novelist to manipulate detail and aspect as a means of controlling and shifting reader attitude as the work progresses. It is possible to make a rhetorical use of elements whose implications will not add up to a logically consistent whole. Clearly such a rhetoric can serve the imaginative purpose of the novel if it is arranged to generate an initial image of life which is then altered by subsequent changes in the handling of character and event, and when the progress of the whole is such as to move the reader from one way of looking at things to another less immediately acceptable view of them. A novelist may meet his readers by providing a view of life which is socially orthodox, familiar, and comforting, then more or less deliberately shift his ground and, in effect, undertake to persuade his audience to adjust or abandon that view in order to accommodate some other less familiar or less comforting one. In such cases, it is not in the sum of its particulars but in the organization of their presentation that the novel will have its unity, and this, I believe, is true of the organization of *The Mayor of Casterbridge*.

The largest elements in *The Mayor of Casterbridge* are four relatively self-contained and structurally similar 'movements' of progressively diminishing lengths, roughly comprising chapters I–XXXI, XXXI–XL, XLI–XLIII, and XLIV–XLV. Each provides a variation on a common pattern: an initial situation which seems to offer some hope for Henchard is followed by events which create doubt, fear, and anxious anticipation for an outcome that comes, finally, as a catastrophe. Furthermore, in each of these succeeding movements there is a reduction in the scope of Henchard's expectations and a corresponding increase in the emphasis which Hardy puts both upon Henchard's anxiety for success and upon the acuteness of his subsequent feeling of failure. Much of our response to Hardy's account of Henchard's final withdrawal and lonely death depends, certainly, upon the cumulative impact of these successively fore-shortened and intensified movements from hope to catastrophe; but the particular tragic response which *The Mayor of Casterbridge* seems calculated to evoke is also the product of other adjustments in detail and emphasis from movement to movement which have the effect of repeatedly shifting our perception of Henchard's character, of the kind of world he inhabits, and of the meaning of the catastrophes which he suffers.

The first and by far the longest of these movements (slightly more than half of the novel) falls into two almost equal parts. The opening fourteen chapters of *The Mayor of Casterbridge* establish a situation which seems to offer hope for Henchard's success. Following the brief prefatory account of Henchard's economic and moral nadir at

Weydon Priors and his resolution to make a 'start in a new direction',[4] Hardy abruptly bridges an intervening eighteen years to reveal the outcome of Henchard's vow; and not only does Henchard reappear transformed into a figure of affluence and social standing, but events now seem to augur his further financial and social success: he gains the commercial support and personal companionship of Farfrae, effects a reconciliation with his lost wife and child, and seems about to find a solution to the awkward aftermath of his affair with Lucetta. Hardy implies, certainly, that Henchard has undergone no equivalent moral transformation; we learn that he is conscientiously abstemious, but is otherwise simply 'matured in shape, stiffened in line, exaggerated in traits; disciplined, thought-marked – in a word, older', and what details contribute to our first impression of the new Henchard – his aloofness, his harsh laugh, the hint of moral callousness in his stiff reply to complaints about his bad wheat – tend to support, as Hardy remarks, 'conjectures of a temperament which would have no pity for weakness, but would be ready to yield ungrudging admiration to greatness and strength. Its producer's personal goodness, if he had any, would be of a very fitful cast – an occasional almost oppressive generosity rather than a mild and constant kindness (v).' Yet, an examination of the following nine chapters will reveal that it is precisely Henchard's fitful personal goodness that Hardy does emphasise. Henchard's consistent if 'rough benignity', his gruff friendliness and frankness with Farfrae, his concern for Lucetta, his efforts to make amends to Susan and Elizabeth Jane, his determination to 'castigate himself with the thorns which these restitutory acts brought in their train', and his humanizing acknowledgements of his own loneliness and need for companionship – these are the most prominent signs of Henchard's character in chapters VI–XIV; they tend to minimize his earlier harshness, so that by chapter XIV, at the high-water mark of Henchard's apparent success, Hardy's bland comment that he was as kind to Susan as 'man, mayor, and churchwarden could possibly be' squares so well with the repeated evidences of Henchard's gruff personal goodness in action that it carries little more than a muted suggestion of stiffness and social pride.

The remaining chapters of the first movement (XV–XXXI) then reverse the course of Henchard's fortunes, and as Hardy gradually increases the sharpness of Henchard's disappointments and anxieties, he also arranges the action so that Henchard's frustrated wrath is vented with increasing vehemence and with more obvious moral culpability on persons who appear to deserve it less and who suffer from it more intensely. In short, the 'temperament which would have no pity for weakness' gradually re-emerges, and by the conclusion of the first movement it is again the dominant feature of Henchard's character. The first sign of this progressive deterioration in Henchard – his grotesque attempt to punish Abel Whittle (XV) – is almost immediately countered by a revelation of Henchard's previous charities to Whittle's mother and by the frankness he displays in his reconciliation with Farfrae. But as the action continues Hardy develops situations which manifest more and more clearly the vehemence and injustice of Henchard's conduct. A first petty annoyance at his loss of popularity turns gradually into the more clearly misplaced and unjustly envious anger which prompts Henchard to dismiss Farfrae and to regard him as an 'enemy'. It is in this context that Hardy supplies an often quoted authorial comment which broadly implies a connection between Henchard's moral stature and his fortune: 'character is fate', Hardy reminds his readers, and he pointedly observes that Farfrae prospers like Jacob in Padan-Aram as he blamelessly pursues his 'praiseworthy course', while the gloomy and Faust-like Henchard has 'quitted the ways of vulgar men without light to guide him on a better way' (XVII).

The chapters which follow seem designed to illustrate this point, for as Henchard's harshness and pitilessness become more apparent, his fortunes decline. What begins in Henchard's impulsive desire for a 'tussle . . . at fair buying and selling' (XVII) develops into his more desperately planned and culpably savage effort to destroy Farfrae's career, 'grind him into the ground', and 'starve him out' (XXVI). Henchard's turning on Farfrae is followed by his more cruelly felt coldness to the unsuspecting Elizabeth Jane, who is the innocent victim of Henchard's anger over the ironic turn of events by which he has discovered the secret of her parentage. And, finally, in his last exasperated effort to best Farfrae, Henchard takes the still more obviously vicious course of wringing an unwilling promise of marriage from Lucetta by mercilessly threatening to reveal their former relations (XXVII). At this point in the action, Hardy reintroduces the furmity woman, whose public exposure of Henchard's past wrong to his wife not only helps to bring about Henchard's fall but also serves to reinforce momentarily the sinister aspect of his character which the previous chapters have made increasingly evident.

Thus, throughout the long first movement of *The Mayor of Casterbridge* Hardy uses both action and authorial comment to shift our impression of Henchard's moral stature in a curve which parallels his economic rise and fall. Nature and chance are repeatedly made to serve what seems to be a larger moral order in the world; Henchard himself comes to feel that some intelligent power is 'bent on punishing him' (XIX) and is 'working against him' (XXVII); and the course of Henchard's career might stand as testimony for the familiar and comforting belief that the wise and good shall prosper and the wicked and rash shall fail. Certainly there is almost a fable-like congruity in the sequence by which Hardy gradually brings Henchard back to something like his moral nadir at Weydon Priors just before public disgrace and bankruptcy come like a retribution and precipitate him to social and economic ruin. Hence, in spite of its really complex and ambiguous cause and effect relationships,[5] the first movement of *The Mayor of Casterbridge* does seem to exemplify the dictum that 'character is fate'; it does so largely because Hardy maintains a general correspondence between the changes in Henchard's apparent moral stature and the changes in his fortunes.

Henchard's fall marks, however, the beginning of another tragic cycle in the novel – a second movement which again opens on a note of rising hope that is followed by a reversal and a falling action which terminates in catastrophe. Hardy clearly intends to leave no doubt about Henchard's fate after the furmity woman has revealed his past: 'On that day – almost at that minute – he passed the ridge of prosperity and honour, and began to descend rapidly on the other side' (XXXI). But having predicted the imminent collapse of Henchard's fortunes, Hardy once more shifts the aspect in which he presents Henchard's character and career; and out of his account of Henchard's failure he contrives to establish a situation which seems to offer renewed hope. Thus he makes the court incident an occasion for a comment which puts Henchard's career in a more favorable light

The amends he had made in after life were lost sight of in the dramatic glare of the original act. Had the incident been well-known of old and always, it might by this time have grown to be lightly regarded as the rather tall wild oat, but well-nigh the single one, of a young man with whom the steady and mature (if somewhat headstrong) burgher of today had scarcely a point in common (XXXI).

Thereafter, Hardy stresses Henchard's generosity and integrity. We learn that it was the failure of a debtor whom Henchard had 'trusted generously' which brought about the final collapse of his fortunes, and the bankruptcy proceedings themselves serve to dramatize Henchard's scrupulous integrity as well as the finer instinct for justice which prompts him to sell his watch in order to repay a needy cottager. In short, Henchard now begins to appear in a character which seems worthy of the general approval of his creditors and the renewed sympathies of his townsmen, who, we are told, come to regret his fall when they have perceived how 'admirably' he had used his energy (XXXI). These signs of hopeful change in Henchard's public reputation are followed in the next chapter by indications of a corresponding change in his private attitudes. Hardy suggests, first, the possibility of Henchard's reconciliation with Farfrae by a scene in which the kindness of Farfrae prompts Henchard to admit, 'I – sometimes think I've wronged 'ee!' and to depart, after shaking hands, 'as if unwilling to betray himself further'. This is followed by Henchard's reconciliation with Elizabeth Jane, who tends him through a brief illness; and the result, Hardy remarks, is a distinct alteration in Henchard's outlook:

The effect, either of her ministrations or of her mere presence, was a rapid recovery . . . and now things seemed to wear a new colour in his eyes. He no longer thought of emigration, and thought more of Elizabeth. The having nothing to do made him more dreary than any other circumstance; and one day, with better views of Farfrae than he had held for some time, and a sense that honest work was not a thing to be ashamed of, he stoically went down to Farfrae's yard and asked to be taken on as a journeyman hay-trusser. He was engaged at once (XXXII).

Through the space of two chapters, then, Hardy repeatedly presents Henchard in ways which not only emphasize his maturity, integrity, and good sense but also suggest the possibility that he may now successfully accommodate himself to his new situation.

But in the following chapters there is an abrupt reversal, a second descending action, and what at first appears to be a second corresponding degeneration of Henchard's character. In rapid succession we are told that Henchard has undergone a 'moral change' and has returned to his 'old view' of Farfrae as the 'triumphant rival who rode rough-shod over him' (XXXII); that Henchard's drinking has brought on a new 'era of recklessness' (XXXIII); and that 'his

sinister qualities, formerly latent' have been 'quickened into life by
his buffetings' (XXXIV). Certainly, the series of progressively heightened crises which follow depend upon and repeatedly dramatize
Henchard's sinister potential for hatred and violence. But they do so
with an important difference: previously Henchard's antagonisms
have been checked by external forces; now Hardy emphasizes the
internal compulsions toward decency and fairness which at critical
moments in the action decisively frustrate Henchard's destructive
intent. Thus the crisis which Henchard precipitates by reading
Lucetta's letters to Farfrae comes to an unexpected conclusion: 'The
truth was that, as may be divined, he had quite intended to effect a
grand catastrophe at the end of this drama by reading out the name:
he had come to the house with no other thought. But sitting here in
cold blood he could not do it. Such a wrecking of hearts appalled
even him' (XXXIV). Twice more Henchard brings matters to the
brink of violence, and in each case the crisis is resolved when he is
prompted by some inner compulsion to desist. In his determination
to defy Farfrae and personally greet the Royal Visitor, Henchard
presses the issue to a point just short of violence, only to be moved
by an 'unaccountable impulse' to respect Farfrae's command and
give way (XXXVII). This incident precipitates Henchard's attack on
Farfrae's life in the hayloft; and once again, at the moment when
Farfrae's life is in his hands, Henchard is so touched by Farfrae's
reproachful accusation that he feels compelled to relent. Instead, he
flings himself down on some sacks 'in the abandonment of remorse'
and takes 'his full measure of shame and self reproach' (XXXVIII).
What seems central to Hardy's characterization of Henchard
throughout these crises, then, is that incapacity for callous destructiveness which repeatedly frustrates his reckless antagonism. Then,
as the action continues through the events which culminate in the
death of Lucetta, it is the frustration of Henchard's attempt to
redeem himself which brings about his personal catastrophe. For
Henchard is 'possessed by an overpowering wish . . . to attempt the
well-nigh impossible task of winning pardon for his late mad
attack' (XXXVIII): he vainly attempts to save Lucetta's life, and
finding himself unable to persuade Farfrae to return to his wife, he is
brought, finally, to the point of despair: 'The gig and its driver
lessened against the sky in Henchard's eyes; his exertions for
Farfrae's good had been in vain. Over this repentant sinner, at least,
there was to be no joy in heaven. He cursed himself like a less

scrupulous Job, as a vehement man will do when he loses self-respect, the last prop under mental poverty' (XL).

When we attend closely to what Hardy has been doing with Henchard's character in chapters XXXIII–XL, it is apparent, then, that although he exploits situations which depend for their effects upon our awareness of Henchard's potential for reckless cruelty, he in fact uses those situations to gradually strip Henchard of the features which earlier in the novel gave rise to 'conjectures of a temperament which would have no pity on weakness'. But more is involved here than a change of the aspect in which Henchard's character appears; there is really a marked change in tragic mode as well – a shift from that fable-like correspondence of fate and character which earlier in the novel seemed to dramatize a connection between Henchard's moral offense and a just retribution which followed upon it. Now something less than an ideal justice seems to govern the grim irony of events, unknown to Henchard, through which his decent attempt to return Lucetta's letters is turned to her destruction by the viciousness of Jopp and his degenerate companions from Mixen Lane; and what Hardy repeatedly dramatizes is Henchard's frustrated incapacity to find either the will to destroy or the means to win pardon. It is, finally, the failure of his well-intentioned acts which brings about Henchard's second catastrophe – that loss of self-respect which verges on despair – and in his second fall he appears no longer as a Faust figure but rather, in Hardy's new image, as a 'less scrupulous Job' and a self-tormented 'repentant sinner' who curses himself for the failure of his own redemptive efforts.

The death of Lucetta marks another major turning point in the novel and the opening of a third cycle from hope to catastrophe for Henchard. Shorn of other interests, he now begins to feel his life centering on his stepdaughter and dreams of a 'future lit by her filial presence' (XLI). By one desperate and unthinking lie he turns away Newson and manages for a while to persevere in the hope that he can fulfill his dream. But just as the furmity woman returned to ruin Henchard by her exposure of his past, so Newson now returns to expose Henchard's lie and dash his hope. But the parallel serves mainly to emphasize a difference, for Henchard appears in a greatly altered character, and Hardy's account of his loss of Elizabeth Jane and his withdrawal from Casterbridge as a self-banished outcast is clearly intended to evoke quite another kind of tragic effect. Hardy now presents Henchard in a character so soberly chastened as to seem 'denaturalized' (XLII). He is reduced to suicidal despair at the thought of losing Elizabeth Jane and to anxiously calculating what he says and does in an effort to avoid her displeasure – so much so, Hardy remarks, that 'the sympathy of the girl seemed necessary to his very existence; and on her account pride itself wore the garments of humility' (XLII). Hence, while he looks forward with dread to living like a 'fangless lion' in the back rooms of his stepdaughter's house, Henchard comes to acknowledge that 'for the girl's sake he might put up with anything; even from Farfrae; even snubbings and masterful tongue scourgings. The privilege of being in the house she occupied would almost outweigh the personal humiliation' (XLIII).

But it is not only Henchard's pathetic subjection to Elizabeth Jane which Hardy stresses; he now directs attention to Henchard's conscious moral struggles (as opposed to those 'unaccountable' impulses which previously checked his drunken recklessness), and he makes increasingly clear that Henchard now thinks and acts with heightened conscientiousness. Thus, when Henchard is again prompted by his perverse instinct to oppose Farfrae, Hardy pointedly reminds his readers that in the past 'such instinctive opposition would have taken shape in action' but that 'he was not now the Henchard of former days'. Instead, Hardy portrays Henchard's struggle against his instinct: Henchard vows not to interfere with Farfrae's courtship of Elizabeth Jane even though he is convinced that by their marriage he will be 'doomed to be bereft of her', and when the impulse returns, he rejects it as a temptation, wondering, 'Why should I still be subject to these visitations of the devil, when I try so hard to keep him away?' (XLII). At the same time, Henchard now suffers through moments of self-doubt and agonized casuistry in which, after the lie to Newson, his 'jealous soul speciously argued to excuse the separation of father and child' (XLI). The problem, Hardy suggests, continues to trouble him:

To satisfy his conscience somewhat, Henchard repeated to himself that the lie which had retained for him the coveted treasure had not been deliberately told to that end, but had come from him as the last defiant word of an irony which took no thought of consequences. Furthermore, he pleaded within himself that no Newson could love her as he loved her, nor would tend her to his life's extremity as he was prepared to do cheerfully (XLII).

And, finally, when Henchard leaves Casterbridge, Hardy makes clear that he goes as a self-condemned man, hoping that Elizabeth Jane will not forget him after she knows all his 'sins' yet assenting both to the fact of his guilt and the appropriateness of his fate: 'I – Cain – go alone as I deserve – an outcast and a vagabond. But my punishment is *not* greater than I can bear!' (LXII).

In view of the crushed submissiveness, remorse, earnest casuistry and conscious moral effort which have come to figure so prominently in Henchard's character, this self-accusation and self-imposed exile is certainly designed to impress us as excessively harsh. But by having Henchard accept an excessive burden of guilt and determine to bear it, Hardy does enable him to achieve a kind of expiation; and although excessiveness is certainly a constant in Henchard, in his third catastrophe we are brought to see in him a kind of excess which makes claims upon our sympathy in a way that his earlier excesses of moral callousness, antagonism, drunkenness, and frustrated violence have not. In short, Henchard now appears to suffer disproportionately, and he has taken on qualities of character which serve to justify on the moral level the pity and sympathy for him which Hardy evokes in other ways by emphasizing his declining health, his morbid sensitivity, his fears of 'friendless solitude', his character as an 'old hand at bearing anguish in silence', and his lack of friends who will speak in his defense.

The final two chapters of *The Mayor of Casterbridge* form a short coda which, on a still lower level, again involves a movement from hope to catastrophe – from that slightest of hopes which prompts Henchard to consider that he need not be separated from Elizabeth Jane to the rebuke which leads to his second departure from Casterbridge and his lonely death. Despite its brevity, this fourth movement has the important function both of further shifting our perception of Henchard's character and situation and of establishing more explicitly the final meaning of his tragedy. Hardy describes Henchard's journey from Casterbridge to Weydon Priors as a kind of pilgrimage carried out 'as an act of penance'. There Henchard mentally relives his past and retraces the foiled course of his career; and from both Henchard's reflections and Hardy's authorial comment upon his situation there emerges a central point – that Henchard's present situation is a consequence of 'Nature's jaunty readiness to support unorthodox social principles'. For as Henchard grimly reflects on the 'contrarious inconsistencies' of Nature which have nullified his recantation of ambition and foiled his attempts to replace ambition with love, Hardy comments on another of those contrarious inconsistencies – that Henchard, as a result of his suffering, has acquired 'new lights', has become capable of 'achieving higher things', and has found a 'wisdom' to do them precisely when an almost malicious machination in things has caused him to lose his zest for doing (XLIV). Henchard does make a final effort to return to Casterbridge and ask forgiveness of Elizabeth Jane, but now, in being condemned and rebuffed by her, it is he who is made to appear more sinned against than sinning. Even Farfrae, toward whom Hardy has been otherwise sympathetic or at least relatively neutral, is momentarily brought forward to contrast with Henchard's sincere repentance by being put in a hypocritical posture, 'giving strong expression to a song of his dear native country, that he loved so well as never to have revisited it' (XLIV), and, most significantly, Elizabeth Jane comes to regret her own harshness and attempts too late to make amends.

It is in the last chapters of the novel, then, that Hardy emphasizes most strongly the disjunction between Henchard's moral stature and the circumstance which has blindly nullified his repentance, his recantation of ambition, and his new capacity for a higher kind of achievement; and in doing so Hardy seems intent on reversing the fable-like correspondence between character and fate which figures so conspicuously in the first half of the novel. If throughout the opening portion of *The Mayor of Casterbridge* both nature and the course of events seem joined in support of the reassuring belief that the good shall prosper and the wicked fail, the remainder of the novel seems designed to reveal with progressively greater clarity that the fable is false. At its conclusion we are told that Elizabeth Jane has learned the 'secret . . . of making limited opportunities endurable' by 'the cunning enlargement . . . of those minute forms of satisfaction that offer themselves to everybody not in positive pain'. Henchard obviously has not learned that secret, and, by contrast, he remains characteristically excessive and tragically mistaken even in his last acts – in 'living on as one of his own worst accusers' and in executing a will which bears testimony to his final acceptance of a terribly disproportionate burden of guilt. But at the same time, by having Henchard persist in these acts, Hardy continues to dramatize his acceptance of a moral responsibility which now tends to set him quite apart from – and above – the indifferent circumstance which has frustrated his effort and contributed to his defeat. It is appropriate, then, that *The Mayor of Casterbridge* should end with the reflections of Elizabeth Jane, who has found the cunning to make the most of limited opportunites, as she gravely ponders the mysterious 'persistence of the unforeseen' in men's destinies and concludes that 'neither she nor any human being deserved less than was given' while 'there were others receiving less who had deserved much more'. Certainly that pointed distinction with which the novel closes – the distinction between what men deserve (which is a question of worth) and what men receive (which may be enlarged and made endurable by self-control, good sense, and cunning stratagems) is central to the final meaning which Hardy puts upon Henchard's tragedy; for although Hardy makes clear that Henchard fails ultimately because he lacks those qualities of character by which he might make the most of his opportunities, he clearly expects, at the same time, to have brought his readers to see that Henchard must finally be classed among those 'others receiving less who had deserved much more'.

There is, then, a marked contrast between that image of a morally ordered world projected by the long opening movement of *The Mayor of Casterbridge* and the more sombre, disenchanted vision of man's predicament with which the novel closes; and what is suggested about the relationship of Henchard's character to his fate by the first part of the novel is clearly inconsistent with the implications of its conclusion. Yet, considered rhetorically, such an arrangement probably worked to Hardy's advantage, for it enabled him to avoid abruptly confronting many of his readers with a view of life which would have sharply conflicted with their own assumptions and attitudes. Instead, Hardy first met his audience on the more readily acceptable ground of the moral fable; only after he had worked out Henchard's rise and fall on this level did he undertake to bring his readers to face the much more grim image of the human condition with which the novel closes, and even then the change was effected gradually, almost imperceptibly, by those various adjustments in detail and emphasis from movement to movement which I have attempted to trace in the preceding pages.

But, however rhetorically advantageous such an arrangement might have been, it need not be assumed to have been the outcome of a deliberate and preconceived plan. I think it more likely, rather, that the progressive changes which I have noted in *The Mayor of Casterbridge* came about in the process of its composition and were the result of Hardy's effort to develop his subject and to work out its implications. There is nothing really surprising in the fact that Hardy began *The Mayor of Casterbridge* with an action which strongly implied a connection between Henchard's moral stature and his fate; for, although Hardy had intellectually rejected the traditional belief in an ethically ordered universe, that belief retained a strong and pervasive hold upon his mind at the level of imagination and feeling, and certainly it shaped some of his most deeply rooted and habitual attitudes towards life.[6] But these attitudes remained at variance with his intellectual commitments, and the gradual shift in aspect and emphasis which takes place throughout the second half of *The Mayor of Casterbridge* suggests that, as composition of the novel progressed, Hardy began to exhaust the line of development which stemmed from his more immediate imaginative grasp of his subject and that thereafter he tended to reflect more deliberately upon the implications of Henchard's fall and did so within the framework of his consciously considered views on man's place in a Darwinian world. Yet it is important to note that even then Hardy's treatment of Henchard's character implies his continued respect for an older, pre-scientific conception of man's dignity and worth as a moral agent, and the conclusion of the novel seems to be as much an affirmation of faith in the transcendent worth of the human person as it is an acknowledgment of man's precarious situation in a blind and uncertain universe.

SOURCE: *Nineteenth-Century Fiction*, vol. 21 (1966–7), pp. 249–62.

NOTES

1. See, for example, James R. Baker, 'Thematic Ambiguity in *The Mayor of Casterbridge*', *Twentieth Century Literature*, I (April 1955), 13–16; Robert B. Heilman, 'Hardy's "Mayor" and the Problem of Intention', *Criticism*, v (Summer 1963), 199–213.

2. John Paterson, '*The Mayor of Casterbridge* as Tragedy', *Victorian Studies*, III (December 1959), 151–72; and Frederick R. Karl, '*The Mayor of Casterbridge*: A New Fiction Defined', *Modern Fiction Studies*, VI (Autumn 1960), 195–213.

3. *The Works of Thomas Hardy*, Wessex Edition (London, 1912), I, xii and xviii.

4. *Works*, Wessex Edition, v, ch. ii. All further citations are to this edition and are indicated by chapter numbers inserted parenthetically in the text.

5. Both Hardy's authorial comments and his handling of the action suggest that Henchard's first downfall is the product of a variety of interconnected causes, some related to Henchard's character (as he is variously prompted by instinctive antagonism, superstitiousness, Southern doggedness, disappointment, unconscious cravings, rashness, rivalry in love) and some more clearly matters of chance (coincidental discoveries, inopportune revelations, the vagaries of the weather): there seems, moreover, no way of establishing any clear causal priority among these.

6. I think that what Delmore Schwartz has had to say about the way belief is involved in Hardy's poetry applies, *mutatis mutandis*, to Hardy's prose fiction as well. See 'Poetry and Belief in Thomas Hardy', *The Southern Review*, VI (Summer 1940), 64–77.

Elaine Showalter The Unmanning of the Mayor of Casterbridge (1979)

In Hardy's career there is a consistent element of self-expression through women; he uses them as narrators, as secretaries, as collaborators, and finally, in the (auto) biography he wrote in the persona of his second wife, as screens or ghosts of himself. Hardy not only commented upon, and in a sense, infiltrated, feminine fictions; he also understood the feminine self as the estranged and essential complement of the male self. In *The Mayor of Casterbridge* (1886), Hardy gives the fullest nineteenth-century portrait of a man's inner life – his rebellion and his suffering, his loneliness and jealousy, his paranoia and despair, his uncontrollable unconscious. Henchard's efforts, first to deny and divorce his passional self, and ultimately to accept and educate it, involve him in a pilgrimage of 'unmanning' which is a movement towards both self-discovery and tragic vulnerability. It is in the analysis of this New Man, rather than in the evaluation of Hardy's New Women, that the case for Hardy's feminist sympathies may be argued.

The Mayor of Casterbridge begins with a scene that dramatises the analysis of female subjugation as a function of capitalism which Engels had recently set out in *The Origins of the Family, Private Property and the State* (1884): the auction of Michael Henchard's wife Susan at the fair at Weydon-Priors. Henchard's drunken declaration that Susan is his 'goods' is matched by her simple acceptance of a new 'owner', and her belief that in paying five guineas in cash for her Richard Newson has legitimised their relationship. Hardy never intended the wife-sale to seem natural or even probable, although he assembled in his Commonplace Book factual accounts of such occurrences from the *Dorset County Chronicle* and the *Brighton Gazette*. The auction is clearly an extraordinary event, which violates the moral sense of the Caster-bridge community when it is discovered twenty years later. But there is a sense in which Hardy recognised the psychological temptation of such a sale, the male longing to exercise his property rights over women, to free himself from their burden with virile decision, to simplify his own conflicts by reducing them to 'the ruin of good men by bad wives' (I, p. 7).

This element in the novel could never have been articulated by Hardy's Victorian readers, but it has been most spiritedly expressed in our century by Irving Howe:

To shake loose from one's wife; to discard that drooping rag of a woman, with her mute complaints and maddening passivity; to escape not by a slinking abandonment but through the public sale of her body to a stranger, as horses are sold at a fair; and thus to wrest, through sheer amoral willfulness, a second chance out of life – it is with this stroke, so insidiously attractive to male fantasy, that *The Mayor of Casterbridge* begins.

The scene, Howe goes on, speaks to 'the depths of common fantasy, it summons blocked desires and transforms us into secret sharers. No matter what judgments one may make of Henchard's conduct, it is hard, after the first chapter, simply to abandon him; for through his boldness we have been drawn into complicity with the forbidden.'

Howe brings an enthusiasm and an authority to his exposition of Henchard's motives that sweeps us along, although we need to be aware both that he invents a prehistory for the novel that Hardy withholds, and that in speaking of 'our' common fantasies, he quietly transforms the novel into a male document. A woman's experience of this scene must be very different: indeed, there were many sensation novels of the 1870s and 1880s which presented the sale of women into marriage from the point of view of the bought wife. In Howe's reading, Hardy's novel becomes a kind of sensation-fiction, playing on the suppressed longings of its male audience, evoking sympthy for Henchard because of his crime, and not in spite of it.

In this exclusive concentration on the sale of the wife, however, Howe, like most of Hardy's critics, overlooks the simultaneous event which more profoundly determines Henchard's fate: the sale of the child. Paternity is a central subject of the book, far more important than conjugal love. Perhaps one reason why the sale of the child has been so consistently ignored by generations of Hardy critics is that the child is female. For Henchard to sell his son would be so drastic a violation of patriarchal culture that it would wrench the entire novel out of shape; but the sale of a daughter – in this case only a 'tiny girl' – seems almost natural. There may even be a suggestion that this too is an act insidiously attractive to male fantasy, the rejection of the wife who has only borne female offspring.

It is the combined, premeditated sale of wife and child which launches Henchard into his second chance. Orphaned, divorced, without mother or sisters, wife or daughter, he has effectively severed all his bonds with the community of women, and re-enters society alone – the new Adam, reborn, self-created, unencumbered, journeying southward without pause until he reaches Casterbridge. Henchard commits his life entirely to the male community, defining his human relationships by the male codes of money, paternity, honour, and legal contract. By his act Henchard sells out or divorces his own 'feminine' self, his own need for passion, tenderness, and loyalty. The return of Susan and Elizabeth-Jane which precipitates the main phase of the novel is indeed a return of the repressed, which forces Henchard gradually to confront the tragic inadequacy of his codes, the arid limits of patriarchal power. The fantasy that women hold men back, drag them down, drain their energy, divert their strength, is nowhere so bleakly rebuked as in Hardy's tale of the 'man of character'. Stripped of his mayor's chain, his master's authority, his father's rights, Henchard is in a sense unmanned; but it is in moving from romantic male individualism to a more complete humanity that he becomes capable of tragic experience. Thus sex-role patterns and tragic patterns in the novel connect.

According to Christine Winfield's study of the manuscript of *The Mayor of Casterbridge*, Hardy made extensive revisions in Chapter 1. The most striking detail of the early drafts was that the Henchard family was originally composed of two daughters, the elder of whom was old enough to try to dissuade Susan from going along with the sale: ' "Don't mother!" whispered the girl who sat on the woman's side. "Father don't know what he's saying." ' On being sold to the sailor Newson, however, Susan takes the younger girl ('her favourite one') with her; Henchard keeps the other. Hardy apparently took this detail from the notice of a wife-sale in the *Brighton Gazette* for 25 May 1826: 'We understand they were country people, and that the woman has had two children by her husband, one of whom he consents to keep, and the other he throws in as a makeweight to the bargain.'

Hardy quickly discarded this cruel opening, and in the final text he emphasises the presence and the sale of a single infant daughter. From the beginning, she and her mother form an intimate unit, as close to each other as Henchard and his wife are separate. Susan speaks not to her husband, but to her baby, who babbles in reply; her face becomes alive when she talks to the girl. In a psychoanalytic study of Hardy, Charles K. Hofling has taken this bond between mother and daughter as the source of Henchard's jealous estrangement, but all the signs in the text point to Henchard's dissociation from the family as his own choice. The personalities of husband and wife are evidenced in all the nuances of this scene, one which they will both obsessively recall and relive. Hardy takes pains to show us Henchard's rigid unapproachability, his body-language eloquent of rejection. In Henchard's very footsteps there is a 'dogged and cynical indifference personal to himself' (I; p. 1); he avoids Susan's eyes and possible conversation by 'reading, or pretending to read' (I; p. 2) a ballad sheet, which he must hold awkwardly with the hand thrust through the strap of his basket. The scene is in marked contrast to Mrs Gaskell's opening in *Mary Barton*, for example, where fathers and brothers help to carry the infants; Hardy plays consciously against the reader's expectation of affectionate closeness. When Susan and Elizabeth-Jane retrace the journey many years later, they are holding hands, 'the act of simple affection' (III; p. 21).

Henchard's refusal of his family antedates the passionate declaration of the auction, and it is important to note that such a sale has been premeditated or at least discussed between husband and wife. There are several references to previous threats: 'On a previous occasion when he had declared during a fuddle that he would dispose of her as he had done, she had replied that she would not hear him say that many times more before it happened, in the resigned tones of a fatalist' (II; p. 17). When Newson asks whether

Susan is willing to go with him, Henchard answers for her: 'She is willing, provided she can have the child. She said so only the other day when I talked o't!' (I; p. 12). After the sale, Henchard tries to evade the full responsibility for his act by blaming it on an evening's drunkenness, a temporary breakdown in reason and control; he even blames his lost wife's 'simplicity' for allowing him to go through with the act: 'Seize her, why didn't she know better than bring me into this disgrace! . . . She wasn't queer if I was. 'Tis like Susan to show such idiotic simplicity' (II; p. 17: ellipsis mine). His anger and humiliation, none the less, cannot undo the fact that the bargain that was struck, and the 'goods' that were divided (Susan takes the girl, Henchard the tools) had been long contemplated. When it was too late, Henchard chiefly regrets his over-hasty division of property: 'She'd no business to take the maid – 'tis my maid; and if it were the doing again she shouldn't have her!' (I; p. 14).

In later scenes, Hardy gives Henchard more elaborated motives for the sale: contempt for Susan's ignorance and naiveté; and, as Henchard recalls on his first pilgrimage to Weydon-Priors, twenty-five years after the fair, his 'cursed pride and mortification at being poor' (XLIV; p. 367). Financial success, in the mythology of Victorian manliness, requires the subjugation of competing passions. If it is marriage that has threatened the youthful Henchard with 'the extinction of his energies' (I; p. 7), a chaste life will rekindle them. Henchard's public auction and his private oath of temperance are thus consecutive stages of the same rite of passage. Henchard's oath is both an atonement for his drunken surrender to his fantasies, and a bargain with success. In Rudyard Kipling's *The Man Who Would Be King* (1899), a similar 'contrack' is made, whereby Peachey Carnehan and Daniel Dravot swear to abjure liquor and women. When Dravot breaks his promise, they are exiled from their kingdom; so too will Henchard be expelled from Casterbridge when he breaks his vows. Save for the romance with Lucetta, in which he appears to play a passive role, Henchard is chaste during his long separation from his wife; he enjoys the local legend he has created of himself as the 'celebrated abstaining worthy' (V; p. 38); the man whose 'haughty indifference to the society of womankind, his silent avoidance of converse with the sex' (XIII; p. 94) is well known. His prominence in Casterbridge is produced by the commercialised energies of sexual sublimation, and he boasts to Farfrae that 'being by nature some-

thing of a woman-hater, I have found it no hardship to keep mostly
at a distance from the sex' (XII; p. 89). There is nothing in
Henchard's consciousness which corresponds to the aching melan-
choly of Hardy's poem 'He abjures love' (1883):

> At last I put off love,
>   For twice ten years
> The daysman of my thought,
>   And hope, and doing.

Indeed, in marrying Susan for the second time, Henchard forfeits
something of his personal magic, and begins to lose power in the
eyes of the townspeople; it is whispered that he has been 'captured
and enervated by the genteel widow' (XIII; p. 94).

Henchard's emotional life is difficult to define; in the first half of
the novel, Hardy gives us few direct glimpses of his psyche, and
soberly refrains from the kind of romantic symbolism employed as
psychological notation by the Brontës and by Dickens – dreams,
doubles, hallucinatory illnesses. But the very absence of emotion,
the 'void' which Hardy mentions, suggests that Henchard has
divorced himself from feeling, and that it is feeling itself which
obstinately retreats from him as he doggedly pursues it. When J.
Hillis Miller describes Henchard as a man 'driven by a passionate
desire for full possession of some other person' and calls the novel 'a
nightmare of frustrated desire', he misleadingly suggests that the
nature and intensity of Henchard's need is sexual. It is an absence
of feeling which Henchard looks to others to supply, a craving
unfocused loneliness rather than a desire towards another person.
Henchard does not seek possession in the sense that he desires the
confidences of others; such reciprocity as he requires, he coerces.
What he wants is a 'greedy exclusiveness' (XLI; p. 338), a title; and
this feeling is stimulated by male competition.

Given Henchard's misogyny, we cannot be surprised to see that
his deepest feelings are reserved for another man, a surrogate
brother with whom he quickly contracts a business relationship that
has the emotional overtones of a marriage. Henchard thinks of
giving Farfrae a third share in his business to compel him to stay; he
urges that they should share a house and meals. Elizabeth-Jane is
the frequent observer of the manly friendship between Henchard
and Farfrae, which she idealises:

She looked from the window and saw Henchard and Farfae in the hay-yard talking, with that impetuous cordiality on the Mayor's part, and genial modesty on the younger man's, that was now so generally observable in their intercourse. Friendship between man and man; what a rugged strength there was in it, as evinced by these two. (xv; p. 110)

Yet Elizabeth-Jane is also an 'accurate observer' who sees that Henchard's 'tigerish affection ... now and then resulted in a tendency to domineer' (XIV; p. 104). It is a tigerish affection that does not respect that other's separateness, that sets its own terms of love and hate. Farfrae's passivity in this relationship is feminine at first, when he is constrained by his economic dependence on Henchard. There is nothing homosexual in their intimacy; but there is certainly on Henchard's side an open, and, he later feels, incautious embrace of homosocial friendship, an insistent male bonding. Success, for Henchard, precludes relationships with women; male camaraderie and, later, contests of manliness must take their place. He precipitately confides in Farfrae, telling him all the secrets of his past, at a point when he is determined to withhold this information from Elizabeth-Jane: 'I am not going to let her know the truth' (XII; p. 92). Despite Henchard's sincerity, the one-sidedness of the exchange, his indifference to Farfrae's feelings if he can have his company, leads the younger man to experience their closeness as artificial, and to resist 'the pressure of mechanized friendship' (XVI; p. 117).

The community of Casterbridge itself has affinities with its Mayor when it is first infiltrated by Farfrae and the women. Like Henchard, it pulls itself in, refuses contact with its surroundings. 'It is huddled all together', remarks Elizabeth-Jane when she sees it for the first time. The narrator goes on: 'Its squareness was, indeed, the characteristic which most struck the eye in this antiquated borough ... at that time, recent as it was, untouched by the faintest sprinkle of modernism. It was compact as a box of dominoes. It had no suburbs – in the ordinary sense. Country and town met at a mathematical line' (IV; pp. 29–30: ellipsis mine). The 'rectangular frame' of the town recalls Hardy's descriptions of the perpendicularity of Henchard's face; entering Casterbridge Susan and Elizabeth-Jane encounter the 'stockade of gnarled trees', the town wall, part of its 'ancient defences', the 'grizzled church' whose bell tolls the curfew with a 'peremptory clang' (IV; pp. 30–2). All these details suggest Henchard, who is barricaded, authoritarian, coercive. He has become, as Christopher Coney tells the women, 'a pillar of the town' (V; p. 39).

Deeply defended against intimacy and converse with women, Henchard is vulnerable only when he has been symbolically unmanned by a fit of illness and depression; his susceptibility to these emotional cycles (the more integrated Farfrae is immune to them) is evidence of his divided consciousness. His romance with Lucetta takes place during such an episode: 'In my illness I sank into one of those gloomy fits I sometimes suffer from, on account o' the loneliness of my domestic life, when the world seems to have the blackness of hell, and, like Job, I could curse the day that gave me birth' (XII; p. 90). Again, when Henchard is living with Jopp, and becomes ill, Elizabeth-Jane is able to penetrate his solitude, and reach his affections. At these moments, his proud independence is overwhelmed by the woman's warmth; he is forced into an emotionally receptive passivity. Yet affection given in such circumstances humiliates him; he needs to demand or even coerce affection in order to feel manly and esteemed.

In health, Henchard determines the conditions of his relationships to women with minimal attention to their feelings. His remarriage to Susan is the product of 'strict mechanical rightness' (XIII; p. 93); his effort to substantiate the union, to give it the appearance of some deeper emotion, is typical of his withholding of self:

Lest she should pine for deeper affection than he could give he made a point of showing some semblance of it in external action. Among other things he had the iron railings, that had smiled sadly in dull rust for the last eighty years, painted a bright green, and the heavily barred, small-paned Georgian sash windows enlivened with three coats of white. He was as kind to her as a man, mayor, and churchwarden could possibly be. (XIV; p. 99)

To Susan, his kindness is an official function, and although he promises her that he will earn his forgiveness by his future works, Henchard's behaviour to women continues to be manipulative and proprietary. He deceives Elizabeth-Jane in the uncomfortable masquerade of the second courtship; he has not sufficient respect for Susan to follow her instructions on the letter about her daughter's true parentage. When he wants Lucetta to marry him, he threatens to blackmail her; when he wants to get rid of Elizabeth-Jane he makes her a small allowance. He trades in women, with dictatorial letters to Farfrae, and lies to Newson, with an ego that is alive only to its own excited claims.

Having established Henchard's character in this way, Hardy introduces an overlapping series of incidents in the second half of the novel which reverses and negates the pattern of manly power and self-possession. These incidents become inexorable stages in Henchard's unmanning, forcing him to acknowledge his own human dependency and to discover his own suppressed or estranged capacity to love. The first of these episodes is the reappearance of the furmity-woman at Petty Sessions, and her public denunciation of Henchard. Placed centrally in the novel (in Chapter XXVIII), this encounter seems at first reading to have the arbitrary and fatal timing of myth; the furmity-woman simply appears in Casterbridge to commit her 'nuisance' and to be arraigned. But the scene in fact follows Henchard's merciless coercion of Lucetta into a marriage she no longer desires. This violation, carried out from rivalry with Farfrae rather than disappointed love, repeats his older act of aggression against human feeling. Thus the declaration of the furmity-woman, the public humbling of Henchard by a woman, seems appropriate. It is for drunk and disorderly behaviour, for disrespect to the church and for profanity that she is accused; and her revelation of Henchard's greater disorder is an effective challenge to the authority of patriarchal law. Hardy's narrative underlines the scene explicitly as forming the 'edge or turn in the incline of Henchard's fortunes. On that day – almost at that minute – he passed the ridge of prosperity and honour, and began to descend rapidly on the other side. It was strange how soon he sank in esteem. Socially he had received a startling fillip downwards; and, having already lost commercial buoyancy from rash transactions, the velocity of his descent in both aspects became accelerated every hour' (XXXI; p. 251). The emphasis at this point is very much on Henchard's fortunes and his bankruptcy; although the furmity-woman's story spreads so fast that within twenty-four hours everyone in Casterbridge knows what happened at Weydon-Priors fair, the one person from whom Henchard has most assiduously kept the secret – Elizabeth-Jane – unaccountably fails to confront him with it. Indeed, Hardy seems to have forgotten to show her reaction; when she seeks him out it is only to forgive his harshness to her. Retribution for the auction thus comes as a public rather than a private shaming; and Henchard responds publicly with his dignified withdrawal as magistrate, and later, his generous performance in bankruptcy.

The next phase of Henchard's unmanning moves into the private sphere. Hearing of Lucetta's marriage to Farfrae, he puts his former threat of blackmail into action, tormenting her by reading her letters to her husband. Henchard cannot actually bring himself to reveal her name, to cold-bloodedly destroy her happiness; but Lucetta, investing him with a more implacable will than he possesses, determines to dissuade him, and so arranges a secret morning meeting at the Roman amphitheatre, which is far more successful than even she had dared to hope:

Her figure in the midst of the huge enclosure, the unusual plainness of her dress, her attitude of hope and appeal, so strongly revived in his soul the memory of another ill-used woman who had stood there and thus in bygone days, had now passed away into her rest, that he was unmanned, and his breast smote him for having attempted reprisals on one of a sex so weak. (XXXV; p. 288)

'Unmanning' here carries the significance of enervation, of a failure of nerve and resolve; and also the intimation of sympathy with the woman's position. The scene is carefully constructed to repeat the earlier meeting in the arena, when the wronged Susan came out to Henchard in all her weakness; Henchard's 'old feeling of supercilious pity for womankind in general was intensified by this suppliant appearing here as the double of the first' (XXXV; p. 289). But Hardy does not allow us such simple sentiments; he intensifies the ironic complexities that make this meeting different. There is certainly a sense in which Lucetta is both touchingly reckless of her reputation, and weak in her womanhood; these elements will come together in the fatal outcome of the skimmington-ride, when her wrecked honour and her miscarriage provide the emotional and physical shocks that kill her. While the Victorian belief in the delicacy of pregnant women, and also the statistical realities of the maternal death rate, are behind this incident (no contemporary reader of *The Mayor of Casterbridge* found it difficult to believe), Hardy obviously intends it symbolically as a demonstration of female vulnerability.

But, in another sense, Henchard is still deceiving himself about women's weakness, and flattering himself about men's strength; his 'supercilious pity' for womankind is obtuse and misplaced. Lucetta's pathetic appearance, her plea of loss of attractiveness, is deliberately and desperately calculated to win his pity and pacify his competitiveness. She is employing 'the only practicable weapon left her as a woman' in this meeting with her enemy. She makes her toilette with the intention of making herself look plain; having missed a night's sleep, and being pregnant ('a natural reason for her slightly drawn look') she manages to look prematurely aged. Skilled at self-production and self-promotion, Lucetta thus turns her hand successfully to this negative strategy, with the result that Henchard ceases to find her desirable, and 'no longer envied Farfrae his bargain'. She has transformed herself into a drooping rag; and Henchard is again eager to get away. Lucetta's cleverest stroke is to remove the stimulus to Henchard's sense of rivalry by telling him that 'neither my husband nor any other man will regard me with interest long' (XXXV; pp. 287–9). Although he is defeated by a woman, Henchard's understanding of women is still constituted by a kind of patriarchal innocence; he is ashamed of himself but for all the wrong reasons.

It is out of this unmanning, out of his disturbed self-esteem which has been deprived of an enemy, that Henchard tries to reassert his legitimate authority, and rebuild his diminished stature, by invading the welcoming ceremonies for the Royal Personage. Defiantly clad in 'the fretted and weather-beaten garments of bygone years', Henchard indeed stands out upon the occasion, and makes himself as prominent and distinctive as Farfrae, who wears 'the official gold chain with great square links, like that round the Royal unicorn' (XXXVII; p. 306). The scene is the necessary preamble to the fight between the two men; Henchard's flag-waving salute to Royalty is really a challenge to Farfrae, the lion against the unicorn. He puts himself in the young mayor's path precisely in order to be snubbed and driven back, to be inflamed so that he can take his revenge in 'the heat of action'. The wrestling-match with Farfrae is the central male contest of the novel – rivalries over business and women resolved by hand-to-hand combat. But in mastering Farfrae, even with one hand tied behind his back, Henchard is again paradoxically unmanned, shamed, and enervated. The sense of Farfrae's indifference to him, the younger man's resistance to even this ultimate and violent coercion of passion, robs Henchard of the thrill of his victory. Again, it is the apparently weaker antagonist who prevails; and in the emotional crisis, roles are reversed so that Farfrae is the winner. As for Henchard,

The scenes of his first acquaintance with Farfrae rushed back upon him – that time when the curious mixture of romance and thrift in the young man's composition so commanded his heart that Farfrae could play upon him as on an instrument. So thoroughly subdued was he that he remained on the sacks in a crouching attitude, unusual for a man, and for such a man. Its womanliness sat tragically on the figure of so stern a piece of virility. (XXXVIII; p. 316)

The rugged friendship between man and man, so impressive when seen from a distance by Elizabeth-Jane, comes down to this regressive, almost foetal, scene in the loft. Henchard has finally crossed over psychically and strategically to the long-repressed 'feminine' side of himself – has declared love for the first time to another person, and accepted the meaning of that victory of the weak over the strong. Thus, as Dale Kramer points out, 'In relation to the pattern of tragedy, the "feminine" Henchard is by his own definition a weakened man.' But again, Henchard's surrender opens him for the first time to an understanding of human need measured in terms of feeling rather than property. In his hasty and desperate lie to Newson, Henchard reveals finally how dependent he has become on ties of love.

Thus the effigy which Henchard sees floating in Ten Hatches Hole, whence he has fled in suicidal despair after the encounter with Newson, is in fact the symbolic shell of a discarded male self, like a chrysalis. It is the completion of his unmanning – a casting-off of the attitudes, the empty garments, the façades of dominance and authority, now perceived by the quiet eye of Elizabeth-Jane to be no more than 'a bundle of old clothes' (XLI; p. 343). Returning home, Henchard is at last able to give up the tattered and defiant garments of his 'primal days', to put on clean linen. Dedicating himself to the love and protection of Elizabeth-Jane, he is humanly reborn.

The final section of the novel fulfils the implications of Henchard's unmanning in a series of scenes which are reversals of scenes in the first part of the book. It is Elizabeth-Jane who assumes ascendancy: 'In going and coming, in buying and selling, her word was law' (XLII; p. 349). He makes her tea with 'housewifely care' (XLI; p. 334). As the 'netted lion' (XLII; p. 349), Henchard is forced into psychological indirection, to feminine psychological manoeuvres, because he does not dare to risk a confrontation: 'He would often weigh and consider for hours together the meaning of such and such a deed or phrase of hers, when a blunt settling question would formerly have been his first instinct' (XLII; p. 351). It is a humbling, and yet educative and ennobling apprenticeship in human sensitivity, a dependence, Hardy writes, into which he had 'declined (or, in another sense, to which he had advanced)' (XLII; p. 351).

In his final self-imposed exile, Henchard carries with him mementoes of Elizabeth-Jane: 'gloves, shoes, a scrap of her handwriting, . . . a curl of her hair' (XLIV; p. 366: ellipsis mine). Retracing his past, he has chosen to burden himself with reminders of womanhood, and to plot his journey in relation to a female centre. Even the circle he traces around the 'centripetal influence' (XLIV; p. 368) of his stepdaughter contrasts with the defended squareness of the Casterbridge he has left behind, the straight grain of masculine direction. Henchard's final pilgrimage, to Elizabeth-Jane's wedding, is, detail by detail, a reliving of the journey made by the women at the beginning of the novel. He enters the town for the last time as they entered at the first: the poor relation, the suppliant, the outsider. 'As a Samson shorn' (XLIV; p. 373) he timidly presents himself at the kitchen-door and from the empty back-parlour awaits Elizabeth-Jane's arrival. As Susan and Elizabeth-Jane watched him preside over the meeting of the Council, so he now must watch his stepdaughter preside over her wedding-party. As Susan was overpowered by the sight of her former husband's glory, and wished only 'to go – pass away – die' (V; p. 37), so is Henchard shamed and overwhelmed by Elizabeth-Jane's moral ascendancy. What is threatened and forgotten in the first instance comes to pass in the second – the rejected guest departs, and neither Elizabeth-Jane nor the reader sees him more.

In a sense which Hardy fully allows, the moral as well as the temporal victory of the novel is Elizabeth-Jane's. It is she to whom the concluding paragraphs are given, with their message of domestic serenity, their Victorian feminine wisdom of 'making limited opportunities endurable', albeit in 'a general drama of pain' (XLV; p. 386). Casterbridge, under the combined leadership of Elizabeth-Jane and Farfrae, is a gentled community, its old rough ways made civil, its rough edges softened. We might read the story of Henchard as a tragic taming of the heroic will, the bending and breaking of his savage male defiance in contest with a stoic female endurance. In such a reading, Henchard becomes a second Heathcliff, who is also overcome by the domestic power of a daughter-figure; like Heathcliff, Henchard is subdued first to the placidities of the grange, then to the grave.

Yet this romantic and nostalgic reading would underestimate Hardy's generosity of imagination. Virginia Woolf, one of Hardy's earliest feminist critics, attributed the 'tragic power' of his characters to 'a force within them which cannot be defined, a force of love or of hate, a force which in the men is the cause of rebellion against life, and in the women implies an illimitable capacity for suffering.' In Henchard the forces of male rebellion and female suffering ultimately conjoin; and in this unmanning Hardy achieves a tragic power unequalled in Victorian fiction. It may indeed be true that Hardy could not be accounted a feminist in the political terms of the 1880s, or the 1970s; but in *The Mayor of Casterbridge* the feminist critic can see Hardy's swerving from the bluff virility of the Rabelais Club, and the misogyny of Gosse, towards his own insistent and original exploration of human motivation. The skills which Henchard struggles finally to learn, skills of observation, attention, sensitivity, and compassion, are also those of the novelist; and they are feminine perhaps, if one contrasts them to the skills of the architect or the statesman. But it is because Hardy dares so fully to acknowledge this side of his own art, to pursue the feminine spirit in his man of character, that his hero, like the great heroines he would create in the 1890s, is more Shakespearean than Victorian.

SOURCE: Extract from *Critical Approaches to the Fiction of Thomas Hardy*, ed. Dale Kramer (Macmillan, London, 1979), pp. 101–14.

TESS OF THE D'URBERVILLES

Kristin Brady Tess and Alec: Rape or Seduction? (1986)

From the time when *Tess of the d'Urbervilles* was first published in 1891, critical response has focused on the closeness of Hardy's narrator to his victimized protagonist, his tendency to act as her advocate and protector even as he subjects her to the terrible fate of his story. Hardy's own recognition of the advocate role is apparent in his notorious subtitle to the novel, 'A Pure Woman Faithfully Presented by Thomas Hardy', and the protective role is implicit in the epigraph from *Two Gentlemen of Verona*: '. . . Poor wounded name! My bosom as a bed shall lodge thee.' Hardy's defence of Tess, this suggests, will be that of a lover rather than of a legal representative. Hardy, in fact, confessed in a letter to Sir George Douglas that 'I . . . lost my heart to her as I went on with her history' and complained to Thomas MacQuoid that 'I have not been able to put on paper all that she is, or was, to me.' Hardy's sense of the incompleteness and inadequacy of the novel seems to have been acute. He complimented Grant Allen on his ability to read 'the *intended* story . . . behind the written one' by 'unconsciously adding out of your own nature all that was necessary to fill up the deficience in my production'. Though there is obviously a touch of false modesty in these remarks, they seem also to reveal both Hardy's intense emotional involvement in the composition of *Tess* and his sense of disappointment that the final product did not fully express all that he had felt and thought while creating it.

Though these feelings of partial failure are by no means unique to Hardy, they seem to have a special application to his situation when writing *Tess of the d'Urbervilles*, a novel whose textual history reveals an unusually complex process of revision and rethinking. As much recent criticism has revealed, Hardy's original portrayal of Tess shows more physical familiarity between Tess and Alec before her loss of virginity in The Chase, while Hardy's own tendency toward partisanship, as well as his emphasis on Tess's victimization, increased in the later stages of the manuscript. These changes are no doubt linked to the difficulties Hardy encountered in trying to find a publisher for the novel's periodical publication. A general disinclination among editors to see female sexuality portrayed frankly, exemplified in Mowbray Morris's irritation at the novel's pervasive 'succulence', seems to have driven Hardy to de-emphasize Tess's sexual responses. By giving increased prominence in the later stages of the manuscript to the villainy of both Alec d'Urberville and Angel Clare, for example, Hardy was able half to suggest that Tess was more a passive victim of male aggression and idealization than an active participant in her own disastrous fate. Mary Jacobus argues that Hardy's original vision of Tess was falsified by the revisions: if Tess is simply a victim, then neither her sexuality nor her moral position in the novel is interesting.

It would be impossible to reclaim the whole original conception of Tess even from the recent scholarly edition of the novel, which traces changes in the extant versions of the manuscript and in all relevant published appearances. Hardy's conception of Tess began to change while he was still writing the novel, and its concluding sections were conceived well after he had begun to intensify her role as victim and his own as defender. The final published novel is thus only an approximation – an approximation not just of one intention but of a whole series of changing intentions as they emerged in Hardy's mind, some clearly in response to the demands of his publishers and audience, others presumably in response to his own growing involvement with his character. What seems to some readers an unevenness or contradictoriness in the final version of the novel is in fact the natural result of the turbulent circumstances surrounding its composition and of its controversial subject matter: not simply seduction, but the sexual responses of a woman who became pregnant by a man she did not love and then recovered sufficiently to feel a strong attraction to another man.

Tess is not, indeed, the typical betrayed maiden, who either forsakes sexual relationships altogether in the aftermath of her moral lapse or pines away hopelessly for her seducer. Elizabeth Gaskell's *Ruth*, in contrast to Tess, devotes the rest of her life after her seduction to good works and to her son, while Beauty of 'Saturday Night in Arcady' (the seduction section of *Tess* that was published separately as a story) differs radically from the novel's heroine in her response to her seducer. Beauty implores him not to desert her and loses all of her former spirit and independence. Her fellow workers observe that 'to him she was deferential thenceforward, that she started when he came into the field and when he joked jokes of the most excruciating quality she laughed with a childlike belief in them'. Such a conclusion to the events at the haytrusser's and in The Chase seems startling to the reader who already knows the novel, for it is inconceivable that Tess would respond in such a way to Alec. What distinguishes her from other seduced maidens is also what makes her such a dangerous subject for fiction: that she could have sexual responses, though of varying intensities and kinds, to two different men.

One can never ignore altogether the serious restrictions on Hardy as he attempted to treat female sexuality in *Tess*, but it would also be simplistic to attribute all the novel's ambivalence to Mrs Grundy. Much recent feminist criticism dwells on the extent to which Hardy's narrator seems himself to exhibit a fundamental ambivalence toward Tess's sexuality. The narrator's undeniably erotic fascination with her takes the form of a visual preoccupation with her physical presence, and it has even been suggested that the narrator derives an almost sadistic pleasure from Tess's suffering, that he shares in part the distorted views of her held by both Alec and Angel, and that he in some sense does himself violate her with his male voice and male eye. By the same token, the narrator seems to retreat from and close his eyes to the most explicit and direct manifestations of the sexuality which so fascinates him. As Penny Boumelha has perceptively remarked, Tess's sexuality is ultimately 'unknowable' and 'unrepresentable' by the narrator, and he withdraws completely from her consciousness at the most crucial points in her life: the moment when she was wakened to Alec's return in The Chase, the weeks following that scene when she was his mistress, the time of the discovery of her pregnancy and the birth of her child, the points when she decided to return to Alec and then to murder him and flee with Angel. Major events often take place between chapters and phases of the book, and are conveyed to the reader only by the narrator's factual reference to their having happened. Indeed, Tess's real thoughts and feelings are rarely presented in the novel, except when she suffers the consequences of her actions. Her moral choices seem obscured in ambivalence, while their results are vividly and dramatically portrayed. The effect of these constant jumps in the narration is that the reader can have a firm sense of Tess's suffering and her role as victim, but a somewhat confused sense of her own participation in her fate. The issue of 'purity' is of course crucial here: if Tess's relationship with Alec was based in any sense on her own sexual desire, regardless of whether she 'loved' him or not, then she is not 'pure' in the rigid Victorian sense of that word; if, on the other hand, Tess was simply the passive victim of Alec's sexual aggression, then the question of her own sexuality becomes insignificant. Tess would then be simply a victim of circumstances, not a woman with complex feelings and responses.

Whether it was from external or internal pressures, Hardy obviously felt he had to walk a tightrope between these two conceptions of Tess. She is both the betrayed maid and the fallen woman, both the scapegoat and the tragic heroine complicitous in her own downfall. The repeated references in the novel to the Persephone myth and to *Paradise Lost* draw together her two roles: raped daughter of Nature sacrificed to the powers of the underworld, and tempted daughter of Nature punished for her act of pride.

While this contradictory portrait can be seen in part as a function of Hardy's own ambivalence about Tess, the results are not entirely negative ones. For although Hardy's portrayal of her never met his intended conception, the book still constitutes a considerable achievement in presenting the conflicting sensations and emotions that can be part of a sexual response. Hardy's own difficulties may, in fact, have contributed to the book's complexity, which lies in the way in which many of Tess's sexual feelings are buried deep within the texture of the narrative. What the novel lost in frankness after Hardy began to revise it may still be found in its rich ambivalences. In his handling of the scenes leading up to Tess's loss of virginity, for example, Hardy is extraordinarily subtle in depicting the sorts of sexual titillation that can be excited by a veteran seducer, especially in a woman like Tess, who has no knowledge or experience of sex. She is temporarily attracted to Alec even as she distrusts him and finds him repellent, and it is this bewildering combination of sensations and emotions that Hardy manages to convey to his Victorian audience.

The central ambivalence in *Tess of the d'Urbervilles* is of course the scene in The Chase, in which the narrator launches into polemics immediately after the description of Alec's discovery of Tess in a sound sleep. The story then leaps into the second phase in the novel,

'Maiden No More' – as if Tess's loss of virginity had taken place on the bare page between the two phases. From the time of the book's publication, the question of whether Tess was raped or seduced has divided critics, and the debate has still not been resolved with perfect clarity. Grindle and Gatrell's 'General Introduction' to the scholarly edition of the novel, for example, uses the words 'rape' and 'seduction' interchangeably, and G. Glen Wickens's fine essay on the Persephone myth speaks of the 'ambiguous moment' when seduction turns into rape. An aspect of the confusion, needless to say, lies not just in Hardy's novel but in the inadequacy of the words themselves. 'Rape' suggests physical force alone, while 'seduction' implies merely the pressure of enticement, and neither of the terms comes close to representing precisely how Alec d'Urberville awakened and then exploited the sexual instincts of Tess Durbeyfield. His most effective pressure, for example – both in The Chase and before her second submission to him at the end of the novel – lies in his appeals to her guilt about her responsibilities to her family. By helping them and so requiring gratitude of her, he makes Tess feel all the more compromised in her rebuffs of his sexual advances. If he did exert physical force on her in The Chase, that would have been just one form of his assault on her person.

It is in the end impossible to ascertain precisely what happened during that September night on The Chase, and Hardy's narrator offers us no real information in his agonized outcry about how 'often the coarse appropriates the finer thus'. Crucial information is offered, however, in chapter XII, in which Tess reveals through her conversations with Alec and her mother a number of facts that ought to guide the reader in understanding what the narrator had left unspoken between the phases: that she had stayed with Alec a number of weeks after her loss of virginity, that she had accepted gifts from him, and that she has come to 'loathe and hate' herself for her 'weakness'. She tells Alec, 'My eyes were dazed by you for a little, and that was all'. In response to her mother's disappointment, Tess then rehearses in her mind the sequence of the whole affair, and here, in an unusual departure from his standard tendency to visualize her responses, the narrator presents her thoughts and memories directly:

Get Alec d'Urberville in the mind to marry her. He marry *her*! On matrimony he had never once said a word. And what if he had? How a convulsive snatching at social salvation might have impelled her to answer him she could not say. But her poor foolish mother little knew her present feeling towards this man. Perhaps it was unusual in the circumstances, unlucky, unaccountable; but there it was; and this, as she had said, was what made her detest herself. She had never wholly cared for him, she did not at all care for him now. She had dreaded him, winced before him, succumbed to adroit advantages he took of her helplessness; then, temporarily blinded by his ardent manners, had been stirred to confused surrender awhile: had suddenly despised and disliked him, and had run away. That was all.

As far as the scene in The Chase is concerned, there is evidence for both the rape and the seduction arguments in this interior mono-logue (it sounds, indeed, more Jamesian than Hardyan), but the more important revelation is that the sexual relationship had continued beyond the single encounter in The Chase. Whether it began as a rape or a seduction, Tess had subsequently 'been stirred to confused surrender awhile'.

It is significant, too, that Hardy expanded this passage as late as the 1892 publication of the novel. Earlier versions had read, 'She had never cared for him, she did not care for him now' – a statement suggesting that Tess's feelings about Alec were always the same. In 1892, however, the sentence was changed to a form that suggests Tess had some attraction to Alec at the beginning: 'She had never *wholly* cared for him, she did not *at all* for him now' (italics mine). In addition, Hardy did not add until 1892 the details that Tess had succumbed to 'a cruel advantage he took of her helplessness; then, temporarily blinded by his flash manners, had been stirred to confused surrender awhile: had suddenly despised and disliked him, and had run away'. Some 1892 deletions are also significant. Until that stage, Tess is described as drinking a cordial that Alec offers her when they arrive at The Chase. This detail can be seen as highlighting both Alec's deviousness and Tess's complicity. In 1892, Hardy also cut an extremely polemical and suggestive passage from The Chase scene:

Already at that hour some sons of the forest were stirring and striking lights in not very distant cottages; good and sincere hearts among them, patterns of honesty and devotion and chivalry. And powerful horses were stamping in their stalls, ready to be let out into the morning air. But no dart or thread of intelligence inspired these men to harness and mount, or gave them by any means the least inkling that their sister was in the hands of the spoiler; and they did not come that way.

The simultaneous addition of a later dialogue among workers at Marlott is a much milder suggestion of rape than this passage, especially since it is spoken by the mouth of gossip or oral tradition: 'A little more than persuading had to do wi' the coming o't, I reckon. There were they that heard a sobbing one night last year in The Chase; and it mid ha' gone hard wi' a certain party if folks had come along.'

What is interesting about these changes is that although Hardy does heighten the villainy of Alec, he also further emphasizes Tess's own reluctant expression of her sexuality. After offering his readers the possibility of seeing rape, he then imposes upon them the necessity of recognizing that she became a kept woman. Significantly, what shocks Tess about this is not the sexual lapse itself, but that she was dazed by and succumbed to a man she 'had never wholly cared for'. The shift in focus is intriguing: in leaving the initial sexual encounter ambiguous while being relatively explicit about later encounters, Hardy de-emphasizes the actual loss of virginity and draws the reader's attention to the issue that most concerns Tess herself: not the manner of the initial penetration but the nature of the whole sexual relationship, from its beginning to its end. This larger topic also encompasses responses that are not sexual, but which bear upon sexual decisions. Indeed, an aspect of the book's complexity is that Hardy does not separate the sexual crises in Tess's life from her other difficulties.

In order to see the relationship between Tess and Alec in this wider context, it is important to turn to the scenes preceding the encounter in The Chase, in which Tess's responses prefigure and emblematize what happened later. To some degree, these scenes objectify in external action precisely the internal events which the narrator shies away from. Some of them – the haytrusser's dance in particular – are as highly stylized, despite their realistic details, as a scene from romance, and bear the burden of expressing indirectly what the novel cannot say outright. These scenes need to be read as one would read Spenser or Milton: by seeing the physical action as emblematic of moral action. Hardy's allusions to Milton in the Talbothays scenes extend beyond the content of his narrative to its very technique, for poised against the narrator's subjective intrusions are moments as emblematically presented as Eve's fall in *Paradise Lost* or the lady's temptation in *Comus*. These scenes of externalized action balance out the polemical presence of the narrator by acting as varied repetitions and comments upon each other. As J. Hillis Miller has pointed out, Tess's life is a constant re-enactment of the same event.

Common to all the important scenes preceding Tess's night in The Chase is the portrayal of a tension in her between passivity and assertion, between submission and independence, between dream and reality. Present in all of the scenes too is an emphasis on Tess's pride, a sense of self that ultimately leads her to the disastrous descent into Trantridge and the 'fall' in The Chase. Hardy's handling of this tension is not simplistic or moralistic, however: Tess's pride cannot be classified as a vice or a weakness in the way that Eve's can in *Paradise Lost*. Milton's methods, but not his values, survive in Hardy's novel.

Emblematic action appears as early as the club-walking scene, in which Tess Durbeyfield is exclusively chosen by the narrative consciousness even as Angel Clare fails to observe her until it is too late. Though nothing of dramatic importance occurs in this scene, it presents many of the aspects of Tess that will figure in important ways later on. She is seen both in representative and in individual terms. Her participation in the 'local Cerealia', in which she appears like a living symbol carrying white flowers and a peeled willow-wand, links her to ancient fertility rites and so locates her both in the timeless continuum of the natural cycle and in the historical world of Wessex. Tess's white dress represents her innocence and virginity, while the red ribbon she wears in her hair and her 'pouted-up deep red mouth' suggest her sexuality (the focus on Tess's mouth is used throughout the novel as a focus for her own passion and her attractiveness to men). These external signs are complemented by the narrator's recognition of Tess's subjective consciousness: she, like the other club-walkers, has a 'private little sun for her soul to bask in; some dream, some affection, some hobby, at least some remote and distant hope which, though perhaps starving to nothing, still [lives] on, as hopes will' (p. 21). The unreality of such dreams is implicit in the description of the varied shades of white in the dresses of the club-walkers, which are seen as a slight clashing of the 'Ideal' and the 'real': the 'pure blanching' white of the young women is contrasted to the 'cadaverous tint' of the old women, 'scourged by time and trouble' (p. 21). Tess, of course, is among the young undisillusioned ones, 'a mere vessel of emotion untinctured by experience'. Her sexual instincts have hardly been awakened:

although she is drawn to Angel Clare's grace of speech and novelty of appearance, she does not concern herself with the attentions of any local suitors and enjoys the dance simply as a physical activity.

Tess seems in this scene a kind of Wessex tabula rasa, an empty surface on which experience will be written; but the tensions already present within her life and her psyche also begin to manifest themselves here. We see Tess both as withdrawn – it is her 'backwardness' that prevents Angel's noticing her before the dance – and as proud. She is mortified by the ludicrous appearance of her father, and responds aggressively to the derisive laughter of her companions: 'Look here; I won't walk another inch with you, if you say any jokes about him!' Tess's tone here is defensive as well as aggressive, and the club-walkers curtail their laughter because they see that she is about to lose her composure. But the narrator's language also suggests the potential danger of a loss of control in Tess: 'Perceiving that they had really pained her they said no more, and order again prevailed. Tess's pride would not allow her to turn her head again, to learn what her father's meaning was, if he had any'. The linking of Tess's sense of pride with a potential loss of order (a Miltonic idea) will figure more clearly in later scenes, as will her sensitivity to the laughter and contempt of others.

The series of incidents culminating in the death of Prince can be linked in interesting ways with the scene in The Chase and with the murder of Alec d'Urberville. There is a fatal penetration in all three scenes, and in each Tess is in a state of reverie or sleep – a state of unconsciousness which is linked by mist and halo imagery to the drunkenness of her parents and the Chaseborough revellers. As she drives the cart toward Casterbridge in chapter 4, Tess lapses into subjective contemplation of her place in the universe:

The mute procession past her shoulders of trees and hedges became attached to fantastic scenes outside reality, and the occasional heave of the wind became the sigh of some immense sad soul, conterminous with the universe in space, and with history in time.

Then, examining the mesh of events in her own life, she seemed to see the vanity of her father's pride; the gentlemanly suitor awaiting herself in her mother's fancy; to see him as a grimacing personage, laughing at her poverty, and her shrouded knightly ancestry. Everything grew more and more extravagant, and she no longer knew how time passed. A sudden jerk shook her in her seat, and Tess awoke from the sleep into which she, too, had fallen.

The association of Tess's 'fall' into sleep with that of little Abraham – who also had indulged in grotesque visions – provides both a parallel and a contrast with the deluded dreams of the Durbeyfield parents: all of them are responding to a far from perfect life, but John and Joan Durbeyfield escape reality through their drinking and romantic notions, while their children sink into nightmarish visions of that same reality. Neither view, of course, is a true one, and Tess pays dearly for her departure into a dream world. In romance, indeed, the act of falling asleep is often a culpable forsaking of responsibility.

At a practical level, however, Tess also suffers from her propensity to take too much responsibility upon herself. She had allowed Abraham to go to sleep because although she 'was not skilful in the management of a horse, . . . she thought that she could take upon herself the entire conduct of the load for the present' (p. 43). She had also 'proudly' refused her mother's suggestion that she ask a 'young feller' from the club-walking to take the hives to Casterbridge: 'O no – I wouldn't have it for the world! . . . And letting everybody know the reason – such a thing to be ashamed of! I think *I* should go if Abraham could go with me to kip me company' (p. 40). In her pride and independence, then, Tess rejects all the help she could have secured to do a job which she was not capable of doing herself. Her pride in this case is more admirable than culpable, and the consequences of her carelessness far exceed the extent of her guilt, but the scene none the less dramatizes Tess's own lack of realism. It is an exact reversal of the recklessness of her parents, who fail to recognize or to worry about their own avoidance of responsibility. In addition to taking too much on herself, Tess also assumes too much blame when things go wrong. After telling Abraham that they live on a blighted planet – thus suggesting that they are not answerable for what happens to them – she then sees the mail-cart accident as entirely her fault, thus suggesting a purely subjective view of external events. What the novel demonstrates, of course, is that neither view offers a full accounting for the complications of human experience: both external events and personal responsibility converge in the life of Tess Durbeyfield.

The trip to Trantridge flows immediately out of the circumstances surrounding the death of Prince. It is guilt at having killed the family's 'breadwinner' – ironically, Hardy's narrator attributes this role to the horse rather than to Tess's father – that chiefly compels her to go there; but again Tess's own pride is also an issue. Here she is torn between two forms of defiance. She is reluctant to follow her mother's suggestion that she assume 'the part of poor relation', but she also cannot countenance her father's deluded dreams of grandeur 'as a reason for staying away':

> "I don't like my children going and making themselves beholden to strange kin," murmured he. "I'm the head of the noblest branch o' the family, and I ought to live up to it."

His reasons for staying away were worse to Tess than her own objections to going.

In earlier scenes, Tess had stood in proud opposition to both her parents. Here she is forced to choose between the shameless opportunism of the one and the feckless vanity of the other. Generally, the heroine of romance must choose in some way between good and evil. Tess's choices are never so clear cut.

Tess's arrival at the d'Urberville estate represents a new and difficult challenge to her independence, for she is confronted for the first time both with wealth and with real sexual aggression. Her response is predictably ambivalent. She has the instinct to detect the vulgar newness of the 'crimson brick lodge' with its 'little fancy farm', but not the experience to see Alec d'Uberville fully as the sham that he is. The club-walking scene had already revealed her attraction to men of a different class from her own, and so Alec d'Uberville represents an exotic world that Tess cannot entirely resist. Although she is disappointed that he does not meet her own romantic expectations of 'an aged and dignified face', she still finds herself in 'awe' (p. 53) of him and responds to all his insinuating invitations with a combination of distrust and fascination. She seems a conflation of the chaste lady in *Comus*, who knows instinctively to resist the lewd enticements of her tempters, and the Eve of *Paradise Lost*, who succumbs to the snake's appeals to her pride and curiosity. In both of Milton's mythical narratives, the woman is offered dangerous food, the acceptance of which itself would constitute a lapse. In this case, Tess accepts 'in a slight distress' Alec's artificially ripened strawberry and then shows its enchanting effects. Alec's food makes her indecisive and submissive: she '[wanders] desultorily . . . eating in a half-pleased, half-reluctant state whatever d'Urberville [offers] her' and obeys 'like one in a dream'. This response alone seems an emblematic prefiguration of Tess's later submission to Alec.

After this initial encounter, Tess's ambivalence about Alec continues to manifest itself. She does not think him handsome, but is gratified to hear that she made a good impression on him. She is unable to express why she does not want to go to Trantridge, but finally succumbs, smiling 'crossly', to the pressure of her mother and siblings. In an ominous fiat, she even consents to let her mother dress her up: 'Very well; I suppose you know best', replied Tess with calm abandonment. And to please her parent the girl put herself quite in Joan's hands, saying serenely, 'Do what you like with me, mother'. The same kind of sudden submission overtakes Tess when she agrees to ride in Alec's gig after looking back at her watching family.

The scenes describing Tess's initiation at Trantridge (chs 8–9) represent an intensification both of her resistance to and of her familiarity with Alec. When he seeks a kiss while they are riding in the gig, she at first openly defies him but then '[pants] miserably' and Alec achieves his 'kiss of mastery'. In a later scene, Tess resists Alec's whistling lesson, only to find herself smiling 'involuntarily' at her 'momentary pleasure of success'. The sexual ambivalence of these scenes is always complicated, too, by Tess's financial reliance on Alec: 'she was more pliable under his hands than a mere companionship would have made her, owing to her unavoidable dependence upon his mother, and, through that lady's comparative helplessness, upon him'. This economic dimension in Alec's sexual aggression will figure again in the Chase scene, as well as in the later scenes at Flintcomb-Ash and Sandbourne.

The Chaseborough dance and its aftermath are the most important emblematic scenes preceding the night in The Chase, and as in the Trantridge scenes, Hardy's language points clearly to the moral action underlying the physical action. Though she never joins this Dionysian dance (as she had eventually joined the more innocent dance of the club-walking), the 'weekly pilgrimages' to Chaseborough still constitute for Tess a kind of rite of passage. Significantly, she had first resisted the invitations of her fellow workers to go to Chaseborough, but had eventually begun to join them in their weekend revels after she had been pressured by 'matrons not much older than herself'. The newest revellers, in other words, seek to initiate Tess into the world of sexuality; and though she does not join them in their celebration of the body, she follows them 'again, and again' out of an attraction to their 'contagious' 'hilariousness' – an escape from 'her monotonous attention to the poultry-farm all the week'. The dance itself is portrayed as another possibility for escape into a dream world: when the couples have been 'suitably matched'. 'the ecstasy and the dream [begin], in which emotion [is] the matter of the universe, and matter but an adventitious intrusion likely to hinder you from spinning where you [want] to'. The idea of emotion as 'the matter of the universe' seems a sensual version of Tess's earlier reverie before Prince's death, in which 'the occasional heave of the wind became the sigh of some immense sad soul, conterminous with the universe'; both ideas impose a subjective feeling onto the objective world. But here, as in the earlier scene, dream and matter collide, and the dreamers are restored to harsh reality: as the dancers tumble upon each other 'in a mixed heap', sexual ecstasy gives way to domestic bickering in the impatient complaints of the newly married woman whose husband had caused the accident. A Miltonic parallel is possible here too: the sexual lapse of Adam and Eve was followed quickly by petty recriminations.

Tess's position during the dance is suggestively emblematic: she stands 'on the momentary threshold of womanhood' poised between the wild sexual frenzy inside the storehouse and 'the wide night of the garden' behind her. The garden seems at first to be emblematic, like the *hortus conclusus*, of virtue and virginity, and Tess's choice seems equally clear: to exclude herself from the dance is to reject the sexual challenge, the antimasque world of chaos and revelry. But the appearance of Alec d'Urberville's 'loud laugh' from 'the shade of the garden' seems to complicate Tess's situation and to alter her choices. The *hortus conclusus* becomes Eve's garden of temptation as Alec's amused outburst unites 'with the titter within the room', and so Tess is surrounded on all sides by titillating sexual laughter which invites participation – a form of the 'contagious' hilarity that had drawn her to Chaseborough in the first place. At this point, however, Tess holds her ground and is reproached by Alec for her stubborn assertion of self: 'Very well, Miss Independence; please yourself'. Like the lady in *Comus*, she does not join in the spirit of the antimasque revellers surrounding her.

The return after the Chaseborough dance, however, provides Tess with a similar set of choices and this time her response is different. As she returns home with the Trantridge revellers (including two of Alec's former mistresses), she continues to keep herself at a remove from the drunken spirit surrounding her: 'They followed the road with a sensation that they were soaring along in a supporting medium, possessed of original and profound thoughts, themselves and surrounding nature forming an organism of which all the parts harmoniously and joyously interpenetrated each other'. But as the treacly snake travels down Car Darch's neck, Tess finally loses her sense of autonomy and yields to the communal ecstasy, not of drink or of sex, but of laughter. The moment is described (ch. 10) in terms that again suggest the antimasque:

> The laughter rang louder: they clung to the gate, to the posts, rested on their staves, in the weakness engendered by their convulsions at the spectacle of Car. Our heroine, who had hitherto held her peace, at this wild moment could not help joining in with the rest.

Here Tess finally joins the surrounding hilarity she had resisted at the Trantridge dance. Her yielding, however, should not be interpreted in any narrow moralistic way. She had been drawn from the beginning to the spirit of laughter among the Trantridge workers, and her act of union with them can even be seen in a positive light as an expression of her vitality and her initiation into the wild complexities of adulthood and sexuality. The fact that the revellers are called 'pilgrims' and carry staves suggests, indeed, that they are joined together by a common density – a human density that Tess ultimately embraces with them.

There is, in fact, a precedent for such a reading in Hawthorne's 'My Kinsman, Major Molineux', a story that may have influenced Hardy when he was constructing this scene in *Tess*. The plots of the two narrative sequences are quite different from each other, but both have the same emphasis on a young person's encounter with the bewildering complexities of an adult world that entices by its ecstatic wildness. In both stories, too, the youthful figure ends his or her isolation from the surrounding frenzy by joining in the derisive and 'convulsive' laughter of figures who seem to inhabit the chaotic universe of the antimasque. Here is the incident as it appears in Hawthorne's story:

> The contagion was spreading among the multitude, when, all at once, it seized upon Robin, and he sent forth a shout of laughter that echoed through the street; every man shook his sides, every man emptied his lungs, but Robin's shout was the loudest there.

It would be wrong, of course, simply to impose a reading of Hawthorne's passage on the analogous excerpt in Hardy, but the parallel is none the less intriguing, and it can be argued at least that both scenes operate in similar ways. The yielding to laughter is seen not simply as a moment of weakness but rather as a complex response to the incongruities of adult experience (Angel Clare's crazed laughter after Tess's confession might be seen in this way too). If Tess is yielding, she may also be undergoing a rite of passage. Her laughter, indeed, may indicate a readiness for the sexual experience, though she has not yet found an appropriate partner. An earlier title for the novel, *Too Late, Beloved*, reflects Hardy's interest in the perversity of circumstances, which often conflict with his characters' desires and intentions.

Tess's encounter with the surrounding wildness does not end, however, as Robin's does, with her explosion of laughter. A rite of passage implies that there will be a more difficult level of existence in the aftermath, and that is certainly true for Tess. When she joins the laughter of the revellers, she immediately becomes the focus for their jealousies and antagonisms. For the first time, she must face in the social world the consequences of Alec's attraction to her. Tess's response is characteristic: 'indignant and ashamed', she feels the desire both to triumph over and to escape 'the whole crew'. When Alec d'Urberville arrives on his horse, Tess discovers the opportunity to satisfy all her conflicting impulses. Assertion and retreat, independence and submission are possible simultaneously in the acceptance of Alec's offer:

coming as the invitation did at the particular juncture when fear and indignation at these adversaries could be transformed by a spring of the foot into a triumph over them she abandoned herself to her impulse, climbed the gate, put her toe upon his instep, and scrambled into the saddle behind him.

The sexual implications of this act are obvious, and were made more emphatic in 1891 when Alec's gig was changed to a horse. Prominent too is the emblematic language suggestive of moral action underlying the physical action. Tess '[abandons] herself to her impulse' and leaves the scene in 'triumph'. And even after she has ridden with Alec 'for some time', she '[clings] to him still panting in her triumph' – a contrast to her miserable panting as she resisted Alec's advances while racing down the hill in his gig. Tess's sexual caution, always present in some degree during her previous encounters with Alec, is now usurped by the pride of triumph.

This act of retreat and defiance, though provoked by different emotions, is connected with Tess's earlier paroxysm of laughter. Both actions, like the sexual act itself, are instinctive responses for which Tess must pay the consequences. The earlier act had seemed sexually neutral, but had initiated Tess into a world of new dangers: the verbal and physical assaults of those sexual rivals who had kept their distance as long as she had isolated herself from their communal rituals. When Tess joins the laughter, she also joins the sexual game – suggested perhaps by the names 'Queen of Diamonds' and 'Queen of Spades' – among her fellow workers. She is then poised for the act of pride that will allow her a triumph in that game.

One triumph leads to another defeat, however, as Car Darch's mother – an experienced player in the sexual game – knows well. Her remark, 'Out of the frying pan into the fire!' and the laughter of the other revellers reveal, indeed, that Tess's 'triumph' is hardly seen as such by them. They take pleasure at the prospect of her initiation into their dark rituals and return home in the same spirit of drunken ecstasy that had inspired their bacchanalian dance.

In the scenes describing Tess's ride to the Chase, Alec gradually reduces her mood of aggressive triumph to one of fretful defeat. Tess herself begins the process as she mentions to Alec her obligation to him for rescuing her: 'I am sure I ought to be much obliged to you'. Alec, however, turns Tess's cautiously polite remark back on her by shifting the conversation to her dislike of kissing him. Throughout the sequence, indeed, Alec subtly connects Tess's various reasons for gratitude to him with his own desire for her. He also takes advantage of Tess's fear of offending him. When she pushes him after he attempts to put his arm around her waist, he reproaches her in hurt tones, manipulates her into a defensive stance, and then aggressively reproaches her. These strategies win for Alec the desired result: 'He settled the matter of clasping his arm round her as he desired – and Tess expressed no further negative.'

Alec employs another manipulative technique in order to cajole Tess out of her indignation when they arrive at the Chase. In a tone 'between archness and real dismay', Tess accuses Alec of treachery, and in response he assumes a reasonable posture, emphasizing that he will take care of her as soon as he finds out where they are. Chastened by his seeming kindness, Tess then allows Alec to play a

chivalrous role and accepts the nest of dead leaves he makes for her.
At this point, Alec knows that Tess is sufficiently weak for him to use
his most effective rhetorical strategy. When he mentions the horse
and gifts he has given her family, Tess is reduced to helpless tears:

> "I'm grateful," she reluctantly admitted. "But I fear I do not –" The
> sudden vision of his passion for herself as a factor in this result so distressed
> her that, beginning with one slow tear, and then following with another, she
> wept outright.

Here Alec has successfully reversed Tess's moment of 'triumph'.
After this moment, she becomes completely passive in her responses
to him, and when he returns to find her sleeping, the tears of
submission are still on her eyelashes. Even before he has wakened
Tess by his sexual advances, whether they lead to rape or seduction, Alec seems to have defeated her spirit of opposition and
independence.

The full implications of all the scenes building up to the sexual
consummation in The Chase are difficult to discover or interpret.
Their emblematic quality suggests the kinds of moral readings one
can give to Milton: like the lady in *Comus*, Tess should reject the
temptation to join in the spirit of the antimasque world; like Eve in
Paradise Lost, she should refuse the appeals to pride made by her
tempter. Because she fails both moral tests, she 'falls' into sin and
suffers the consequences. And in keeping with the Miltonic pattern,
the sin of pride is followed by the sexual lapse. The complexity of the
whole narrative, however, militates against such a judgmental
reading. In Hardy's novel, the sexual act is ultimately seen as
natural, not as sinful or intrinsically evil, and pride is often a
necessary and instinctive assertion of self.

This discrepancy between Hardy's use of an emblematic method
that invites a strictly moral reading and his emphatic insistence –
through both the content of his narrative and the tone of his narrator
– that such a reading of Tess's experience is misguided and limiting,
provides him with an effective ironic device. Hardy takes a form that
expresses exactly those values he seeks to question and, by an
ironic inversion of that form, undermines those values. In the
Chaseborough and Chase scenes (the similarity in names suggests
the link between the experiences of the two places – the haytrusser's
dance is a communal version of the coupling in The Chase), Tess's
choices are not clearly defined. If there is a sinister quality in the

Chaseborough revellers, there is also a vitality in them which Tess cannot help responding to. If her decision to go off with Alec is impulsive, it is not so in a sinful or evil way. It is part, rather, of her instinctive and natural responses to life. The use of emblematic machinery thus serves to emphasize how inadequate the old moral values are in fostering an understanding of the experience of sex. And it is understanding, rather than moral judgement, that Hardy ultimately elicits from his reader.

In the final analysis, the scenes preceding the incident in The Chase do not provide a conclusive answer to the question of whether Tess was raped or seduced by Alec d'Urberville. Instead, they point to the reductive thinking about sex that such a question could represent, especially in Hardy's Victorian audience. If he had clearly described a rape, then his readers could have concluded that Tess did not herself have any sexual response to Alec; if he had described Tess as submitting completely to Alec's sexual attentions, then they might have dismissed her as unworthy of their sympathies. Instead, Hardy retains their interest and sympathy by leaving the sexual consummation in The Chase engulfed in fog, darkness, and silence. In doing so, he also turns his readers' attentions to the whole range of Tess's sexual responses to a man who is both attractive and repellent to her. The ambivalence in the scene in The Chase is an expression of the complexity and the contradictoriness of the sexual experience itself.

SOURCE: *Thomas Hardy Annual*, No. 4, ed. Norman Page (Macmillan, London, 1986), pp. 127–45.

David Lodge Tess, Nature, and the Voices of Hardy (1966)

Thomas Hardy might be described as an 'in-spite-of' novelist. That is, he figures in literary criticism and literary history as a great novelist 'in spite of' gross defects, the most commonly alleged of which are his manipulation of events in defiance of probability to produce a tragic–ironic pattern, his intrusiveness as authorial commentator, his reliance on stock characters, and his capacity for writing badly. In my view, the last of these alleged faults involves all the others, which, considered in the abstract as narrative strategies, are not necessarily faults. If we have reservations about them in Hardy's work, it must be because of the way they are articulated – or inadequately articulated.

Does Hardy write badly? One method of trying to answer such a question is that of Practical Criticism: the critical analysis of a passage extracted from its context. I therefore begin by citing an example of Practical Criticism *avant la lettre* performed by Vernon Lee upon five hundred words taken at random from *Tess of the d'Urbervilles*.[1] The unsatisfactoriness of her conclusions, I suggest, can only be made good by returning the passage to its context – the whole novel, and by trying to define the linguistic character of the novel in terms of its literary purpose. Using the perspective thus established, I turn to the consideration of another passage from the novel, one which has attracted a good deal of conflicting commentary. My intention is primarily to try and define as clearly as possible the sense in which the author of *Tess* may be said to 'write badly'; and to show that the consideration of this question, even when based on the close examination of short extracts, must inevitably involve us in the consideration of the meaning and artistic success of the novel as a whole.

The passage discussed by Vernon Lee is from Chapter XVI, the first chapter of the third 'Phase' of the novel, entitled 'The Rally'. It follows immediately after Tess, on her journey from her home at Marlott in the Vale of Blackmoor to the dairy of Talbothays, where she hopes to make a new start after her seduction by Alec d'Urberville, breaks into the 148th Psalm; and it describes her descent into the valley of the Var:

However, Tess found at least approximate expression for her feelings in the old *Benedicite* that she had lisped from infancy; and it was enough. Such high contentment with such a slight initial performance as that of having started towards a means of independent living was a part of the Durbeyfield temperament. Tess really wished to walk uprightly, while her father did nothing of the kind; but she resembled him in being content with immediate and small achievements, and in having no mind for laborious effort towards such petty social advancement as could alone be effected by a family so heavily handicapped as the once powerful d'Urbervilles were now.

There was, it might be said, the energy of her mother's unexpended family, as well as the natural energy of Tess's years, rekindled after the experience which had so overwhelmed her for the time. Let the truth be told – women do as a rule live through such humiliations, and regain their spirits, and again look about them with an interested eye. While there's life there's hope is a conviction not so entirely unknown to the 'betrayed' as some amiable theorists would have us believe.

Tess Durbeyfield, then, in good heart, and full of zest for life, descended the Egdon slopes lower and lower towards the dairy of her pilgrimage.

The marked difference, in the final particular, between the rival vales now showed itself. The secret of Blackmoor was best discovered from the heights around; to read aright the valley before her it was necessary to descend into its midst. When Tess had accomplished this feat she found herself to be standing on a carpeted level, which stretched to the east and west as far as the eye could reach.

The river had stolen from the higher tracts and brought in particles to the vale all this horizontal land; and now, exhausted, aged, and attenuated, lay serpentining along through the midst of its former spoils.

Not quite sure of her direction Tess stood still upon the hemmed expanse of verdant flatness, like a fly on a billiard table of indefinite length, and of no more consequence to the surroundings than that fly. The sole effect of her presence upon the placid valley so far had been to excite the mind of a solitary heron, which, after descending to the ground not far from her path, stood with neck erect, looking at her.

Suddenly there arose from all parts of the lowland a prolonged and repeated call –

'Waow! waow! waow!'

From the furthest east to the furthest west the cries spread by contagion, accompanied in some cases by the barking of a dog. It was not the expression of the valley's consciousness that beautiful Tess had arrived, but the ordinary announcement of milking-time – half-past four o'clock, when the dairy men set about getting in the cows.

The interested reader will find it rewarding to read Vernon Lee's commentary in its entirety, but I must confine myself to extracts from it. Her basic objection to this passage is 'that we are *being told about* the locality, not what is necessary for the intelligence of the situation'[2] – the 'then', she argues, poses falsely as a connective between the description of the valley and the meditative commentary that precedes it[3] – and that even as a straightforward description it is awkwardly and untidily written:

Notice how he tells us the very simple fact of how Tess stops to look round: 'Tess ... stood still upon the hemmed expanse of verdant flatness, like a fly on a billiard-table of indefinite length.' '*Hemmed* expanse,' that implies that the expanse had limits; it is, however, compared to a billiard-table 'of indefinite length'. Hardy's attention has slackened, and really he is talking a little at random. If he visualized that valley, particularly from above, he would not think of it, which is bounded by something on his own higher level (*hemmed*, by which he means *hemmed in*), in connection with a billiard table which is bounded by the tiny wall of its cushion. I venture to add that if, at the instant of writing, he were feeling the variety, the freshness of a valley, he would not be comparing it to a piece of cloth, with which it has only two things in common, being flat and being green; the utterly dissimilar flatness and greenness of a landscape and that of a billiard-table.

We are surely in the presence of slackened interest, when the Writer casts about for and accepts any illustration, without realizing it sufficiently to reject it. Such slackening of attention is confirmed by the poor structure of the sentence, 'a fly on a billiard-table of indefinite length *and* of no more consequence to the surroundings than that fly'. The *and* refers the 'of no more consequence' in the first instance to the billiard-table. Moreover, I venture to think the whole remark was not worth making: why divert our attention from Tess and her big, flat valley, surely easy enough to realize, by a vision of a billiard-table with a fly on it? Can the two images ever grow into one another? is the first made clearer, richer, by the second? How useless all this business has been is shown by the next sentence: 'The sole effect of her presence upon the placid valley so far had been to excite the mind of a solitary heron, which, after descending to the ground not far from her path, stood, with neck erect, looking at her.' Leave out all about the billiard-table, and the sentences coalesce perfectly and give us all we care to know.[4]

Vernon Lee's discussion of the rest of the passage is equally severe, finding everywhere a 'general slackening of attention, the vagueness showing itself in the casual distribution of the subject matter; showing itself, as we . . . see in lack of masterful treatment of the Reader's attention, in utter deficiency of logical arrangement. These are the co-related deficiencies due to the same inactivity and confusion of thought'.[5] In her closing remarks, however, Vernon Lee glaringly declines to accept the critical conclusions which follow from her analysis:

The woolly outlines, even the uncertain drawing, merely add to the impression of primeval passiveness and blind, unreasoning emotion; of inscrutable doom and blind, unfeeling Fate which belong to his whole outlook on life. And the very faults of Hardy are probably an expression of his solitary and matchless grandeur of attitude. He belongs to a universe transcending such trifles as Writers and Readers and their little logical ways.[6]

This disingenuous conclusion conceals either a failure of nerve before the Great Reputation, or an admission that the total effect of *Tess* is rather more impressive than the analysis of the extract suggests. I suspect that the latter is the case, and that if we consider the peculiarities of the passage in the context of the whole novel we shall arrive at a view of Hardy somewhere between the semi-illiterate blunderer exposed by Vernon Lee's commentary and the majestic figure transcending ordinary critical standards postulated in her conclusion. Such a consideration must start with an attempt to describe the function of the 'author's voice' in *Tess*, and proceed to discuss the attitudes of that author to Nature.

Underlying all Vernon Lee's criticism we can detect a prejudice against omniscient narration and in favour of Jamesian 'presentation'; against 'telling' and in favour of 'showing'. Just how dangerously narrowing and exclusive such prescriptive interpretation of Jamesian precept and practice can be, has been fully and persuasively argued by Wayne Booth in *The Rhetoric of Fiction*. But to note the existence of this element in Vernon Lee's approach to Hardy by no means disposes of her objections for a candid appraisal of *Tess* will reveal a fundamental uncertainty about the author's relation to his readers and to his characters, an uncertainty which is betrayed again and again in the language of the novel.

Tess, we are told, 'spoke two languages: the dialect at home, more or less; ordinary English abroad and to persons of quality' (III). To some extent the same is true of Hardy as narrator. There is the Hardy who can recreate dialect speech with flawless authenticity, who shows how closely he is in touch with the life of an agrarian community through being in touch with its idiom; and there is the Hardy speaking to 'the quality' in orotund sentences of laboured syntax and learned vocabulary, the Hardy who studied *The Times*, Addison, and Scott to improve his style.[7] It is probably the second Hardy who is responsible for the most spectacular stylistic lapses. But to regard the second Hardy as a regrettable excrescence superimposed upon the first, 'true', Hardy would be mistaken. For while one aspect of the novelist's undertaking in *Tess* demands a quality of immediacy , of 'felt life', achieved through his empathetic identification with his characters, particularly his heroine – in other words, the voice of the first Hardy – other aspects demand a quality of distance, both of time and space, through which the characters can be seen in their cosmic, historical and social settings – in other words, the voice of the second Hardy. And some of the most effective passages in the book – the description of the mechanical thresher, for instance (XLVII) – are articulated by this second Hardy.

Several accents are mingled in this voice. The author here is a combination of sceptical philosopher, and local historian, topographer, antiquarian, mediating between his 'folk' – the agricultural community of Wessex – and his readers – the metropolitan 'quality'. About the sceptical philosopher critics have had much to say, and most of them have regretted his presence. But if we reject such intrusions *qua* intrusions, we must reject other kinds of intrusion in the novel, in which case we shall not be left with very much in our hand. On the whole I think it will be found that these intrusions offend when they are crudely expressed. The sentence in Vernon Lee's passage, 'While there's life there's hope is a conviction not so entirely unknown to the "betrayed" as some amiable theorists would have us believe', for example, alienates rather than persuades the reader because it attempts to overthrow a social–moral cliché (that sexual betrayal is irredeemable) by nothing more potent than a proverbial cliché ('while there's life there's hope') and an ironic cliché ('amiable'). Compare the bitingly effective comment on the burial of Tess's child:

> So the baby was carried in a small deal box, under an ancient woman's shawl, to the churchyard that night, and buried by lantern-light, at the cost of a shilling, and a pint of beer to the sexton, in that shabby corner of God's allotment where He lets the nettles grow, and where all unbaptized infants, notorious drunkards, suicides and others of the conjecturally damned are laid. (XIV)

There is much to admire in this sentence. It begins with a subdued literal description of the pathetic particulars of the child's burial. A hint of irony appears in the shilling and the pint of beer. This becomes overt in the axis of the sentence which marks the transition from impersonal narration to comment – 'That shabby corner of God's allotment where He lets the nettles grow' – where, through the conventional idea that the churchyard is ground dedicated to God, He is held responsible for the behaviour of His earthly representatives – is presented, in fact, as a cynically careless smallholder, a stroke which has particular appropriateness in the agrarian environment of the story. The irony is sustained and intensified in the conclusion of the sentence, in the grouping of unbaptized infants with drunkards and suicides, and in the juxtaposition of the cool 'conjecturally' with the uncompromising 'damned', which effectively shocks us into awareness of the arrogance and inhumanity of presuming to forecast the eternal destiny of souls.

The author of *Tess* as local historian has received less attention than the author as sceptical philosopher, but his presence is unmistakable. The title-page tells us that the story of Tess is 'Faithfully Presented by Thomas Hardy'; and the explanatory note to the first edition of 1891 describes the novel, rather equivocally, 'as an attempt to give artistic form to a true sequence of things'. Although no dates are specified in the novel, we are often made to feel that Tess's story is not taking place in a continuum in which author and reader keep pace with the action and, so to speak, discover its outcome with the protagonists; but that it is already finished, that it took place in living memory, and is being reported to us by someone who lived in the locality, who knew her, though only slightly, who has received much of his information at second-hand, and whose account is one of imaginative reconstruction:

The name of the eclipsing girl, whatever it was, has not been handed down. (II)

. . . the stopt-diapason note which her voice acquired when her heart was in her speech, and which will never be forgotten by those who knew her. (XIV)

It was said afterwards that a cottager of Wellbridge, who went out late that night for a doctor, met two lovers in the pastures, walking very slowly, without converse, one behind the other, as in a funeral procession, and the glimpse he obtained of their faces seemed to denote that they were anxious and sad. (XXXV)

This voice of the author as local historian, dependent upon secondary sources, is in a state of uneasy co-existence with the voice of the author as creator and maker, as one acquainted with the deepest interior processes of his characters' minds. The uneasiness manifests itself notably in Hardy's hesitation about how far to attempt an imitation of the verbal quality of Tess's consciousness. Often he does not attempt it at all: the morning after Angel's sleep-walking, for instance, we are told that, 'It just crossed her mind, too, that he might have a faint recollection of his tender vagary, and was disinclined to allude to it from a conviction that she would take amatory advantage of the opportunity it gave her to appealing to him anew not to go' (XXXVII). That Hardy was not entirely happy about using vocabulary and syntax so far removed from Tess's natural idiom is suggested by this quotation: 'She thought, *without actually wording the thought*, how strange and godlike was a composer's power, who from the grave could lead through sequences of emotion, which he alone had felt at first, a girl like her who had never heard of his name. . . .' (XIII – *my italics*). Of course, in the strict sense, there is no 'real' Tess, and everything we know about her proceeds from the same source. But in terms of literary illusion, the distinction between Tess's consciousness and the author's articulation of it is a real one. Consider for example the account of her disappointment at the appearance of Alec d'Urberville:

> She had dreamed of an aged and dignified face, the sublimation of all the d'Urberville lineaments, furrowed with incarnate memories representing in hieroglyphic the centuries of her family's and England's history. But she screwed herself up to the work in hand, since she could not get out of it, and answered –
> 'I came to see your mother, sir.' (V)

The first sentence is a consciously literary paraphrase of Tess's vague, romantic expectations; whereas the second sentence is tough, simple and idiomatic, precisely rendering the verbal quality of Tess's consciousness. Each sentence is written in a mode which is legitimate and effective. But the transition between the two is too abrupt: a slight disturbance and confusion is created in the movement of the language, of a kind which we experience persistently in Hardy. It is particularly noticeable when he employs free indirect speech, for it would appear that the novelist who uses this device is obliged to be particularly faithful to the linguistic quality of his character's consciousness – the omission of the introductory verb 'he thought', 'he said', etc., seems to break down the literary convention by which we accept that the writer and his characters operate on quite different levels of discourse. Here is an example: 'Was once lost always lost really true of chastity? she would ask herself. She might prove it false if she could veil bygones. The recuperative power which pervaded organic nature was surely not denied to maiden-hood alone' (XV). The structure of the last sentence indicates that it is a rendering, in free indirect speech, of Tess's thought; but its vocabulary belongs to the voice of the authorial commentator.

This duality in the presentation of Tess's consciousness is par-
alleled in the treatment of Nature (understanding Nature in its
general cosmic sense and more specific sense of landscape, the earth,
flora and fauna). Ian Gregor has commented acutely on the
contradiction that exists in *Tess* between a 'Rousseauistic view of
Nature' as essentially life-giving, healthy, opposed to the inhibiting,
destructive forces of society and convention which alone generate
human misery, and the 'deterministic [view] which Hardy runs
alongside it', in which the world appears as a 'blighted star' and the
three dairymaids in love with Angel 'writhed feverishly under the
oppressiveness of an emotion which they neither expected nor
desired'.[8] This contradiction applies not only to generalizations
about Nature, but also to the treatment of landscape, and Gregor's
own assertion that 'at every stage of the tale interior states are
visualized in terms of landscape'[9] must be qualified. It would be
difficult to refute Vernon Lee's point that in the passage she quotes
the description of the landscape does *not* reflect Tess's interior state
of mind. On the other hand, we must not assume that such a
relationship between character and setting is a necessary feature of
imaginative prose, or that Hardy failed to establish it through
incompetence. The truth of the matter is rather more complex.

No attentive reader can fail to note how persistently Tess is
associated and identified with Nature, on several different levels. On
the social level, in terms of the rural/urban or agrarian/industrial
antithesis on which the values of the novel are largely based, she is a
'daughter of the soil' (XIX), almost timeless and anonymous – 'Thus
Tess walks on; a figure which is part of the landscape, a fieldswoman
pure and simple, in winter guise' (XLII) (the present tense here
having an effect of timelessness rather than of immediacy) – quasi-
symbolic 'object . . . foreign to the gleaming cranks and wheels' of
the railway engine (XXX). In religious or spiritual terms, Tess is a
Nature-worshipping pagan. Her beliefs are 'Tractarian as to phrase-
ology' 'but Pantheistic as to essence' (XXVII). 'You used to say at
Talbothays that I was a heathen', says Tess to Angel, as she lies on a
stone 'altar' at Stonehenge, 'So now I am at home' (LVIII). 'Did they
sacrifice to God here?' she asks later. 'No . . . I believe to the sun', he
replies (LVIII). And we may recall here, that at their second embrace
at Talbothays the sun had shone through the window 'upon her
inclining face, upon the blue veins of her temple, upon her naked
arm, and her neck, and into the depths of her hair' (XXVII).

This schematic association of Tess with Nature is enforced by insistent allusion, literal and figurative, to flora and fauna. Early in the novel she appears with 'roses at her breast; roses in her hat; roses and strawberries in her basket to the brim' (VI). Her hair is 'earth-coloured' (V), her mouth 'flower-like' (XIV), and her breath tastes 'of the butter and eggs and honey on which she mainly lived' (XXXVI). She is compared to a 'plant' (XXVII) and a 'sapling' (XX); the dew falls on her as naturally as on the grass (XX). To Angel, 'her arm, from her dabbling in the curds, was cold and damp to his mouth as new-gathered mushrooms' (XXVIII). While her physical appearance finds its metaphorical equivalents in the vegetable world, her behaviour is often compared to that of animals, particularly cats and birds. She 'wears the look of a wary animal' (XXXI). 'There was something of the habitude of the wild animal in the unreflecting instinct with which she rambled on' (XLI). She is as unresponsive to sarcasm as a 'dog or cat' (XXXV). She listens to Angel's harp like a 'fascinated bird', and moves through an overgrown garden 'as stealthily as a cat' (XIX). After sleep, 'she was as warm as a sunned cat' (XXVII). When she is happy her tread is like 'the skim of a bird which has not quite alighted' (XXXI). She faces d'Urberville with 'the hopeless defiance of the sparrow's gaze before its captor twists its neck' (XLVII).

This network of imagery and reference encourages us to think of Tess as essentially 'in touch' with Nature. Her character is defined and justified by metaphors of flora and fauna, and the changing face of the earth both directs and reflects her emotional life. At such moments we are least conscious of the literary *persona* of the author, and of his distance from the story. But it is equally true that Nature is quite indifferent to Tess and her fate. It is simply 'there', the physical setting against which the story takes place, described by the local historian with a wealth of geological and topographical detail, its moral neutrality emphasized by the sceptical philosopher.

This is surely the case in the passage quoted by Vernon Lee, particularly the two paragraphs beginning, 'The marked difference, in the final particular, between the rival vales now showed itself'. These paragraphs have the very tone of the guide-book, the tone of the parallel description of the Vale of Blackmoor: 'It is a vale whose acquaintance is best made by viewing it from the summits of the hills that surround it – except perhaps during the droughts of summer. An unguided ramble into its recesses in bad weather is apt to engender dissatisfaction with its narrow, tortuous, and miry ways' (II). But this earlier description is deliberately and clearly detached from the narrative, most obviously by its use of the present tense. Whereas in the passage quoted by Vernon Lee there is a fumbling attempt to relate the guide-book view to Tess. It is true that the two valleys might present themselves to Tess as in some sense 'rivals', but not in such impersonal, topographical terms.

A similar problem is raised by the simile of the fly, of which Vernon Lee asks, 'Why divert our attention from Tess and her big, flat valley, surely easy enough to realise, by a vision of a billiard table with a fly on it?' The answer surely is that Hardy, having got Tess into the valley, wants to give us, not a horizontal picture of the situation from her point of view, but a vertical, bird's eye picture; and he wants to do so in order to bring out her defencelessness, her isolation, her insignificance, in the eye of impersonal nature. (One is reminded of the later description of Flintcomb, in which the earth and the sky are compared to two vacant faces, 'the white face looking down on the brown face, and the brown face looking up at the white face, without anything standing between them but the two girls crawling over the surface of the former like flies' (XLIII), and even of the lines from *Lear* quoted in the Preface to the Fifth and later editions: 'As flies to wanton boys are we to the gods;/They kill us for their sport.') The trouble, once again, is that the structure of the sentence is confused and misleading. 'Not quite sure of her direction Tess stood still . . .' arouses expectations that any subsequent image will define her sense of uncertainty, whereas it does nothing of the sort. This confusion in the handling of the point of view, with its consequent disturbance of tone and meaning, is the essential basis of Vernon Lee's criticism; and I do not see how it can be dismissed, here or elsewhere in the novel.

On the other hand her critique can be challenged on two grounds. Firstly, she does not seem to have given her text the careful attention which close criticism demands. Her transcription of the passage (from an unspecified 'cheap edition') runs together the three paragraphs beginning 'Tess Durbeyfield, then', 'The marked difference', and 'The river had stolen', and adds on the following sentence to make one paragraph ending with 'fly'. This considerably increases the confusion in the point of view. For in my text the first of these three paragraphs stands as a self-contained statement of Tess's mood and action, which seems to have a sufficient logical connection with the preceding commentary to justify the use of the connective 'then'; and the third stands as a self-contained statement of the geological history of the valley. The attempt to provide some transition between the two in the second paragraph remains, however, a muddle.*

A more significant limitation of Vernon Lee's critique is her assumption that landscape in fiction must be vividly realized in sensuous terms, and reflect characters' states of consciousness. The fly and billiard table image does neither of these things, and is dismissed as the mechanical gesture of a nodding writer. She does not consider the possibility that it is a deliberately homely and bathetic image, designed to dissociate us from Tess at this point, to check any tendency to find reassurance in the identification of Tess's renewed hope with the fertile promise of the valley.

Ruskin called such identification the 'pathetic fallacy', and Hardy's ambiguous treatment of Nature throughout *Tess* might be formulated as his inability to decide whether the pathetic fallacy was fallacious or not. For of course it is Hardy himself who has encouraged us to make this kind of identification between Tess and her environment. A page or two before the passage quoted by Vernon Lee, we have the following description of Tess on a summit overlooking the valley into which she later descends:

The bird's eye perspective before her was not so luxuriantly beautiful, perhaps, as that other one which she knew so well; yet it was more cheering. It lacked the intensely blue atmosphere of the rival vale, and its heavy soils and scents; the new air was clear, bracing, ethereal. The river itself, which nourished the grass and cows of these renowned dairies, flowed not like the streams in Blackmoor. Those were slow, silent, often turbid; flowing over beds of mud into which the incautious wader might sink and vanish unawares. The Froom waters were clear as the pure River of Life shown to the Evangelist, rapid as the shadow of a cloud, with pebbly shallows that prattled to the sky all day long. There the water-flower was the lily; the crowfoot here.

Either the change in the quality of the air from heavy to light, or the sense of being amid new scenes where there were no invidious eyes upon her, sent up her spirits wonderfully. Her hopes mingled with the sunshine in an ideal photosphere which surrounded her as she bounded along against the soft

---

* Vernon Lee also omits from her transcription the line 'Waow! waow! waow!'; and when quoting the sentence with the fly simile a second time, she omits the comma after *length*, which removes the grammatical ambiguity of which she complains.

south wind. She heard a pleasant voice in every breeze, and in every bird's note seemed to lurk a joy. (XVI).

Here we have the 'rivalry' of the two valleys defined in a quite different way, a way that is verbally related to Tess's sensuous and emotional experience (the pedantic 'photosphere' striking the only incongruous note). The suggestions of hope and recovery are unmistakable, and appropriate to the first chapter of a 'Phase' of the novel entitled 'The Rally'. And yet, as Tess descends this same valley, the 'Froom waters . . . clear as the pure river of life shown to the Evangelist', become a river exhausted by aeons of geological activity, and we are sharply reminded that Tess was of not the slightest consequence to her natural surroundings, that the sudden burst of sound 'was not the expression of the valley's consciousness that lovely Tess had arrived'. 'Who in his senses would have thought that it was?' asks Vernon Lee. The answer is surely, a Romantic poet – Wordsworth, perhaps, to whom Hardy twice alludes in sarcastic asides elsewhere in the novel (III and LI). Hardy's undertaking to defend Tess as a pure woman by emphasizing her kinship with Nature[*] perpetually drew him towards the Romantic view of Nature as a reservoir of benevolent impulses, a view which one side of his mind rejected as falsely sentimental. Many Victorian writers, struggling to reconcile the view of Nature inherited from the Romantics with the discoveries of Darwinian biology, exhibit the same conflict, but it is particularly noticeable in Hardy.

A passage which seems especially revealing in this respect is that which describes Tess's gloomy nocturnal rambling in the weeks following her seduction, where she is explicitly shown entertaining the pathetic fallacy, and her mistake explicitly pointed out by the author:

On these lonely hills and dales her quiescent glide was of a piece with the element she moved in. Her flexuous and stealthy figure became an integral part of the scene. At times her whimsical fancy would intensify natural processes around her till they seemed a part of her own story. Rather they became a part of it; for the world is only a psychological phenomenon, and what they seemed they were. The midnight airs and gusts, moaning

---

[*] In the Preface to the 5th edition (1895), Hardy says of readers who had objected to the description of Tess as a 'pure' woman: 'They ignore the meaning of the word in Nature.'

amongst the tightly-wrapped buds and bark of the winter twigs, were formulae of bitter reproach. A wet day was the expression of irremediable grief at her weakness in the mind of some vague ethical being whom she could not class definitely as the God of her childhood, and could not comprehend as any other.

But this encompassment of her own characterization, based on shreds of convention, peopled by phantoms and voices antipathetic to her, was a sorry and mistaken creation of Tess's fancy – a cloud of moral hobgoblins by which she was terrified without reason. It was they that were out of harmony with the actual world, not she. Walking among the sleeping birds in the hedges, watching the skipping rabbits on a moonlit warren, or standing under a pheasant-laden bough, she looked upon herself as a figure of Guilt intruding into the haunts of Innocence. But all the while she was making a distinction where there was no difference. Feeling herself in antagonism she was quite in accord. She had been made to break an accepted social law, but no law known to the environment in which she fancied herself such an anomaly. (XIII)

Here we have two paragraphs, one describing Tess's subjective state of mind, and the second describing the objective 'reality'. We are meant to feel that the second cancels out the first, that 'guilt' is a fabrication of social convention, something unknown to the natural order which Tess distorts by projecting her own feelings into it. It seems to me, however, that there is an unresolved conflict in Hardy's rhetoric here. Not only are the 'midnight airs and gusts, moaning amongst the tightly wrapped buds and bark of the winter twigs' images of sorrow and remorse too moving and impressive to be easily overthrown by the rational arguments of the second paragraph; we are explicitly told that 'the world is only a psychological [i.e. subjective] phenomenon', in which case the view expressed in the second paragraph is as 'subjective' as that expressed in the first, and has no greater validity. If Tess felt herself in antagonism she *was* in antagonism. But in fact 'antagonism' is a clumsy formulation of the experience so delicately expressed in the first paragraph. That Nature should present its most sombre aspect to Tess when she is most desolate is, in a way, evidence of how deeply she is 'in accord' with Nature. There are many other places in the book where Hardy 'intensifies natural processes around Tess till they seem part of her story', without suggesting that she is deceiving herself, e.g. – 'She was wretched – O so wretched. . . . The evening sun was now ugly to her like a great inflamed wound in the sky. Only a solitary cracked-voiced reed-sparrow greeted her from the bushes by the river, in a sad, machine-made tone, resembling that of a past friend whose friendship she had outworn.' (XXI)

There is further ambiguity about the 'actual world' of nature with which, according to the author, Tess is in accord without realizing it. Is she mistaken in thinking herself guilty, or Nature innocent, or both? Elsewhere in the novel it is true to say that when Nature is not presented through Tess's consciousness, it is neither innocent nor guilty, but neutral; neither sympathetic nor hostile, but indifferent. When Tess and her young brother are driving their father's cart through the night, 'the cold pulses' of the stars 'were beating in serene dissociation from these two wisps of human life' (IV). The birds and rabbits skip happily and heedlessly round the defenceless Tess at her seduction (XI); and the Valley of the Var has no interest in her arrival. Is not Tess more human in preferring a sad but sympathetic Nature to a gay but indifferent one?

Hardy, then, here undermines our trust in the reliability of Tess's response to Nature, which is his own chief rhetorical device for defending her character and interesting our sympathies on her behalf. Without this winterpiece, which the author dismisses as a delusion of Tess's mind, we would lose the significance of Tess's renewal of energy in the spring which urges her towards the Valley of the Var and her 'rally':

A particularly fine spring came round, and the stir of germination was almost audible in the buds; it moved her, as it moved the wild animals, and made her passionate to go . . . some spirit within her rose automatically as the sap in the twigs. It was unexpended youth, surging up anew after its temporary check, and bringing with it hope, and the invincible instinct towards self-delight. (XV)

But of course the instinct is, in the event, vincible . . . and so we return to the basic contradiction pointed out by Ian Gregor, of which he says: 'the small measure in which this confusion, which is central to the theme of the novel, really decreases its artistic compulsion, suggests how effectively the latter is protected against the raids of philosophic speculation'.[10] I find myself in some disagreement with this verdict for, as I have tried to show, the confusion is not merely in the abstractable philosophical content of the novel, but inextricably woven into its verbal texture. . . .

SOURCE: David Lodge, *Language of Fiction* (1966), extract from chapter IV.

NOTES

1. Vernon Lee, *The Handling of Words and Other Studies in Literary Psychology* (London, 1923), pp. 222–41. Vernon Lee's method does not of course anticipate I. A. Richards' procedure in *Practical Criticism* (London, 1929) exactly. His is primarily pedagogic in purpose; hers, critical. He deals with complete short poems, the context from which they are extracted being historical knowledge of the poem's origins; she deals with extracts from novels which are identified, though they are not discussed as wholes. The similarity resides mainly in their mutual reliance on the close analysis of limited pieces by reference to certain constant assumptions about good literary language.

2. Lee, *The Handling of Words*, p. 224.

3. Ibid. p. 233.

4. Ibid. pp. 227–8.

5. Ibid. p. 234.

6. Ibid. pp. 240–1.

7. Douglas Brown, *Thomas Hardy* (London, 1954; reprinted 1961), p. 103.

8. Ian Gregor and Brian Nicholas, *The Moral and the Story* (London, 1962), pp. 143–4.

9. Ibid. p. 137.

10. Ibid. p. 144.

Tony Tanner Colour and Movement in *Tess of the d'Urbervilles* (1968)

'the discontinuance of immobility in any quarter suggested confusion' (*The Return of the Native*)

'the least irregularity of motion startled her' (*Tess of the d'Urbervilles*)

I

Every great writer has his own kind of legibility, his own way of turning life into a language of particular saliences, and in Hardy this legibility is of a singularly stark order. If we can think of a novelist as creating, among other things, a particular linguistic world by a series of selective intensifications of our shared vocabulary, then we can say that Hardy's world is unusually easy to read. The key words in his dialect, to continue the image, stand out like braille. It is as though some impersonal process of erosion had worn away much of the dense circumstantial texture of his tales, revealing the basic resistant contours of a sequence of events which Hardy only has to point to to make us see – like ancient marks on a barren landscape. And Hardy above all does make us see. Just as he himself could not bear to be touched, so he does not 'touch' the people and things in his tales, does not interfere with them or absorb them into his own sensibility. When he says in his introduction to *Tess of the d'Urbervilles* that 'a novel is an impression, not an argument', or in his introduction to *Jude the Obscure* that 'like former productions of his pen, *Jude the Obscure* is simply an endeavour to give shape and coherence to a series of seemings, or personal impressions', we should give full stress to the idea of something seen but not tampered with, something scrupulously watched in its otherness, something perceived but not made over. Hardy's famous, or notorious, philosophic broodings and asides are part of his reactions as a watcher, but they never give the impression of violating the people and objects of which his tale is composed. Reflection and perception are kept separate (in Lawrence they often tend to merge), and those who complain about the turgidity of his thoughts may be overlooking the incomparable clarity of his eyes.

II

This illusion that the tale exists independently of Hardy's rendering of it *is* of course only an illusion, but it testifies to art of a rather special kind. For all Henry James's scrupulous indirectness, Hardy's art is more truly impersonal. He goes in for graphic crudities of effect which James would have scorned, yet, as other critics have testified, the result is an anonymity which we more commonly associate with folk-tale, or the ballads. By graphic crudity of effect I am referring, for instance, to such moments as when Tess, shortly after being seduced, encounters a man who is writing in large letters 'THY, DAMNATION, SLUMBERETH, NOT.' There are commas between every word 'as if to give pause while that word was driven well home to the reader's heart'. This is not unlike Hardy's own art which is full of prominent notations, and emphatic pauses which temporarily isolate, and thus vivify, key incidents and objects. On the level of everyday plausibility and probability it is too freakish a chance which brings Tess and the painted words together at this point. In the vast empty landscapes of Hardy's world, peoples' paths cross according to some more mysterious logic – that same imponderable structuring of things in time which brought the *Titanic* and the iceberg together at one point in the trackless night sea. (See the poem 'The Convergence of the Twain'.) A comparable 'crudity' is discernible in the characterisation which is extremely schematic, lacking in all the minute mysteries of individual uniqueness which a writer like James pursued. *Angel* Clare is indeed utterly ethereal; his love is 'more spiritual than animal'. He even plays the harp! On the other hand Alec d'Urberville is almost a stage villain with his 'swarthy complexion ... full lips ... well-groomed black moustache with curled points', his cigars and his rakish way with his fast spring-cart. If we turn from character to plot sequence we see at once that the overall architecture of the novel is blocked out with massive simplicity in a series of balancing phases – The Maiden, Maiden No More; The Rally, The Consequence; and so on. Let it be conceded at once that Hardy's art is not subtle in the way that James and many subsequent writers are subtle. Nevertheless I think it is clear that Hardy derives his great power from that very 'crudity' which, in its impersonal indifference to plausibility and rational cause and effect, enhances the visibility of the most basic lineaments of the tale.

III

I want first to concentrate on one series of examples which show how this manifest visibility works. For an artist as visually sensitive as Hardy, colour is of the first importance and significance, and there is one colour which literally catches the eye, and is meant to catch it, throughout the book. This colour is red, the colour of blood, which is associated with Tess from first to last. It dogs her, disturbs her, destroys her. She is full of it, she spills it, she loses it. Watching Tess's life we begin to see that her destiny is nothing more or less than the colour red. The first time we (and Angel) see Tess, in the May dance with the other girls, she stands out. How? They are all in white except that Tess 'wore a red ribbon in her hair, and was the only one of the white company who would boast of such a pronounced adornment'. Tess is marked, even from the happy valley of her birth and childhood. The others are a semi-anonymous mass; Tess already has that heightened legibility, that eye-taking prominence which suggests that she has in some mysterious way been singled out. And the red stands out because it is on a pure white background. In that simple scene and colour contrast is the embryo of the whole book and all that happens in it.

This patterning of red and white is often visible in the background of the book. For instance 'The ripe hue of the red and dun kine absorbed the evening sunlight, which the white-coated animals returned to the eye in rays almost dazzling, even at the distant elevation on which she stood.' This dark red and dazzling white is something seen, it is something there; it is an effect on the retina, it is a configuration of matter. In looking at this landscape Tess in fact is seeing the elemental mixture which conditions her own existence. In the second chapter Tess is described as 'a mere vessel of emotion untinctured by experience'. The use of the word 'untinctured' may at first seem surprising; we perhaps tend to think of people being shaped by experience rather than coloured by it – yet the use of a word connected with dye and paint is clearly intentional. In her youth Tess is often referred to as a 'white shape' – almost more as a colour value in a landscape than a human being. And on the night of her rape she is seen as a 'white muslin figure' sleeping on a pile of dead leaves; her 'beautiful feminine tissue' is described as 'practically blank as snow'. The historic precedent for what is to happen to this vulnerable white shape is given at the start when we read that 'the Vale was known in former times as the Forest of White Hart, from a curious legend of King Henry III's reign, in which the killing by a certain Thomas de la Lynd of a beautiful white hart which the king had run down and spared, was made the occasion of a heavy fine'. Against all social injunctions, white harts are brought down. And in Tess's case the 'tincturing' – already prefigured in the red ribbon – starts very early.

The next omen – for even that harmless ribbon is an omen in this world – occurs when Tess drives the hives to market when her father is too drunk to do the job. When she sets out the road is still in darkness. Tess drifts, sleeps, dreams. Then there is the sudden collision and she wakes to find that Prince, their horse, has been killed by another cart. 'The pointed shaft of the cart had entered the breast of the unhappy Prince like a sword, and from the wound his life's blood was spouting in a stream and falling with a hiss on the road. In her despair Tess sprang forward and put her hand upon the hole, with the only result that she became splashed from face to skirt with the crimson drops. Then she stood helplessly looking on. Prince also stood firm and motionless as long as he could, till he suddenly sank down in a heap.' It is possible to say different things about this passage. On one level the death of the horse means that the family is destitute, which means in turn that Tess will have to go begging to the d'Urbervilles. Thus, it is part of a rough cause and effect economic sequence. But far more graphic, more disturbing and memorable, is the image of the sleeping girl on the darkened road, brutally awakened and desperately trying to staunch a fatal puncture, trying to stop the blood which cannot be stopped and only getting drenched in its powerful spurts. It adumbrates the loss of her virginity, for she, too, will be brutally pierced on a darkened road far from home; and once the blood of her innocence has been released, she too, like the stoical Prince, will stay upright as long as she can until, all blood being out, she will sink down suddenly in a heap. Compressed in that one imponderable scene we can see her whole life.

After this Tess is constantly encountering the colour red – if not literal blood, manifold reminders of it. When she approaches the d'Urberville house we read: 'It was of recent erection – indeed almost new – and of the same rich red colour that formed such a contrast with the evergreens of the lodge.' And the corner of the house 'rose like a geranium bloom against the subdued colours around'. Tess, with her red ribbon, also stood out against 'the subdued colours around'. Mysteriously, inevitably, this house will play a part in her destiny. And if this red house contains her future rapist, so it is another red house which contains her final executioner, for the prison where she is hanged is 'a large red-brick building'. Red marks the house of sex and death. When first she has to approach the leering, smoking Alec d'Urberville, he forces roses and strawberries on her, pushing a strawberry into her mouth, pressing the roses into her bosom. Hardy, deliberately adding to the legibility I am describing, comments that d'Urberville is one 'who stood fair to be the blood-red ray in the spectrum of her young life'. On the evening of the rape, Tess is first aware of d'Urberville's presence at the dance when she sees 'the red coal of a cigar'. This is too clearly phallic to need comment, but it is worth pointing out that, from the first, d'Urberville seems to have the power of reducing Tess to a sort of trance-like state, he envelopes her in a 'blue narcotic haze' of which his cigar smoke is the most visible emblem. On the night of the rape, at the dance, everything is in a 'mist', like 'illuminated smoke'; there is a 'floating, fusty *débris* of peat and hay' stirred up as 'the panting shapes spun onwards'. Everything together seems to form 'a sort of vegeto-human pollen'. In other words it becomes part of a basic natural process in which Tess is caught up simply by being alive, fecund, and female. D'Urberville is that figure, that force, at the heart of the haze, the mist, the smoke, waiting to claim her when the dance catches her up (we first saw her at a dance and she can scarcely avoid being drawn in). It is in a brilliant continuation of this blurred narcotic atmosphere that Hardy has the rape take place in a dense fog, while Tess is in a deep sleep. Consciousness and perception are alike engulfed and obliterated. When Tess first leaves d'Urberville's house she suddenly wakes up to find that she is covered in roses; while removing them a thorn from a remaining rose pricks her chin. 'Like all the cottagers in Blackmoor Vale, Tess was steeped in fancies and prefigurative superstitious; she thought this an ill omen.' The world of the book is indeed a world of omens (*not* symbols) in which things and events echo and connect in patterns deeper than lines of rational cause and effect. Tess takes it as an omen when she starts to bleed from the last rose pressed on her by Alec. She is right; for later on she will again wake up to find that he has drawn blood – in a way which determines her subsequent existence.

After the rape we are still constantly seeing the colour red. The man who writes up the words promising damnation is carrying 'a tin pot of red paint in his hand'. As a result 'these vermilion words shone forth'. Shortly after, when Tess is back at home, Hardy describes a sunrise in which the sun 'broke through chinks of cottage shutters, throwing stripes like red-hot pokers upon cupboards, chests of drawers, and other furniture within'. (The conjunction of sun-light and redness is a phenomenon I will return to.) And Hardy goes on: 'But of all ruddy things that morning the brightest were two broad arms of painted wood ... forming the revolving Maltese cross of the reaping-machine.' We will later see Tess virtually trapped and tortured on a piece of red machinery, and her way will take her past several crosses until she finds her own particular sacrificial place. When Tess is working in the fields her flesh again reveals its vulnerability. 'A bit of her naked arm is visible between the buff leather of the gauntlet and the sleeve of her gown; and as the day wears on its feminine smoothness becomes scarified by the stubble, and bleeds.' Notice the shift to the present tense: Hardy makes us look at the actual surfaces – the leather, the sleeve, the flesh, the blood. One of the great strengths of Hardy is that he knew, and makes us realise, just how very much the surfaces of things mean.

Of course it is part of the whole meaning of the book that there is as much red inside Tess as outside her. Both the men who seek to possess her see it. When Tess defies d'Urberville early on, she speaks up at him, 'revealing the red and ivory of her mouth'; while when Angel watches her unawares, 'she was yawning, and he saw the red interior of her mouth as if it had been a snake's'. When Angel does just kiss her arm, and he kisses the inside vein, we read that she was such a 'sheaf of susceptibilities' that 'her blood (was) driven to her finger ends'. Tess does not so much act as re-act. She would be content to be passive, but something is always disturbing her blood, and all but helplessly she submits to the momentums of nature in which, by her very constitution, she is necessarily involved. As for example when she is drawn by Angel's music 'like a fascinated bird' and she makes her way through, once again, a misty atmosphere ('mists of pollen') of uncontrollable swarming fertility and wide-spread insemination. It is a place of growth, though not wholly a place of beauty. There are 'tall blooming weeds' giving off 'offensive smells' and some of the weeds are a bright 'red'. 'She went stealthily as a cat through this profusion of growth, gathering cuckoo-spittle on her skirts, cracking snails that were underfoot, staining her hands with thistle-milk and slugslime, and rubbing off upon her naked arms sticky blights which though snow-white on the apple-tree trunks, made *madder* stains on her skin...' (my italics). In some of the earlier editions (certainly up to the 1895 edition) that final phrase was 'blood-red stains on her skin'; only later did Hardy change 'blood-red' to 'madder', a crimson dye made from a climbing plant. This change clearly reveals that he intended us once again to see Tess's arm marked with red, though he opted for a word which better suggested something in nature staining, 'tincturing', Tess as she pushes on through 'this profusion of growth'. And once again Hardy presents us with redness and snow-whiteness in the same scene – indeed, in the same plant.

After Tess has been abandoned by Angel and she has to renew her

endless journeying the red omens grow more vivid, more violent.
She seeks shelter one night under some bushes and when she wakes
up: 'Under the trees several pheasants lay about, their rich plumage
dabbled with blood; some were dead, some feebly twitching a wing,
some staring up at the sky, some pulsating quickly, some contorted,
some stretched out – all of them writhing in agony, except for the
fortunate ones whose torture had ended during the night by the
inability of nature to bear more'. There is much that is horribly
apposite for Tess in these bloody writhings. (It is worth noting that
Hardy uses the same word to describe the torments of the onset of
sexual impulse; thus he describes the sleeping girls at Talbothays
who are all suffering from 'hopeless passion'. 'They writhed feverishly under the oppressiveness of an emotion thrust on them by cruel
Nature's law – an emotion which they had neither expected nor
desired.' The writhings of life are strangely similar to the writhings
of death.) Looking at the dying birds Tess reprimands herself for
feeling self-pity, saying 'I be not mangled, and I be not bleeding'.
But she will be both, and she, too, will have to endure until she
reaches 'the inability of nature to bear more'. Like the white hart
and the pheasants she is a hunted animal; hunted not really by a
distinct human individual, but by ominous loitering presences like
the cruel gun-men she used to glimpse stalking through the woods
and bushes – a male blood-letting force which is abroad. Later
when she makes her fruitless trek to Angel's parents she sees 'a piece
of blood-stained paper, caught up from some meat-buyer's dust
heap, beat up and down the road without the gate; too flimsy to rest,
too heavy to fly away, and a few straws to keep it company'. It is
another deliberate omen. Tess, too, is blood-stained, she, too, is beat
up and down the road without the gate; too flimsy to rest, too heavy
(no door opens to her); and she, too, very exactly, is too flimsy to rest,
too heavy to fly away. (cf. Eustacia Vye's envy of the heron. 'Up in
the zenith where he was seemed a free and happy place, away from
all contact with the earthly ball to which she was pinioned; and she
wished that she could arise uncrushed from its surface and fly as he
flew then.') The blood-stained piece of paper is not a clumsy symbol;
it is one of a number of cumulative omens. When Alec d'Urberville
renews his pressure on Tess, at one point she turns and slashes him
across the face with her heavy leather gauntlet. 'A scarlet oozing
appeared where her blow had alighted and in a moment the blood
began dropping from his mouth upon the straw.' (Notice again the

conjunction of blood and straw.) The man who first made her bleed now stands bleeding from the lips. Blood has blood, and it will have more blood. We need only to see the scene – there, unanalysed, unexplained; a matter of violent movement, sudden compulsions. Hardy spends more time describing the glove than attempting to unravel the hidden thoughts of these starkly confronted human beings. Few other writers can so make us feel that the world is its own meaning – and mystery, requiring no interpretative gloss. Seeing the heavy glove, the sudden blow, the dripping blood, we see all we need to see.

At one point shortly before her marriage, Tess comes into proximity with a railway engine. 'No object could have looked more foreign to the gleaming cranks and wheels than this unsophisticated girl, with the round bare arms...' This feeling that her vulnerable flesh is somehow menaced by machinery is realised when she is later set to work on that 'insatiable swallower', the relentless threshing machine. It is a bright red machine, and the 'immense stack of straw' which it is turning out is seen as 'the *faeces* of the same buzzing red glutton'. Tess is 'the only woman whose place was upon the machine so as to be shaken bodily by its spinning'. She is beaten into a 'stupefied reverie in which her arm worked on independently of her consciousness' (this separation, indeed severance, of consciousness and body is a crucial part of Tess's experience). Whenever she looks up 'she beheld always the great upgrown straw-stack, with the men in shirt-sleeves upon it, against the grey north sky; in front of it the long red elevator like a Jacob's ladder, on which a perpetual stream of threshed straw ascended...'. There it is. We see Tess, trapped and stupefied in the cruel red man-made machine. Whenever she looks up in her trance of pain and weariness she sees – the long red elevator, the growing heap of straw, the men at work against the grey sky. It is a scene which is, somehow, her life: the men, the movement, the redness, the straw (blood and straw seem almost to be the basic materials of existence in the book – the vital pulsating fluid, and the dry, dead stalks). At the end of the day she is as a 'bled calf'. We do not need any enveloping and aiding words; only the legibility of vibrant, perceived detail.

The end of the book is sufficiently well known, but it is worth pointing out how Hardy continues to bring the colour red in front of our eyes. The landlady who peeps through the keyhole during Tess's anguish when Angel has returned reports that, 'her lips were bleeding from the clench of her teeth upon them'. It is the landlady who sees 'the oblong white ceiling, with this scarlet blot in the midst', which is at once the evidence of the murder and the completion of a life which also started with a red patch on a white background, only then it was simply a ribbon on a dress. The blood stain on the ceiling has 'the appearance of a gigantic ace of hearts'. In that shape of the heart, sex and death are merged in utmost legibility. After this we hardly need to see the hanging. It is enough that we see Tess climb into a vast bed with 'crimson damask hangings', not indeed in a home, for she has no home, but in an empty house to be 'Let Furnished'. And in that great crimson closed-in bed she finds what she has wanted for so long – rest and peace. Apart from the last scene at Stonehenge, we can say that at this point the crimson curtains do indeed fall on Tess; for if she was all white at birth, she is to be all red at death. The massed and linking red omens have finally closed in on Tess and her wanderings are over.

Tess is a 'pure woman' as the subtitle, which caused such outrage, specifically says. The purest woman contains tides of blood (Tess is always blushing), and if the rising of blood is sexual passion and the spilling of blood is death, then we can see that the purest woman is sexual and mortal. Remember Tess watching Prince bleed to death – 'the hole in his chest looking scarcely large enough to have let out all that animated him'. It is not a large hole that Alec makes in Tess when he rapes her, but from then on the blood is bound to go on flowing until that initial violation will finally 'let out all that animated her'. Hardy is dealing here with the simplest and deepest of matters. Life starts in sex and ends in death, and Hardy constantly shows how closely allied the two forms of blood-letting are in one basic, unalterable rhythm of existence.

IV

I have suggested that the destiny of Tess comes to us as a cumulation of visible omens. It is also a convergence of omens and to explain what I mean I want to add a few comments on the part played in her life by the sun, altars and tombs, and finally walking and travelling. When we first see Tess with the other dancing girls we read that they are all bathed in sunshine. Hardy, ever conscious of effects of light, describes how their hair reflects various colours in the sunlight. More, 'as each and all of them were warmed without by the sun, so each of them had a private little sun for her soul to bask in'. They are creatures of the sun, warmed and nourished by the sources of all heat and life. Tess starts sunblessed. At the dairy, the sun is at its most active as a cause of the fertile surgings which animate all nature. 'Rays from the sunrise drew forth the buds and stretched them into stalks, lifted up sap in noiseless streams, opened petals, and sucked out scents in invisible jets and breathings.' This is the profoundly sensuous atmosphere in which Tess, despite mental hesitations, blooms into full female ripeness. Hardy does something very suggestive here in his treatment of the times of day. Tess and Angel rise very early, before the sun. They seem to themselves 'the first persons up of all the world'. The light is still 'half-compounded, aqueous', as though the business of creating animated forms has not yet begun. They are compared to Adam and Eve. As so often when Tess is getting involved with the superior power of a man, the atmosphere is misty, but this time it is cold mist, the sunless fogs which precede the dawn. In this particular light of a cool watery whiteness, Tess appears to Angel as 'a visionary essence of woman', something ghostly, 'merely a soul at large'. He calls her, among other things, Artemis (who lived, of course, in perpetual celibacy). In this sunless light Tess appears to Angel as unsexed, sexless, the sort of non-physical spiritualised essence he, in his impotent spirituality, wants. (At the end he marries 'a spiritualized image of Tess'.) But Tess is inescapably flesh and blood. And when the sun does come up, she reverts from divine essence to physical milkmaid: 'her teeth, lips and eyes scintillated in the sunbeams, and she was again the dazzlingly fair dairymaid only...' (That placing of 'only' is typical of the strength of Hardy's prose.) Soon after this, the dairyman tells his story of the seduction of a young girl; 'none of them but herself seemed to see the sorrow of it'. And immediately we read, 'the evening sun was now ugly to her, like a great inflamed wound in the sky'. Sex is a natural instinct which however can lead to lives of utter misery. The same sun that blesses, can curse.

Tess drifts into marriage with Angel (her most characteristic way of moving in a landscape is a 'quiescent glide'), because 'every wave of her blood ... was a voice that joined with nature in revolt against her scrupulousness', but meanwhile 'at half-past six the sun settled down upon the levels, with the aspect of a great forge in the heavens'. This suggests not a drawing-up into growth, but a slow inexorable downward crushing force, through an image linked to that machinery which will later pummel her body. It is as though the universe turns metallic against Tess, just as we read when Angel rejects her that there is in him a hard negating force 'like a vein of metal in a soft loam'. This is the metal which her soft flesh runs up against. Other omens follow on her journey towards her wedding. Her feeling that she has seen the d'Urberville coach before; the postillion who takes them to church and who has 'a permanent running wound on the outside of his right leg'; the ominous 'afternoon crow' and so on. I want to point to another omen, when the sun seems to single out Tess in a sinister way. It is worth reminding ourselves that when Angel finally does propose to Tess she is quite sun-drenched. They are standing on the 'red-brick' floor and the sun slants in 'upon her inclining face, upon the blue veins of her temple, upon her naked arm, and her neck, and into the depths of her hair'. Now, on what should be the first night of her honeymoon we read: 'The sun was so low on that short, last afternoon of the year that it shone in through a small opening and formed a golden staff which stretched across to her skirt, where it made a spot like a paint-mark set upon her'. She has been marked before – first, with the blood of a dying beast, now with a mark from the setting sun. We find other descriptions of how the sun shines on Tess subsequently, but let us return to that crimson bed which, I suggested, effectively marked the end of Tess's journey. 'A shaft of dazzling sunlight glanced into the room, revealing heavy, old-fashioned furniture, crimson damask hangings, and an enormous four-poster bedstead....' The sun and the redness which have marked Tess's life, now converge at the moment of her approaching death. Finally Tess takes her last rest on the altar of Stonehenge. She speaks to Angel – again, it is before dawn, that sunless part of the day when he can communicate with her.

'Did they sacrifice to God here?' asked she.
'No', said he.
'Who to?'
'I believe to the sun. That lofty stone set away by itself is in the direction of the sun, which will presently rise behind it.'

When the sun does rise it also reveals the policemen closing in, for it is society which demands a specific revenge upon Tess. But in the configuration of omens which, I think, is the major part of the book,

Tess is indeed a victim, sacrificed to the sun. The heathen temple is fitting, since of course Tess is descended from Pagan d'Urberville, and Hardy makes no scruple about asserting that women 'retain in their souls far more of the Pagan fantasy of their remote forefathers than of the systematized religion taught their race at a later date'. This raises an important point. Is Tess a victim of society, or of nature? Who wants her blood, who is after her, the policemen, or the sun? Or are they in some sadistic conspiracy so that we see nature and society converging on Tess to destroy her? I will return to this question.

To the convergence of redness and the sun we must add the great final fact of the altar, an altar which Tess approaches almost gratefully, and on which she takes up her sacrificial position with exhausted relief. She says (I have run some of her words to Angel together): 'I don't want to go any further, Angel. ... Can't we bide here? ... you used to say at Talbothays that I was a heathen. So now I am at home ... I like very much to be here.' Fully to be human is partly to be heathen, as the figure of Tess on the altar makes clear. (And after all what did heathen originally mean? – someone who lived on the heath; and what was a pagan? – someone who lived in a remote village. The terms only acquire their opprobrium after the advent of Christianity. Similarly Hardy points out that Sunday was originally the sun's day – a spiritual superstructure has been imposed on a physical source.) Tess's willingness to take her place on the stone of death has been manifested before. After she returns from the rape we read 'her depression was then terrible, and she could have hidden herself in a tomb'. On her marriage night, Angel sleepwalks into her room, saying 'Dead! Dead! Dead! ... My wife – dead, dead!' He picks her up, kisses her (which he can now only manage when he is unconscious), and carries her over a racing river. Tess almost wants to jog him so that they can fall to their deaths: but Angel can negotiate the dangers of turbulent water just as he can suppress all passion. His steps are not directed towards the movement of the waters but to the stillness of stone. He takes Tess and lays her in an 'empty stone coffin' in the 'ruined choir'. In Angel's life of suppressed spontaneity and the negation of passional feeling, this is the most significant thing that he does. He encoffins the sexual instinct, then lies down beside Tess. The deepest inclinations of his psyche, his very being, have been revealed.

Later on, when things are utterly desperate for Tess's family and

they literally have no roof over their heads, they take refuge by the
church in which the family vaults are kept (where 'the bones of her
ancestors – her useless ancestors – lay entombed'). In their exhaustion they erect an old 'four-post bedstead' over the vaults. We see
again the intimate proximity of the bed and the grave. This sombre
contiguity also adumbrates the ambiguous relief which Tess later
finds in her crimson four-post-bed which is also very close to death.
On this occasion Tess enters the church and pauses by the 'tombs of
the family' and 'the door of her ancestral sepulchre'. It is at this
point that one of the tomb effigies moves, and Alec plays his insane
jest on her by appearing to leap from a tomb. Again, we are invited
to make the starkest sort of comparison without any exegesis from
Hardy. Angel, asleep, took Tess in his arms and laid her in a coffin.
Alec, however, seems to wake up from the tomb, a crude but
animated threat to Tess in her quest for peace. Angel's instinct
towards stillness is countered by Alec's instinct for sexual motion.
Together they add up to a continous process in which Tess is simply
caught up. For it is both men who drive Tess to her death: Angel by
his spiritualised rejection, Alec by his sexual attacks. It is notable
that both these men are also cut off from any fixed community; they
have both broken away from traditional attitudes and dwellings.
Angel roams in his thought; Alec roams in his lust. They are both
drifters of the sort who have an unsettling, often destructive impact
in the Hardy world. Tess is a pure product of nature; but she is
nature subject to complex and contradictory pressures. Angel wants
her spiritual image without her body (when he finds out about her
sexual past he simply denies her identity, 'the woman I have been
loving is not you'); Alec wants only her body and is indifferent to
anything we might call her soul, her distinctly human inwardness.
The effect of this opposed wrenching on her wholeness is to induce a
sort of inner rift which develops into something we would now call a
schizophrenia. While still at Talbothays she says one day: 'I do
know that our souls can be made to go outside our bodies when we
are alive.' Her method is to fix the mind on a remote star and 'you
will soon find that you are hundreds and hundreds o' miles away
from your body, which you don't seem to want at all'. The deep
mystery by which consciousness can seek to be delivered from the
body which sustains it, is one which Hardy had clearly before him.
That an organism can be generated which then wishes to repudiate
the very grounds of its existence obviously struck Hardy as provid-

ing a very awesome comment on the nature of nature. Tess is robbed of her integrated singleness, divided by two men, two forces. (This gives extra point to the various crosses she passes on her travels; the cross not only indicating torture, but that opposition between the vertical and the horizontal which, as I try to show, is ultimately the source of Tess's – and man's – sufferings in Hardy.) It is no wonder that when Alec worries and pursues her at the very door of her ancestors' vault, she should bend down and whisper that line of terrible simplicity – 'Why am I on the wrong side of this door?' (A relevant poem of great power is 'A Wasted Illness' of which I quote three stanzas which are very apt for Tess:

> 'Where lies the end
> To this foul way?' I asked with weakening breath.
> Thereupon ahead I saw a door extend –
>   The door to Death.
>
>   It loomed more clear:
> 'At last!' I cried. 'The all-delivering door!'
> And then, I know not how, it grew less near
>   Than theretofore.
>
>   And back slid I
> Along the galleries by which I came,
> And tediously the day returned, and sky,
>   And life – the same.)

Tess at this moment is utterly unplaced, with no refuge and no comfort. She can only stumble along more and rougher roads; increasingly vulnerable, weary and helpless, increasingly remote from her body. Her only solution is to break through that 'all-delivering door', the door from life to death which opens on the only home left to her. This she does, by stabbing Alec and then taking her place on the ritual altar. She has finally spilled all the blood that tormented her; she can then abandon the torments of animateness and seek out the lasting repose she has earned.

V

This brings me to what is perhaps the most searching of all Hardy's preoccupations – walking, travelling, movement of all kinds. Some-where at the heart of his vision is a profound sense of what we may call the mystery of motion. *Tess of the d'Urbervilles* opens with a man staggering on rickety legs down a road, and it is his daughter we shall see walking throughout the book. Phase the Second opens, once again, simply with an unexplained scene of laboured walking. 'The basket was heavy and the bundle was large, but she lugged them along like a person who did not find her especial burden in material things. Occasionally she stopped to rest in a mechanical way by some gate or post; and then, giving the baggage another hitch upon her full round arm, went steadily on again'. Such visualised passages carry the meaning of the novel, even down to the material burdens which weigh down that plump, vulnerable flesh: the meaning is both mute and unmistakable. At the start of Phase the Third, again Tess moves: 'she left her home for the second time'. At first the journey seems easy and comfortable in 'a hired trap'; but soon she gets out and walks, and her journey again leads her into portents of the life ahead of her. 'The journey over the intervening uplands and lowlands of Egdon, when she reached them, was a more troublesome walk than she had anticipated, the distance being actually but a few miles. It was two hours, owing to sundry turnings, 'ere she found herself on a summit commanding the long-sought-for vale. . . .' The road to the peaceful vale of death is longer and harder than she thinks. Always Tess has to move, usually to harsher and more punishing territories, and always Hardy makes sure we *see* her. After Angel has banished her: 'instead of a bride with boxes and trunks which others bore, we see her a lonely woman with a basket and a bundle in her own porterage. . . .' Later she walks to Emminster Vicarage on her abortive journey to see Angel's parents. She starts off briskly but by the end she is weary, and there are omens by the way. For instance, from one eminence she looks down at endless little fields, 'so numerous that they look from this height like the meshes of a net'. And again she passes a stone cross, Cross-in-Hand, which stands 'desolate and silent, to mark the site of a miracle, or murder, or both'. (Note the hint of the profound ambivalence and ambiguity of deeds and events.) At the end of this journey there is nobody at home and there follows the incident of Tess losing her walking boots, another physical reminder that the walking gets harder and harder for her. 'Her journey back was rather a meander than a march. It had no sprightliness, no purpose; only a tendency.' Her movements do get more laden throughout, and by the end Hardy confronts us with one of the strangest phenomena of existence

– motion without volition. (Interestingly enough, Conrad approaches the same phenomenon in *The Secret Agent* where walking is also the most insistent motif.) The only relief in her walking is that as it gets harder it also approaches nearer to darkness. Thus when she is summoned back to her family: 'She plunged into the chilly equinoctial darkness ... for her fifteen miles' walk under the steely stars'; and later during this walk from another eminence she 'looked from that height into the abyss of chaotic shade which was all that revealed itself of the vale on whose further side she was born'. She is indeed returning home, just as Oedipus was returning home on all his journeyings. Perhaps the ultimate reduction of Tess, the distillation of her fate, is to be seen when she runs after Angel having murdered Alec. Angel turns round. 'The tape-like surface of the road diminished in his rear as far as he could see, and as he gazed a moving spot intruded on the white vacuity of its perspective.' This scene has been anticipated when Tess was working at Flintcomb-Ash: 'the whole field was in colour a desolate drab; it was a complexion without features, as if a face, from chin to brow, should be only an expanse of skin. The sky wore, in another colour, the same likeness; a white vacuity of countenance with the lineaments gone. So these two upper and nether visages confronted each other all day long ... without anything standing between them but the two girls crawling over the surface of the former like flies.' In both cases we see Tess as a moving spot on a white vacuity. And this extreme pictorial reduction seems to me to be right at the heart of Hardy's vision.

VI

To explain what I mean I want to interpose a few comments on some remarkable passages from the earlier novel, *The Return of the Native*. Chapter I describes the vast inert heath. Chapter II opens 'Along the road walked an old man'. He in turn sees a tiny speck of movement – 'the single atom of life that the scene contained'. And this spot is a 'lurid red'. It is, of course, the reddleman, but I want to emphasise the composition of the scene – the great stillness and the tiny spot of red movement which is the human presence on the heath. Shortly after, the reddleman is scanning the heath (Hardy's world is full of watching eyes) and it is then that he first sees Eustacia Vye. But how he first sees her is described in a passage which seems to me so central to Hardy that I want to quote at length.

> There the form stood, motionless as the hill beneath. Above the plain rose the hill, above the hill rose the barrow, and above the barrow rose the figure. Above the figure there was nothing that could be mapped elsewhere than on a celestial globe.
>
> Such a perfect, delicate, and necessary finish did the figure give to the dark pile of hills that it seemed to be the only obvious justification of their outline. Without it, there was the dome without the lantern; with it the architectural demands of the mass were satisfied. The scene was strangely homogeneous. The vale, the upland, the barrow, and the figure above it amounted to unity. Looking at this or that member of the group was not observing a complete thing, but a fraction of a thing.
>
> The form was so much like an organic part of the entire motionless structure that to see it move would have impressed the mind as a strange phenomenon. Immobility being the chief characteristic of that whole which the person formed portion of, the discontinuance of immobility in any quarter suggested confusion.
>
> Yet that is what happened. The figure perceptibly gave up its fixity, shifted a step or two, and turned round.

Here in powerful visual terms is a complete statement about existence. Without the human presence, sheer land and sky seem to have no formal, architectural significance. The human form brings significant outline to the brown mass of earth, the white vacuity of sky. But this moment of satisfying formal harmony depends on stillness, and to be human is to be animated, is to move. Hardy's novels are about 'the discontinuance of immobility'; all the confusions that make up his plots are the result of people who perceptibly give up their fixity. To say that this is the very condition of life itself is only to point to the elemental nature of Hardy's art. All plants and all animals move, but much more within rhythms ordained by their native terrain than humans – who build things like the *Titanic* and go plunging off into the night sea, or who set out in a horse and cart in the middle of the night to reach a distant market, in both cases meeting with disastrous accidents. Only what moves can crash. Eustacia moves on the still heath, breaking up the unity: there is confusion ahead for her. Not indeed that the heath is in a state of absolute fixity; that would imply a dead planet: 'the quality of repose appertaining to the scene ... was not the repose of actual stagnation, but the apparent repose of incredible slowness'. Hardy often reminds us of the mindless insect life going on near the feet of his bewildered human protagonists; but to the human eye, which after all determines the felt meaning of the perceptible world, there is a movement which is like stillness just as there is a motion which seems to be unmitigated violence. The 'incredible slowness' of the heath, only serves to make more graphic the 'catastrophic dash' which ends the lives of Eustacia and Wildeve. And after the 'catastrophic dash' – 'eternal rigidity'.

The tragic tension between human and heath, between motion and repose, between the organic drive away from the inorganic and, what turns out to be the same thing, the drive to return to the inorganic, provides Hardy with the radical structure of his finest work. The human struggle against – and temporary departure from – the level stillness of the heath, is part of that struggle between the vertical and the horizontal which is a crucial part of Hardy's vision. We read of the 'oppressive horizontality' of the heath, and when Eustacia comes to the time of her death Hardy describes her position in such a way that it echoes the first time we saw her, and completes the pattern of her life. She returns to one of those ancient earthen grave mounds, called barrows. 'Eustacia at length reached Rainbarrow, and stood still there to think ... she sighed bitterly and ceased to stand erect, gradually crouching down under the umbrella as if she were drawn into the Barrow by a hand from underneath.' Her period of motion is over; her erect status above the flatness of the heath terminates at the same moment; she is, as it were, drawn back into the undifferentiated levelness of the earth from which she emerged. At the same time, you will remember, Susan is tormenting and burning a wax effigy of Eustacia, so that while she seems to be sinking back into the earth Hardy can also write 'the effigy of Eustacia was melting to nothing'. She is losing her distinguishing outline and features. Hardy describes elsewhere how a woman starts to 'lose her own margin' when working the fields. Human life is featured and contoured life: yet the erosion of feature and contour seems to be a primal activity of that 'featureless convexity' of the heath, of the earth itself.

VII

This feeling of the constant attrition, and final obliteration, of the human shape and all human structures, permeates Hardy's work.

Interviewed about Stonehenge he commented that 'it is a matter of wonder that the erection has stood so long', adding however that 'time nibbles year after year' at the structure. Just so he will write of a wind 'which seemed to gnaw at the corners of the house'; of 'wooden posts rubbed to a glossy smoothness by the flanks of infinite cows and calves of bygone years'. His work is full of decaying architecture, and in *The Woodlanders* there is a memorable picture of the calves roaming in the ruins of Sherton Castle, 'cooling their thirsty tongues by licking the quaint Norman carving, which glistened with moisture'. It is as though time, and all the rest of the natural order, conspired to eat away and erase all the structures and features associated with the human presence on, or intrusion into, the planet. Of one part of the heath Hardy says, in a sentence of extraordinarily succinct power, 'There had been no obliteration, because there had been no tending'. Tess working at Flintcomb-Ash in a landscape which is 'a complexion without features', and Tess running after Angel, 'a moving spot intruding on the white vacuity', is a visible paradigm of the terms of human life – a spot of featured animation moving painfully across a vast featureless repose. Like Eustacia, and like her wounded horse Prince, having remained upright as long as possible, she, too, simply 'ceases to stand erect' and lies down on the flat sacrificial stone, as though offering herself not only up to the sun which tended her, but to the obliterating earth, the horizontal inertia of which she had disturbed.

Life is movement, and movement leads to confusion. Tess's instinct is for placidity, she recoils from rapid movements. Yet at crucial times she finds herself in men's carriages or men's machines. She has to drive her father's cart to market and Prince is killed. Alec forces her into his dog-cart which he drives recklessly at great speed. Of Tess we read 'the least irregularity of motion startled her' and Alec at this point is disturbing and shaking up blood which will only be stilled in death. Angel, by contrast, takes Tess to the wedding in a carriage which manages to suggest something brutal, punitive, and funereal all at once – 'It had stout wheel-spokes, and heavy felloes, a great curved bed, immense straps and springs, and a pole like a battering-ram.' All these man-made conveyances, together with the ominous train, and that 'tyrant' the threshing machine, seem to threaten Tess. And yet she is bound to be involved in travelling, and dangerous motion, because she has no home. At the beginning the parson telling Tess's father about his noble lineage says an ominous

thing. To Jack's question, 'Where do we d'Urbervilles live?' he
answers: 'You don't live anywhere. You are extinct – as a county
family.' Tess does not live anywhere. The one home she finds, Angel
turns her out of. That is why she is bound to succumb to Alec. He
provides a place but not a home. Alec takes her to Sandbourne, a
place of 'detached mansions', the very reverse of a community. It is
a 'pleasure city', 'a glittering novelty', a place of meretricious
fashion and amusement. "Tis all lodging-houses here. . . .' This is
the perfect place for the modern, deracinated Alec. It is no place at
all for Tess, 'a cottage girl'. But we have seen her uprooted, forced to
the roads, ejected from houses, knocking on doors which remain
closed to her; we have seen the process by which she has become an
exhausted helpless prey who is finally bundled off to a boarding
house. Her spell in this place is a drugged interlude; she seems
finally to have come to that state of catatonic trance which has been
anticipated in previous episodes.

Angel realises that 'Tess had spiritually ceased to recognize the
body before him as hers – allowing it to drift, like a corpse upon the
current, in a direction dissociated from its living will'. Tess has been
so 'disturbed' by irregularities of motion, so pulled in different
directions, that she really is sick, split, half dead. Hardy was very
interested in this sort of split person – for instance, people with
primitive instincts and modern nerves, as he says in another book –
and we can see that Tess is subjected to too many different
pressures, not to say torments, ever to achieve a felicitous wholeness
of being.

VIII

This brings me to a problem I mentioned earlier. We see Tess
suffering, apparently doomed to suffer; destroyed by two men, by
society, by the sun outside her and the blood inside her. And we are
tempted to ask, what is Hardy's vision of the *cause* of this tale of
suffering. Throughout the book Hardy stresses that Tess is damned,
and damns herself, according to man-made laws which are as
arbitrary as they are cruel. He goes out of his way to show how
Nature seems to disdain, ignore or make mockery of the laws which
social beings impose on themselves. The fetish of chastity is a
ludicrous aberration in a world which teems and spills with such
promiscuous and far-flung fertility every year (not to say a brutal

caricature of human justice in that what was damned in the woman was condoned in the man). So, if the book was an attempt to show an innocent girl who is destroyed by society though justified by Nature, Hardy could certainly have left the opposition as direct and as simple as that. Social laws hang Tess; and Nature admits no such laws. But it is an important part of the book that we feel Nature itself turning against Tess, so that we register something approaching a sadism of *both* the man-made *and* the natural directed against her. If she is tortured by the man-made threshing machine, she is also crushed by the forge of the sun; the cold negating metal in Angel is also to be found in the 'steely stars'; the pangs of guilt which lacerate her are matched by the 'glass splinters' of rain which penetrate her at Flintcomb-Ash. Perhaps to understand this feeling of almost universal opposition which grows throughout the book, we should turn to some of Hardy's own words, when he talks of 'the universal harshness ... the harshness of the position towards the tempera-ment, of the means towards the aims, of today towards yesterday, of hereafter towards today'. When he meditates on the imment dis-appearance of the d'Urberville family he says, 'so does Time ruthlessly destroy his own romances'. This suggests a universe of radical opposition, working to destroy what it works to create, crushing to death what it coaxes into life. From this point of view society only appears as a functioning part of a larger process whereby the vertical returns to the horizontal, motion lapses into stillness and structure cedes to the unstructured. The policemen appear as the sun rises: Tess is a sacrifice to both, to all of them. Hardy's vision is tragic and penetrates far deeper than specific social anomalies. One is more inclined to think of Sophocles than, say, Zola, when reading Hardy. The vision is tragic because he shows an ordering of existence in which nature turns against itself, in which the sun blasts what it blesses, in which all the hopeful explorations of life turn out to have been a circuitous peregrination towards death. 'All things are born to be diminished' said Pericles at the time of Sophocles; and Hardy's comparable feeling that all things are tended to be obliterated, reveals a Sophoclean grasp of the bed-rock ironies of existence.

Tess is the living demonstration of these tragic ironies. That is why she who is raped lives to be hanged; why she who is so physically beautiful feels guilt at 'inhabiting the fleshy tabernacle with which Nature had endowed her'; why she who is a fertile source of life comes to feel that 'birth itself was an ordeal of degrading personal compulsion, whose gratuitousness nothing in the result seemed to justify'. It is why she attracts the incompatible forces represented by Alec and Angel. It is why she who is a lover is also a killer. Tess is gradually crucified on the oppugnant ironies of circumstance and existence itself, ironies which centre, I have suggested, on the fact of blood, that basic stuff which starts the human spot moving across the white vacuity. Blood, and the spilling of blood; which in one set of circumstances can mean sexual passion and the creation of life, and in another can mean murderous passion and death – two forms of 'red' energy intimately related – this is the substance of Tess's story. And why should it all happen to her? You can say, as some people in the book say fatalistically, 'It was to be'. Or you could go through the book and try to work out how Hardy apportions the blame – a bit on Tess, a bit on society, a bit on religion, a bit on heredity, a bit on the Industrial Revolution, a bit on the men who abuse her, a bit on the sun and the stars, and so on. But Hardy does not work in this way. More than make us judge, Hardy makes us see; and in looking for some explanation of why all this should happen to Tess, our eyes finally settle on that red ribbon marking out the little girl in the white dress, which already foreshadows the red blood stain on the white ceiling. In her beginning is her end. It is the oldest of truths, but it takes a great writer to make us experience it again in all its awesome mystery.

IX

Hardy specifically rejected the idea of offering any theory of the universe. In his General Preface to his works, he said 'Nor is it likely, indeed, that imaginative writings extending over more than forty years would exhibit a coherent scientific theory of the universe even if it had been attempted – of that universe concerning which Spencer owns to the "paralyzing thought" that possibly there exists no comprehension of it anywhere. But such objectless consistency never has been attempted....' Hardy 'theorizes' far less than Lawrence, but certain images recur which serve to convey his sense of life – its poignancy and its incomprehensibility – more memorably than any overt statement. Death, the sudden end of brilliance and movement, occupied a constant place in his thoughts. 'The most prosaic man becomes a poem when you stand by his grave and think of him' he once wrote; and the strange brightness of ephemeral creatures is something one often meets in his fiction – pictorially, not philosophically. 'Gnats, knowing nothing of their brief glorification, wandered across the shimmer of this pathway, irradiated as if they bore fire within them, then passed out of its line, and were quite extinct.' Compare with that the description of the girls returning from the dance: 'and as they went there moved onward with them ... a circle of opalized light, formed by the moon's rays upon the glistening sheet of dew. Each pedestrian could see no halo but his or her own....' Hardy is often to be found stressing the ephemeral nature of life – 'independent worlds of ephemerons were passing their time in mad carousal', 'ephemeral creatures, took up their positions where only a year ago other had stood in their place when these were nothing more than germs and inorganic particles' – and it often seems that the ephemeral fragments of moving life are also like bubbles of light, temporary illuminations of an encroaching darkness. One of the greatest scenes in all of Hardy is in *The Return of the Native* when Wildeve and Venn, the reddleman, gamble at night on the heath. Their lantern makes a little circle of light which draws things out of the darkness towards it. 'The light of the candle had by this time attracted heath-flies, moths and other winged creatures of night, which floated round the lantern, flew into the flame, or beat about the faces of the two players.' Much more suggestively as they continue to throw dice: 'they were surrounded by dusky forms about four feet high, standing a few paces beyond the rays of the lantern. A moment's inspection revealed that the encircling figures were heath-croppers, their heads being all towards the players, at whom they gazed intently.' When a moth extinguishes the candle, Wildeve gathers glow worms and puts them on the stone on which they are playing. 'The incongruity between the men's deeds and their environment was great. Amid the soft juicy vegetation of the hollow in which they sat, the motionless and the uninhabited solitude, intruded the chink of guineas, the rattle of dice, the exclamations of the reckless players.' Again, it is one of those scenes which seems to condense a whole vision of human existence – a strange activity in a small circle of light, and all round them the horses of the night noiselessly gathering at the very perimeter. And in *Tess of the d'Urbervilles* Hardy develops this scene into a metaphor of great power. He is describing how Tess's love for Angel sustains her: 'it enveloped her as a photosphere, irradiated her into forgetfulness of her past sorrows, keeping back the gloomy spectres that would persist in their attempts to touch her – doubt, fear, moodiness, care, shame. She knew that they were waiting like wolves just outside the circumscribing light, but she had long spells of power to keep them in hungry subjection there.... She walked in brightness, but she knew that in the background those shapes of darkness were always spread.'

I have singled out this image not only because I think there is something quintessentially Hardyan in it, but also because I think it is an image which profoundly influenced D. H. Lawrence. Here is a final quotation, taken from the culmination of perhaps his greatest novel, *The Rainbow*. Ursula is trying to clarify her sense of her own presence in the world.

This world in which she lived was like a circle lighted by a lamp. This lighted area, lit up by man's completest consciousness, she thought was all the world: that here all was disclosed for ever. Yet all the time, within the darkness she had been aware of points of light, like the eyes of wild beasts, gleaming, penetrating, vanishing. And her soul had acknowledged in a great heave of terror only the outer darkness. This inner circle of light in which she lived and moved, wherein the trains rushed and the factories ground out their machine-produce and the plants and the animals worked by the light of science and knowledge, suddenly it seemed like the area under an arc lamp, wherein the moths and children played in the security of blinding light, not even knowing there was any darkness, because they stayed in the light.

But she could see the glimmer of dark movement just out of range, she saw the eyes of the wild beasts gleaming from the darkness, watching the vanity of the camp fire and the sleepers; she felt the strange, foolish vanity of the camp, which said 'Beyond our light and our order there is nothing', turning their faces always inwards toward the sinking fire of illuminating consciousness, which comprised sun and stars, and the Creator, and the System of Righteousness, ignoring always the vast shapes that wheeled round about, with half-revealed shapes lurking on the edge....
Nevertheless the darkness wheeled round about, with grey shadow-shapes of wild beasts, and also with dark shadow-shapes of the angels, whom the light fenced out, as it fenced out the more familiar beasts of darkness.

Lawrence, more insistent as to the torments and sterilities of consciousness, confidently ascribes positive values to the shapes prowling around the perimeter of the circle of light. But Lawrence's *interpretation* – itself an act of consciousness – of the population of the dark, is only something overlayed on the *situation*, that irreducible configuration which is to be found, I suggest, at the heart of Hardy's work. 'She walked in brightness, but she knew that in the background those shapes of darkness were always spread.'

SOURCE: *Critical Quarterly*, 10 (Autumn 1968).

JUDE THE OBSCURE

Rosemary Sumner   Jude and Sue: the Psychological Problems of Modern Man and Woman   (1981)

Hardy's creation of Sue is one of his most remarkable achievements. This character is, as J. I. M. Stewart has said, 'virtually a point of major innovation in prose fiction'. With her, Hardy is exploring further aspects of personality already developed in Knight and Angel, but in comparison with Sue, these earlier attempts look like merely tentative trial runs. With Sue, he made tremendous advances on all fronts: he explored psychological problems in greater depth than ever before; he dealt with taboo subjects with clarity and honesty; he raised questions about mental health and psychological balance which were to become central in psychological and educational writing and in novels during the following 30 years and beyond; he began to touch on possible new ways of conceiving character in the novel which were to be developed by his successors; and he rendered Sue's personality with concreteness, vividness and immediacy. In the combination of these elements Hardy achieved the peak of his art as a novelist because he here fuses most completely the analytical and creative aspects of characterisation. As we read about Sue, we are fully conscious of her psychological problems, but she is never merely a clinical case; Hardy makes us experience her mode of being. We cannot fully appreciate what Hardy is doing without grasping intellectually the problematic nature of her personality and simultaneously entering into it imaginatively.

The many qualities she has in common with Knight and Angel – their abstemiousness, especially in sexual matters, and their consequent claims to virtue, their rationality – make clear that these particular psychological characteristics have interested Hardy for a long time; with Sue, he reaches a fuller and more profound understanding and realisation of them. The structure of *Jude the Obscure* allows this further treatment. In *Tess of the d'Urbervilles* Angel is subordinate. His major psychological upheaval in Brazil is given cursory treatment so as to avoid shifting the balance of the book away from Tess. In *Jude the Obscure* Sue carries equal weight to Jude in the structure of the novel, and this seems to have been the intention from the start. In the manuscript there is, in the early part, a lot of detail about Sue's life as the niece of the head of a Christminster College, and early ideas for a title included 'The Simpletons', 'The Malcontents' and 'Hearts Insurgent'. It seems reasonable to assume that Hardy expected to give more or less equal prominence to Sue and Jude, thus allowing himself the scope to carry out that exploration in depth of her psychological problems which he could not allow himself with Angel. With this fuller treatment, Hardy has space to present Sue dramatically instead of, as often with Angel, through analytical summary. Most of the analysis of Sue is done by herself, or by Jude and Phillotson as they grope towards an understanding of her, or by Arabella, in her limited but shrewd assessments. Thus the whole treatment of Sue is more complete and more extreme than that of Angel. By dealing with a woman rather than a man, Hardy was challenging contemporary opinion more sharply, since women's sexual feelings (if they were admitted to exist) were regarded as an even more indelicate subject than men's. Sue's problems are more extreme than Angel's and eventually develop into mental illness, so that in this respect Hardy is going much further than he has gone before. Also, since he manages to make Sue more interesting, more attractive and more neurotic than Knight and Angel, he achieves a sense of greater intensity, of a more extreme personality with her than with the earlier characters. The originality of the portrait lies in the detailed examination of Sue's particular kind of psychological complexity; the strength lies in the way these insights are used to create a vivid and living character whose emotions we can experience vicariously.

A close reading of the book reveals that as well as being intuitively sympathetic to Sue's feelings, Hardy is consciously aware that he is exploring regions of great psychological complexity; but there is also external evidence which substantiates this point. One of the most valuable contributions to our understanding of *Jude the Obscure* and especially of the character of Sue is Edmund Gosse's review which

Hardy said was 'the most discriminating that has yet appeared'.
Gosse stressed the importance of Sue in the book:

The 'vita sexualis' of Sue is the central interest of the book, and enough is
told about it to fill the specimen tables of a German specialist. Fewer
testimonies will be given to her reality than Arabella's because hers is a
much rarer case. But her picture is not less admirably drawn; Mr Hardy
has, perhaps, never devoted so much care to the portrait of a woman. She is
a poor, maimed 'degenerate', ignorant of herself and of the perversion of her
instincts, full of febrile, amiable illusions, ready to dramatise her empty life,
and play at loving though she cannot love. Her adventure with the
undergraduate has not taught her what she is: she quits Phillotson still
ignorant of the source of her repulsion; she lives with Jude, after a long,
agonising struggle, in a relationship that she accepts with distaste, and
when the tragedy comes, her children are killed, her poor, extravagant brain
slips one grade further down and she sees in this calamity the chastisement
of God. What has she done to be chastised? She does not know but supposes
it must be her abandonment of Phillotson, to whom, in a spasm of self-
abasement and shuddering with repulsion, she returns without a thought for
the misery of Jude. It is a terrible study in pathology, but of the splendid
success of it, of the sustained intellectual force implied in the evolution of it,
there cannot, I think, be two opinions.

In a further letter, ten days after his first appreciative response to
the review, Hardy wrote again to Gosse saying 'you are quite right'
but, nevertheless, modifying Gosse's comments to some extent. He
referred to Sue's 'abnormalism' and spoke of her sexual instinct as
'unusually weak and fastidious', yet said that it was 'healthy, as far
as it goes'. Later in the same letter, he said, 'Sue is a type of woman
which has always had an attraction for me, but the difficulty of
drawing the type has kept me from attempting it until now'. It seems
that while Hardy felt that Gosse had fully understood his intentions
with Sue, he hesitated to endorse phrases like 'a terrible study in
pathology'; this would indeed equate it with 'the specimen tables of
a German specialist'. Sue's attractiveness for Hardy, stated in this
letter, is evident in the whole conception of the character. His great
achievement with Sue is that she is simultaneously a suitable case
for analysis, and a living, changing, 'unstatable' woman, evoking
vivid and changing responses from those who know her.

It is interesting to consider here Havelock Ellis's review of *Jude the
Obscure*, since he too played down the neurotic element: 'Sue is
neurotic, some critics say; it is fashionable to play cheerfully with

terrible words you know nothing about. "Neurotic" these good people say by way of dismissing her, innocently unaware that many a charming "urban miss" of their own acquaintance would deserve the name at least as well'. I think these comments can be attributed primarily to Hardy's achievement in conveying Sue's attractiveness and charm, also to the fact that many of her attitudes are (in spite of her revolutionary claims) those of the ideal Victorian maiden, wishing to 'ennoble some man to high aims' and to elevate him out of his masculine 'grossness', so that she did appear perhaps as one among many 'charming urban misses'. Ellis is also claiming superior and specialised knowledge of neuroses, but his later psychological writings classify people very similar to Sue as distinctly neurotic:

We have to recognise that while in its more moderate demands an ideal of sexual abstinence remains within the sphere of sanity, it tends to pass beyond that sphere in its more extravagant demands. The conception of sexual abstinence . . . fails even to evoke any genuine moral motives, for it is exclusively self-regarding and self-centred . . . moreover in this special matter of sex, it is inevitable that the needs of others, and not merely the needs of the individual himself, should determine action.

This might well be a summary of Sue's behaviour. Ellis's description of 'exclusively self-regarding and self-centred behaviour' exactly fits her treatment of the undergraduate, of Phillotson, of Jude. It would not be an exaggeration to say that she practises sexual abstinence 'passing beyond the sphere of sanity' with the undergraduate and Phillotson, and even with Jude, it is the self-centred need to keep him from Arabella which makes her consent to go to bed with him eventually, although in eloping with him she told him she had 'resolved to trust you to set my wishes above your gratification'. The neurotic nature of Sue's attitude to marriage is emphasised by a comparison with Sally in 'Interlopers at the Knap' (*Wessex Tales*), who decides quite calmly and rationally after one disappointment that she does not wish to marry. Hardy shows her decision to be a sensible one; he appreciates her unconventionality and independence, and enjoys the discomfiture and incredulity of the somewhat despised suitor. This mature, well-balanced woman's refusal to conform to the expected pattern of behaviour contrasts with Sue's neurotic advances and retreats. This rather slight story shows that Hardy made a clear distinction between a sane rational rejection of marriage and the neurotic, hovering on the brink, shifting between rejection and acceptance of Sue.

Surprisingly, Lawrence is among those who failed to recognise the real nature of Sue's conflicts. This is probably because he is far more concerned in his 'Study of Thomas Hardy' to work out his own philosophy and development as a novelist than to assess Hardy's. The study is interesting and illuminating because it shows the affinity between the two novelists and the powerful impact Hardy made on Lawrence, but, as he said, 'it is the story of my heart' and thus illuminates Lawrence more than Hardy. He has some interesting comments on Sue, but simplifies Hardy's treatment of her sexuality. He says she is completely sexless, 'scarcely a woman at all', and argues that she should have been left intact. 'She had a being special and beautiful. . . . She was not a woman. . . . Why was there no place for her? . . . . If we had reverence for what we are, our life would take real form, and Sue would have a place, as Cassandra had a place.' This part of his argument suggests that Sue's sexual problems come almost exclusively from the outside, from the men who love her and from a society which cannot accept the existence of sexless beings. This argument cannot be sustained in the light of Sue's repeated attempts to attract men. Nor can Hardy possibly be construed as saying that society forces a sex life on its unwilling members. Much of the novel is an indictment of a society which restricts, condemns and denies sexuality. Possibly Lawrence is here really expressing second thoughts on Miriam (the essay was written in 1914, the year after the publication of *Sons and Lovers*). The character he creates out of Sue has some resemblances to Miriam, in her high evaluation of learning and knowing (though Sue is far more intellectual and widely read than Miriam) and also in the way he imagines she treats her children. He says Sue 'would not be satisfied till she had them crushed on her breast'. In fact, Sue only shows an interest in her children when they are dead. She attends to their physical needs, but otherwise seems to have little contact with them. She talks to Little Father Time who is old enough to take part in an intellectual discussion, but the total impression, created largely by omission, is of a cool, detached mother. It is only when they are dead and buried that she becomes passionate about them, struggling hysterically to get to them in their coffins. This is characteristic of all her human relationships. When there is a barrier (Jude is outside the window, or she is communicating with him by letter, or he is departing for the last time), she can feel affectionate, even passionate. Lawrence is using Hardy as a springboard to stimulate his own imagination rather than analysing his art as a novelist.

A close reading of *Jude the Obscure* makes it clear that Hardy with great insight and sympathy, is carefully building up a picture of a personality precariously balanced on the edge of sanity. As Havelock Ellis says, she is not 'a monstrosity', but Hardy has created convincingly the weaknesses in her personality, 'the channels of least resistance along which the forces of life most impetuously rush', and which in the end undermine her precarious balance. Sue is the culmination of several attempts of this kind – Boldwood, Knight, Angel, possibly Clym – but she is the most complex and the most vital and, as he said to Gosse, exceptionally difficult to depict. One of the difficulties was the ban on saying anything honestly about sexual relationships in contemporary fiction. 'Candour in English Fiction' makes it clear that Hardy regarded this as one of the major obstacles to the writing of serious fiction. His final novel is a determined attempt to break down these taboos on 'those issues which are not to be mentioned in respectable magazines and select libraries'. He is far more explicit in his treatment of Sue's sexual difficulties than his letter to Gosse suggests. There he says,

One point illustrating this I could not dwell upon: that, though she had children, her intimacies with Jude have never been more than occasional, even when they were living together (I mention that they occupy separate rooms, except towards the end) and one of her reasons for fearing the marriage ceremony is that she fears it would be breaking faith with Jude to withhold herself at pleasure, or altogether, after it; though while uncontracted she feels at liberty to yield herself as seldom as she chooses.

But in fact all this is very clear in the book itself. Hardy stresses her intellectual fascination with sex in her 'daring' views on 'The Song of Songs': 'I hate such humbug as could attempt to plaster over with ecclesiastical abstractions such ecstatic, natural human love as lies in that great and passionate song'. The implications of this come out quite clearly in her account of her relations with the undergraduate: 'he wanted me to be his mistress, but I wasn't in love with him – and on my saying I should go away if he didn't agree to *my* plan, he did so. We shared a sitting-room for fifteen months.' Already here she is showing her delight in arousing love and her inability to reciprocate it and her mixture of guilt and self-righteousness because of this.

While weeping and accusing herself of cruelty, she says, 'People say I must be cold-natured – sexless – on account of it. But I won't have it! Some of the most passionately erotic poets have been the most self-contained in their daily lives,' and a little later she speaks of wanting 'to ennoble some man to high aims'. This attempt to justify herself for alternately attracting and repulsing her lovers is of course a rationalisation of something Hardy suggests is not wholly involuntary. The marriage 'rehearsal' with Jude on her wedding morning is deliberately contrived by this 'epicure of the emotions'. Her sadism is directed towards both lovers. She wilfully tortures Jude by taking his arm for the first time that morning and forcing him through what is almost a mock marriage; then she taunts Phillotson with the fact that they have done this. Between the two episodes, she masochistically expresses remorse for what she had done. Jude thinks, 'Possibly she would go on inflicting such pains again and again, and grieving for the sufferers again and again, in all her colossal inconsistency'.

The immediate cause of her marrying Phillotson is jealousy at the news of Jude's marriage, but Hardy hints at other reasons too. He stresses Phillotson's age, his restrained, subdued manner. He also shows how Sue retreats whenever Jude becomes demonstrative. He seems to be implying that Sue feels she can marry Phillotson because she hopes that he will not make any sexual demands on her (and Jude thinks that she does not know what marriage means). Hardy makes it clear to the reader that any such expectations are false. He says of Phillotson's celibacy, 'It was a renunciation forced upon him by his academic purpose, rather than a distaste for women which had hitherto kept him from closing with one of the sex in matrimony'. If she had any such hope, it is fading by the evening of the wedding, when 'she has the manner of a scared child'. After the wedding, Hardy unambiguously underlines the physical repulsion Sue feels. Shortly after the marriage, she defends a hypothetical woman 'who didn't like to live with her husband . . . merely because she had a feeling against it – a physical objection – a fastidiousness'. A little later, she is admitting, 'It is a torture to me to live with him as a husband'. This feeling on Sue's part is explicable enough. Hardy has made it quite clear that she is not in love with Phillotson. She has committed herself to the marriage for a number of largely negative reasons – annoyance at Jude's marriage, fear of public opinion after her expulsion from college, and a failure to imagine what marriage is likely to entail. The fact that she has not foreseen that the sexual relationship may be a problem is perhaps more revealing than her dismay when actually confronted by Phillotson as a lover. She is educated, emancipated, independent, and presumably is not simply ignorant of the facts of marriage. Yet she repressed all thoughts about this aspect of it until it was too late. This suggests a tendency to repression which is often a feature of neurosis and throws some light on her return to Phillotson's bed at the end of the novel.

There seem to me absolutely no grounds for assuming that Phillotson has 'some unexplained sexual peculiarities'. Lerner and Holmstrom argue that the book is ambiguous on this point, that 'a novelist who has begun to be outspoken must not stop halfway'. Admittedly, there are two hints that Phillotson might be abnormal sexually, one coming from Aunt Drusilla: 'There be certain men here and there no woman can stomach. I should have said he was one'. But Aunt Drusilla is hardly an unbiased judge since she is a spinster with a lifelong hatred of marriage. The other suggestion comes from Widow Edlin:

'What is it you don't like about him?' asked Mrs Edlin curiously. 'I cannot tell. It is something . . . I cannot say.'

But this only shows that the 'normal' Mrs Edlin could not sense anything she 'couldn't stomach' in Phillotson. All the other evidence points to Phillotson being tolerant, long-suffering, generous, but annoyed, disappointed and hurt by Sue's horror of a sexual relationship with him. There is, perhaps, a hint that the marriage was not consummated; when Jude and Sue meet for the first time after it, 'she seemed unaltered – he could not say why'. Hardy's intention is not clear here, but there is otherwise no ambiguity about Sue's relations with Phillotson; physically, she cannot stand him, she would rather sleep in a cupboard among spiders than with him, she jumps out of a window to escape him. Lerner and Holmstrom ask, 'Is Hardy portraying the sufferings of a woman who has found herself with a physically incompatible mate, or a frigid woman? The difference is surely important, and it implies a further question, what were her sexual relations with Jude like?'. They do not answer the question, but Hardy does. He not only shows both relationships in considerable detail, but he makes explicit comments: 'the ethereal, fine-nerved, sensitive girl, quite unfitted by temperament

and instinct to fulfil the conditions of the matrimonial relationship
with Phillotson, possibly with scarce any man'. (It is, incidentally,
noteworthy that when Sue is weeping and saying that Aunt Drusilla
is right about Phillotson, she says 'perhaps I ought not to have
married', not 'perhaps I ought not to have married him'.)

   Of course, there is a difference in her relationship with Jude, for,
as Arabella says, 'She cares for him – as much as she is able to'. But
Hardy, nevertheless, builds up a clear picture of her feeling of dislike
for any sexual relationship. She wishes that Eve had not fallen 'so
that some harmless form of vegetation might have peopled Paradise'. She asks Jude to elope with her, then demands separate rooms.
Hardy gives an outspoken conversation between them with no
'stopping short'. Sue, obviously, is evasive. The dialogue would be
very unconvincing if she were not. But Hardy manages to convey the
important point quite clearly in spite of this. At first she says that
she is timid, then that Phillotson has been so generous that, 'I would
rather not be other than a little rigid' (the tortuous negative
effectively conveys her nervous tension). Then she admits, 'My
nature is not so passionate as yours'. She tells Jude that Phillotson
'was too resigned almost' at letting her go. Here Hardy brings in
something he emphasises at every opportunity – Sue's incessant
hunger to be loved, even though she knows she can give almost
nothing in return. The conversation continues:

'If I loved him ever so little as a wife, I'd go back to him even now'. 'But you
don't, do you?' 'It is true – O so terribly true – I don't.' 'Nor me neither, I
half fear', he said pettishly, 'Nor anybody perhaps! Sue, sometimes when I
am vexed with you, I think you are incapable of real love . . . .'
'. . . . My liking for you is not as some women's perhaps. But it is a delight in
being with you, of a supremely delicate kind, and I don't want to go further
and risk it by – an attempt to intensify it! . . . . I resolved to trust you to set
my wishes above your gratification.'

Here Hardy makes Sue express very clearly her distaste for and fear
of sexual intercourse. Her attitude is conveyed with delicacy and
subtlety, but the reader cannot misunderstand what she is saying.
Had he made her any more explicit, he would have falsified her
character. This stilted, rational piece of self-analysis is characteristic and credible. She has what Lawrence calls 'sex in the head'
rather than the sexlessness he attributes to her, enjoys talking about
love and sex, but gets frightened as soon as a physical relationship

seems to be a possibility. Lerner and Holmstrom's suggestion that Hardy ought to have answered the question, 'Is she frigid? Yes or No?' has something of the crudity of a sex manual or a lawcourt beside Hardy's complex rendering of Sue's conflicting emotions.

Far from 'stopping short', Hardy continues to show Sue's fears of sex. When Jude and Sue are both divorced and free to marry one another, Sue says, 'I would much rather go on . . . only meeting by day. It is so much sweeter – for the woman at least, and when she is sure of the man'. Eventually, of course, she does go to bed with Jude, but this is solely in order to keep him for herself when Arabella threatens her security. She does it saying, 'I am not a cold-blooded sexless creature, am I, for keeping you at such a distance?'

But they do not get married. They do not even share a bedroom. Hardy unobtrusively indicates this on the night of Father Time's arrival: 'Jude had just retired to bed and Sue was about to enter her chamber adjoining when she heard the knock and came down'. This is the point that Hardy said he 'could not dwell on' in the letter to Gosse. But he succeeds in making it clear enough that Sue had not wholeheartedly accepted Jude as a lover. 'A fortnight or three weeks' after Arabella's influential visit, he shows Sue's jealousy of her aroused again by the sight of Little Father Time. Jude comments, 'Jealous little Sue! I withdraw all my remarks about your sexlessness'. Hardy certainly intends us to notice the timing of this remark, and later implies that the situation of those first two or three weeks is not much improved after years of living together, when Jude says she is 'not quite so impassioned perhaps as I could wish'. Hardy further increases the impression that their sexual relationship has not had much positive impact on Sue by showing her, after she has accepted Little Father Time and told him to call her mother, saying, 'I feel myself getting intertwined with my kind'. Yet making love with Jude has not made her feel this.

So far then Hardy has given a sympathetic portrait of an extremely complex personality for whom some calamitous experience is likely to be traumatic. While enabling us to experience what it is like to be Sue, what it is like to know and love her and be exasperated by her, he has simultaneously outlined the symptoms of psychological weakness which will make any disastrous event traumatic for her. Her particular kind of psychological problem was perhaps particularly prevalent among women at that time, possibly partly as a result of the growing opportunities for education and partial emancipation – a situation which tended to arouse new hopes and frustrate them at the same time. Freud devised what he called a 'parable' about two girls which gives in outline the kind of contrast Hardy embodied in Sue and Arabella. Freud's story describes how as little girls the daughters of a landlord and his caretaker play with one another and have sex play together. As they get older the landlord's daughter is kept busy being educated and cannot play with her friend. The caretaker's child continues the same kind of play with other children, sees sexual activity going on at home, has a boyfriend at puberty, soon a lover, marries young, has children and takes it all for granted. For the other girl, life is more difficult:

The well-brought-up, intelligent and high-minded girl has completely repressed her sexual impulses ... [she] came under the influence of education and accepted its demands. From the suggestions offered to it, her ego constructed ideals of feminine purity and abstinence which are incompatible with sexual activity; her intellectual education reduced her interest in the feminine part which she was destined to play. Owing to this higher moral and intellectual development of her ego, she came into conflict with the demands of her sexuality.

It is interesting that Hardy and Freud in their portraits of contrasting women are pinpointing precisely the same point of contrast. The kind of woman they are both describing – educated and inhibited – is the modern woman of the late nineteenth and early twentieth century (Freud's account was written in 1917). It is an indication of Hardy's awareness and sensitivity that he was able to observe and understand such psychological problems and then create a character which embodies them more than twenty years before Freud diagnosed them through psychoanalysis. This is a further example of Hardy giving imaginative life to the kind of knowledge about human nature which was explored in a different way with the development of psychoanalysis.

Hardy said that Sue was a type of woman who had always interested him, and this seems to be true of Freud also. Many of the qualities which Hardy portrays so vividly in Sue as she experiences and inflicts joy and anguish were found also by Freud in the neurotic women he analysed. She is similar to those 'narcissistic' women whose needs do not 'lie in the direction of loving but of being loved'. 'Strictly speaking, it is only themselves that such women love with an intensity comparable to that of a man's love for them'. Such a woman's attitude towards men is cool and she causes her lovers 'doubts of her love and complaints of her enigmatic nature'. Hardy gives a beautiful illustration of Sue's narcissism when she tries to get Jude to quote from 'Epipsychidion', and eventually recites the lines herself, applying them to herself and saying that they are 'too flattering'. Freud's, 'They are plainly seeking themselves as love objects', parallels this. Sue reveals that she regards this as an admirable emotional state when she claims that 'some of the most passionately erotic poets have been the most self-contained in their daily lives'. Freud uses the words 'self-containment' and 'inaccessibility' to describe this aspect of narcissism.

Freud maintained that masochism is an element in narcissism since 'masochism is actually sadism turned round upon the subject's own ego'. As we have seen, Sue continually tortures first her lovers, then herself for having caused them pain. Freud analyses this behaviour:

We have every reason to believe that sensations of pain, like other unpleasurable sensations, trench upon sexual excitation and produce a pleasurable condition, for the sake of which the subject will even willingly experience the unpleasure of pain. When once feeling pains has become a masochistic aim, the sadistic aim of *causing* pain can arise retrogressively; for while these pains are being inflicted on other people, they are enjoyed masochistically by the subject through his identification of himself with his suffering object. In both, of course, it is not the pain itself that is enjoyed, but the accompanying sexual excitation – so that this can be done especially conveniently from the sadistic position.

Much of this applies to Sue, that 'epicure of the emotions' who tantalises and tortures Jude and Phillotson on her wedding day, and before and after. Some of the characteristics, however, do not manifest themselves clearly until after the traumatic experience of the children's deaths, when her whole life is directed towards trying to maintain her precarious mental balance.

The deaths of the children is one of those melodramatic episodes for which Hardy is often criticised. There are obviously some weaknesses in the treatment of it, but the sense of violence and shock is essential to his design. If Sue's psychological vulnerability is to be fully exposed, he must show her precariously built up defences being broken down. He shows the breakdown into hysteria, the frantic struggle at the graveside, then the gradual building of fresh defences, the creation of the neurotic personality as a defence against insanity. All her former qualities are still there; her feelings remain basically the same, though grotesquely exaggerated; it is only the ideas, the theories that change fundamentally. Her sexual fears, her guilt, her masochism persist, increasing wildly: 'We should mortify the flesh, – the terrible flesh – the curse of Adam!'; 'I should like to prick myself all over with pins and bleed out the badness that is in me'; she attempts to cope with fear and guilt by a complete reversal of her intellectual position, saying, 'It is no use fighting against God'. Hardy shows her adopting a harsh, rigid form of Christianity as a way of achieving some kind of self-control; it has to be harsh, because for her nothing milder would be effective.

It is wholly convincing that she should attempt to deal with her emotional problems by self-punishment and rationality. It is reminiscent of Angel's attempt at his time of crisis to solve the problem by thinking, till he was 'ill with thinking; eaten out with thinking; withered by thinking'. Sue, similarly, applies her intellect to the problem, and comes up with some self-analysis which is strikingly accurate as far as it goes. She tells Jude:

Your wickedness was only the natural man's desire to possess the woman. Mine was not the reciprocal wish till envy stimulated me to oust Arabella. I had thought I ought in charity to let you approach me – that it was damnably selfish of me to torture you as I did my other friend. But I shouldn't have given way if you hadn't broken me down by making me fear you would go back to her. . . . At first, I did not love you Jude; that I own. When I first knew you I merely wanted you to love me. I did not exactly flirt with you, but that inborn craving that undermines some women's morals almost more than unbridled passion – the craving to attract and captivate, regardless of the injury it may do to the man – was in me; and when I found I had caught you I was frightened. And then – I don't know how it was – I couldn't bear to let you go – possibly to Arabella again – and so I got to love you Jude. But you see, however fondly it ended, it began in the selfish and cruel wish to make your heart ache for me without letting mine ache for you.

That she understands herself as far as this, including her sadistic impulses (she uses the word 'torture') may at first sight seem incompatible with her psychological state. But it is, I think, another example of Hardy's insight into psychological complexities. Such perception on Sue's part is in keeping with her former 'sparkling intellect', such close self-observation is part of her 'self-containment'; it is also this which enables her to survive the traumatic experience of the children's deaths combined with her own neuroses without collapsing totally and permanently – which the scene at the graveside shows to have been a possibility. She uses her intellectual recognition of her own guilt to justify her self-punishment (while hardly noticing that Jude will be punished too). Her behaviour is a continuation, in an even more obsessive form, of what it was in the past. When she turns Jude out of the house, she kisses him, and rejects him simultaneously:

'Goodnight', he said, and turned to go. 'Oh but you shall kiss me!' said she, starting up, 'I can't – bear – '.

Thus she builds up her self-protective barriers by forcing Jude to agree to living elsewhere, and then from behind these barriers, demands demonstrations of love.

In their arguments, Sue has always switched from discussion to emotion as soon as they verged on any criticism of herself. Jude feels she is utterly changed, but in fact she has only increased her former tendency to use emotional blackmail when things seemed to be going badly for her. In argument, she has always put her points ruthlessly, sometimes almost contemptuously, adopting a stance of moral superiority. She quotes some words of J. S. Mill to Phillotson and demands to know, 'Why can't you act upon them? I wish to always'. (The poor man moans, 'What do I care about J. S. Mill! I only want to lead a quiet life'.) From the heights of her knowledge and understanding she analyses the intellectual phases Jude is going through: 'You are in the Tractarian stage now . . . let me see – when was I there? In the year eighteen hundred and –'. Yet though she can be so sarcastic and never pulls her punches, she becomes hypersensitive when the argument is going against her, and hastily withdraws from it, usually making her opponent seem guilty at the same time. During one of the long discussions on marriage, Sue has made her points as vigorously as Jude has, but when he begins to say that he really fears she cannot love and that women who 'play the game of elusiveness' too often 'go unlamented to their graves', she 'acquired a guilty look; and she suddenly replied in a tragic voice, "I don't like you so well today as I did Jude! . . . you are not nice – too sermony"'. She then switches round to extreme self-accusation. The same pattern is repeated in the later arguments after the deaths of the children, the main differences being that she starts using emotion as a weapon earlier and her expressions of guilt are far more intense.

During her last meeting with Jude, she performs almost a caricature of her earlier actions by repelling him as long as he begs her to come back to him, but as soon as he starts telling her he will never come to see her again and that 'she is not worth a man's love', ' "I can't endure you to say that" she burst out . . . "Don't, don't scorn me! Kiss me, O kiss me lots of times" '. When he does so, her response is, 'Now I'll hate myself for ever for my sin', and she sends him away, coughing into the rain.

Her attitude to physical sexual relationships also remains basically unchanged even though the outcome in behaviour seems completely contradictory. It is characteristic that, when she has sent the dying Jude away and decided, 'I am going to make my conscience right on my duty to Richard – by doing a penance, the ultimate thing', it is then, for the first time, when she will never see Jude again that she says, 'I love him – O, grossly'. This is the first time that she has ever admitted to any 'grossness' in herself. She immediately follows this with her decision to go to bed with Phillotson, 'shuddering' and 'with a look of aversion . . . and clenched teeth'; this epitomises her conscious attitude towards sexual intercourse as something terrifying and 'gross'. She sees her decision as a way of enabling herself to cope with her otherwise overwhelming sense of guilt, ostensibly guilt because she left Phillotson in the first place, then guilt because she has kissed Jude, and probably above all, guilt because of the 'grossness' of her feelings for him.

Phillotson is very hesitant about admitting her to his bedroom, asks if she realises what she is letting herself in for, and leaves her waiting on the threshold while he fetches a testament on which he makes her swear that she will not see Jude again. Her persistence in the face of all this is characteristic; it is when she is being rebuffed that she demands love.

We do not necessarily have to accept Sue's interpretation of her behaviour as simply a way of expiating her guilt. As we have seen, her self-analysis has been extremely accurate in many respects, but Jude repeatedly feels that since the deaths of the children her intellect has been destroyed: 'Her once clear vision was dimmed'; 'bereavement seemed to have destroyed her reasoning faculty'. Her desire to punish herself is understandable, however unreasonable; she does it by wearing herself out scrubbing the stairs 'since eight' and simultaneously washing away her guilt. Hardy often shows neuroses emerging in minor typical modes of behaviour which are very effective in giving substance and actuality to the psychological states he is describing (Boldwood's clothes fetishism is a comparable example of his use of a clinical symptom). However, scrubbing the stairs all evening is a different matter from forcing herself on a hesitant man, while shrinking, clenching her teeth, but managing to utter no cry.

If at this point, we return to Freud, we find a possible interpretation of this episode which differs from Sue's explanation of her motives but corresponds more closely with Hardy's total treatment of her. Freud says:

Of the many symptomatic pictures in which obsessional neurosis appears, the most important turn out to be those provoked by the pressure of excessively strong sadistic sexual impulses (perverse therefore in their aim). The symptoms, indeed in accordance with the structure of an obsessional neurosis, serve predominantly as a *defence* against these wishes or give expression to the struggle between satisfaction and defence. But satisfaction does not come off too badly either; it succeeds in roundabout ways in putting itself into effect in the patient's behaviour and is preferably directed against themselves and makes them into self-tormenters.

Freud is here talking about people who find a substitute for the sexual act, but Sue's 'prostituting' herself to Phillotson is just as much an 'abnormal method of sexual excitation' as any other perverse inclination. Freud's suggestion that such people are creating a defence against strong sexual impulses does not fit in with Sue's own view of her refinement and elevating 'freedom from grossness' but it does give a more plausible explanation of her repeated attracting and repulsing than any she offers herself.

I have up to this point been arguing that Hardy's psychological insight is fully conscious, that he is interested in and aware of psychological theory as well as being particularly able to enter imaginatively into the mode of being of psychologically disturbed characters. With Sue, I think, we have an example of an intuitive glimpse of an idea which has not been fully formulated though it has been embodied in the novel. Hardy does not at any point in the novel state explicitly that Sue's aversion to sexual relationships derives from exceptionally strong drives which have been suppressed. All the characters, including Sue herself, assume the opposite. Yet the story shows her continually creating cliff-hanging situations (by living with the undergraduate, by marrying Phillotson, by eloping with Jude) in which the possibility of a sexual relationship is always present but kept at bay. In the description of the return to Phillotson, her aversion is shown to be so violent that it seems almost incredible that she would go through with it; if, however, Hardy has intuitively sensed that people like Sue have violent but repressed sex drives which they are terrified of, then the shuddering and clenched teeth fit the total picture. As Freud said, 'satisfaction does not come off too badly either'. Later in the same work, he accounts for this by saying, 'It seems that an accumulation of narcissistic libido beyond a certain amount is not to be tolerated'. The step from Sue's admission of her feelings about Jude – 'I love him – O grossly!' to Phillotson's bed is explicable in this way.

Whether we accept Freud's theory as psychologically accurate or not, there is much in the novel to suggest that Hardy was thinking on similar lines. Sue cannot allow her sexual feelings into her consciousness, but Hardy shows them emerging in other ways. When she says, 'I should like to prick myself all over with pins and bleed out the badness that is in me', the image is a sexual, as well as a masochistic one. This advanced, modern young woman is totally incapable of telling Little Father Time about childbirth; she will never express feelings of love except when their fulfilment has become impossible. (Even on the happy day at the Agriculture Show, when Jude tries to get her to say that she is happy 'because *we* have come' to the show, she replies, 'You are always trying to make me confess to all sorts of absurdities. Because I am improving my mind, of course'.) At the time, these responses seem to support her own view that she is too refined for sex, but her later developments cast doubt on this. That she should choose sex as punishment, and actually force herself upon Phillotson at a time when she has managed to set up the kind of situation which she has always apparently sought – living with a man who loves and admires her but makes no sexual demands on her – makes her explanation suspect. It is worth remembering also that it is at the point when she has established precisely the same Platonic relationship in her first marriage to Phillotson that she decides to leave him for Jude. Freud says that we must not 'judge everything as it appears to the ego of the neurotic subject'; certainly by the last chapters of the book we accept that Sue's 'once clear vision is dimmed'. Hardy's treatment of the story suggests 'the repressed and repudiated demands of sexuality', and also that this repudiation is not prompted by the straightforward distaste which she claims, since she follows each successful repudiation by seeking a new set-up where a sexual relationship will become a possibility again.

SOURCE: Extract from *Thomas Hardy: Psychological Novelist* (Macmillan, London, 1981), pp. 165–82.

R. P. Draper Hardy's Comic Tragedy: *Jude the Obscure* (1990)

In *Unsent Letters*, a series of semi-fictional, semi-biographical letters, Malcolm Bradbury reflects on his time as a young man in the Nottingham of the 1950s, where the youthful avant-garde of the day cadged drinks in the milk bars 'and, sitting on park benches, wrote their novels, all of which began: "The agony continues, unabated."'[1] These were, surely, the spiritual heirs of Hardy's long-suffering and much-protesting Jude Fawley. However, Bradbury's inarticulately angry young men had less excuse than Hardy's articulate stonemason; and it has to be admitted that, great though its charms may be, Nottingham does not quite possess the air of hoary antiquity combined with romantic idealisation that makes the Christminster (alias Oxford) of *Jude the Obscure* such a potent symbol of history and convention fused into the same fatally attractive environment.

Christminster is inhabited by people and by ghosts. The ghosts are literary figures whose writings have so shaped the image of the place for Jude that it becomes an elusive fabrication of inter-textuality, represented by the anthology with which chapter 1 of part 2 ('At Christminster') concludes – its farrago of 'memorable words' from Arnold, Sir Robert Peel, Gibbon, Browning, Newman, Keble, Addison, and Bishop Ken sounding in his ears as he falls asleep on his first night there. The people are working men and women whom Jude later comes to see as the real citizens: 'These struggling men and women before him were the reality of Christminster, though they knew little of Christ or Minster.'[2] But if this statement seems to imply that a kind of progress is made from literary illusion to sociological enlightenment, that impression is misleading. Jude never actually banishes the ghosts altogether. Alternation between dream and reality becomes the pendulum on which his nature swings, and which likewise provides the pattern of the novel's plot. 'The agony' in this proleptic novel 'continues, unabated' because of this permanent condition of instability, which in itself is a manifestation of the psychology of the avant-garde. Thus another hard-won insight of Jude's is that he and Sue were in advance of their day: 'The time was not ripe for us!' he says, toward the end of their catastrophic partnership. 'Our ideas were fifty years too soon to be any good to us' (p. 419). To be part of the avant-garde is to dream a dream of a better world, but also to bump up constantly against the unreformed, and almost, it seems, unregenerate, nature of the real world, so that, as Jude goes on to say, the resistance inevitably encountered by advanced ideas brings 'reaction' (which he attributes to Sue) and 'recklessness and ruin' (which he sees as the consequence for himself).

Such words suggest a somewhat ambiguous attitude towards avant-gardism: and if I have begun by treating what many readers regard as the most tragic of Hardy's novels in a somewhat comic manner it is because it seems to me a moot point whether *Jude the Obscure* should be designated as comedy or tragedy. Perhaps it did to Hardy, too, for when the novel was serialised in *Harper's New Monthly Magazine* (prior to publication in book form), the first instalment appeared under the title 'The Simpletons' and the second under the changed title of 'Hearts Insurgent' (see 'Note on the Text', p. 438). This ambiguity continues in the character of the work as we have it in the published version, where Hardy opts for the more neutral title *Jude the Obscure*. Thus from one point of view Jude can be seen as a heroic figure struggling to realise a noble ambition to become an enlightened scholar, who is defeated by the inert, selfish condition of the society in which he has the misfortune to find himself, while from another he appears as a foolishly inveterate idealist who seems quite incapable of learning from experience. His career is a remarkable series of seesaws, deliberately intended, it would seem from one of the letters to Edmund Gosse that are included in the *Life*, to illustrate a contrast:

The 'grimy' features of the story go to show the contrast between the ideal life a man wished to lead, and the squalid real life he was fated to lead. The throwing of the pizzle, at the supreme moment of his [Jude's] young dream, is to sharply initiate this contrast. But I must have lamentably failed, as I feel I have, if this requires explanation and is not self-evident. The idea was meant to run all through the novel. It is, in fact, to be discovered in *everybody*'s life, though it lies less on the surface perhaps than it does in my poor puppet's.[3]

In the actual presentation of this particular scene (part 1, chapter 6) the contrast between ideal and real is more like Fielding than Greek tragedy, with Arabella as a very plausible Molly Seagrim. In this connection Hardy himself, reacting to some adverse reviews, says: 'As to the "coarse" scenes with Arabella, the battle in the schoolroom, etc., the newspaper critics might, I thought, have sneered at them for their Fieldingism rather than for their Zolaism', and he adds that he has 'felt akin locally to Fielding, so many of his scenes having been laid down this way [he writes from Max Gate, near Dorchester], and his home near' (*Life*, p. 273). Furthermore, Jude's self-communings not only have the exaggerated air of a man in cloud-cuckoo land, but also come near to being comically blasphemous: 'Yes, Christminster shall be my Alma Mater; and I'll be her beloved son, in whom she shall be well pleased' (p. 58). What follows may be the gods' revenge on hubris, but, if so, it comes in the form of a rapid descent from the sublime to the ridiculous, which is more like Augustan bathos: 'On a sudden something smacked him sharply in the ear, and he became aware that a soft cold substance had been flung at him, and had fallen at his feet' – a something which he immediately recognises as 'the characteristic part of a barrow-pig'.

Nor is this the first time that such a thing happens to Jude. How seriously Hardy intended his phrase *my poor puppet* (in the extract from the *Life* quoted above) I am not sure, but it has a certain appropriateness. One of the first scenes in the novel has young Jude failing in his task of defending Farmer Troutham's corn and luxuriating in the sense that a 'magic thread of fellow-feeling united his own life' with that of the birds, only to become all at once 'conscious of a smart blow upon his buttocks, followed by a loud clack, which announced to his surprised senses that the clacker [with which he should have been scaring off the birds] had been the instrument of offence used' (p. 35). It is much the same when Jude's earnest attempt to con the Greek New Testament (signalled to the reader with deliberate pomp by isolating its title in the text in capitalised Greek lettering) is abruptly displaced by the sex instinct aroused in him by Arabella, which 'seemed to care little for his reason and his will, nothing for his so-called elevated intentions, and moved him along, as a violent schoolmaster a schoolboy he has seized by the collar' (p. 64).

There are touches of this comic exaggeration in the presentation of Sue as well. Aunt Drusilla, for example, illustrates Sue's naughtiness as a young girl with a tale of how she walked into a pond with her petticoats pulled up above her knees, saying: 'Move on, aunty! This is no sight for modest eyes!' (p. 130). This preludes her teasing perversity as a woman who provokes her lovers, but denies them satisfaction. The extraordinary psychology underlying such coy behaviour has excited much excellent critical comment (including Robert B. Heilman's celebrated article, and Rosemary Sumner's and Rosemary Morgan's more recent books),[4] and Hardy himself elaborates on it with the care of one fascinated. In the preface of the 1912 edition of *Jude* he cites – with evident gratification – the opinion of a German reviewer who told him 'that Sue Bridehead, the heroine, was the first delineation in fiction of the woman who was coming into notice in her thousands every year – the woman of the feminist movement – the slight, pale "bachelor" girl – the intellectualised, emancipated bundle of nerves that modern conditions were producing, mainly in cities as yet; who does not recognise the necessity for most of her sex to follow marriage as a profession, and boast themselves as superior people because they are licensed to be loved on the premises.' Yet in places, at least, the narrator of the novel finds her a subject for ironic banter rather than sociological comment – as when he observes that 'Sue's logic was extraordinarily compounded, and seemed to maintain that before a thing was done it might be right to do, but that being done it became wrong; or, in other words, that things which were right in theory were wrong in practice' (p. 239).

The Hardy of such wry little satires-of-circumstance poems as 'Ah, Are You Digging on My Grave?' and 'The Curate's Kindness' is also present in *Jude the Obscure*. For example, the story of Jude and the composer of 'The Foot of the Cross' might well have been turned into verse; and though the pun with which the composer dismisses music ('But music is a poor staff to lean on') may not be a very good one, there is something ludicrous about the eagerness with which he produces his wine list as a practical, commercial alternative.

The difference, however, between Hardy the poet in this vein and Hardy the novelist is that the novelist widens the listener's or reader's response. There is a significant change in the musician's manner when he discovers that Jude is a poor man rather than a prosperous potential buyer, and the effect of the disclosure on Jude is to make him abandon his hope of finding a mentor capable of giving his miseries a sympathetic hearing. The reader takes in these reactions; they modify the undoubted sense of the comic in the episode; and in the still-wider context of Jude's career the comedy dissolves into that recurrent pattern of illusion and disillusion which makes Jude more representative of the vanity of human wishes – a Johnsonian figure driven on to pursue the beckoning ideal, but doomed perpetually to disappointment.

The comedy, then, may be regarded as something embittered by the prevailing tone of disenchantment. This does not take us far enough, however. There is a more frustratingly tragic power at work. The comically external force that repeatedly makes its violent impact on Jude is the other side of a tragic force that seems arbitrarily to take over the novel and produce a plot 'almost geometrically constructed'. This is a phrase, yet again, taken from one of the letters to Gosse (10 November 1895; *Life*, p. 271). These letters show Hardy fully conscious of what he is doing – though sometimes admitting, sometimes denying, premeditation. The one dated 20 November 1895 is perhaps the most specific: 'Of course the book is all contrasts – or was meant to be in its original conception. Alas, what a miserable accomplishment it is, when I compare it with what I meant to make it! – e.g. Sue and her heathen gods against Jude's reading the Greek testament; Christminster academical, Christminster in the slums; Jude the saint, Jude the sinner; Sue the Pagan, Sue the saint; marriage, no marriage, &c., &c.' (*Life*, pp. 272–3).

These are contrasts which are not only juxtapositions, like the descent from dream to pizzle, or Jude's dying recitation from the Book of Job interrupted by cheering from the spectators at the Remembrance games, but also reversals in the fates of the two central figures, so contrived that they appear forever mismatched. The teasing character of Sue seen against this background becomes the expression of an ironic power that is itself perverse. The result is an enormous elaboration of the *X*-pattern that Hardy has already employed in *The Return of the Native* where Clym Yeobright and

Eustacia Vye encounter each other when they are set on opposite courses – he to return to his native heath, she to do all she can to escape it. In *Jude the Obscure* the principals change intellectual places to their mutual frustration: Sue begins as the sceptic and disbeliever, Arnoldian Hellenist and opponent of convention, respectability and puritanical duty, but after the deaths of her children she undergoes a nervous collapse that is followed by reaction towards the conformity she had previously despised ('Sue the Pagan, Sue the saint'). Jude, Gothic rather than Hellenic both in his ideals and in his trade as stonemason, begins as devotèe of Christminster; modulates to highly orthodox Christianity, during which phase he hopes to become a priest ('Jude the saint'); and then – partly as a result of his disillusioning encounters with reality, but even more, and with intense irony, as a result of his absorption of Sue's liberalism – swings round to more modern ideas, becoming a sceptic and finally a complete opponent of the conventional establishment of his day ('Jude the sinner').

The 'marriage, no marriage' part of this design is still more strikingly 'geometric' in execution: first Jude is married *to* the intellectually incompatible Arabella, and Sue *to* the sexually incompatible Phillotson; then Sue is divorced *from* Phillotson, and Jude *from* Arabella, to form a liaison with each other that is 'no marriage', yet spiritually a perfect one (in terms of the plot, this is the junction of their *X*); and finally Sue, under the influence of her masochistic reversion to orthodoxy, is married again *to* Phillotson, and Jude, under the influence of his weakness for drink, is married again *to* Arabella. Though the pattern sometimes strains the reader's credulity, it powerfully reinforces the sense generated throughout the novel that man's, and woman's, aspirations are mockingly out of tune with the actual shape of their lives.

There are also hints in the novel (supported again by one of Hardy's comments to Gosse on 'a doom or curse of hereditary temperament' [*Life*, p. 271]) that the destiny that misshapes the lives of Jude and Sue might be linked with inherited tendencies. Aunt Drusilla warns them that the family has a bad history of wedlock, and on the eve of their abortive attempt at marrying – largely for the sake of Little Time – their wedding 'guest', Mrs Edlin, tells them an ill-omened tale of marriage break-up that leads to the boy's comically solemn warning: 'If I was you, mother, I wouldn't marry father!' (p. 301). Sue likewise reacts to Mrs Edlin's 'horrid' story with the comment 'It makes me feel as if a tragic doom overhung our family, as it did the house of Atreus' (p. 302) – though as Sue is somewhat prone to exaggeration, this makes only a qualified effect; and Jude's rejoinder, 'Or the house of Jeroboam', followed by 'said the quondam theologian', lessens rather than strengthens its force. Thus if heredity is an issue, it lacks the seriousness of a centrally tragic idea. It is at best just a minor contribution to the sense that the celestial cards are stacked against Jude and Sue.

Sue's 'tragic doom' is, in fact, a phrase that sounds a little out of tune with the curious music of *Jude the Obscure*. Dark and gloomy notes are recurrent, and the reader is given the impression that even when things appear to be going right for Jude and Sue, they won't stay that way for long. To heighten that effect, Hardy has a habit of undercutting even the limited intervals of happiness in their lives, as when the carefree excursion made by Jude and Sue to the Great Wessex Agricultural Show is rounded off with a characteristic *memento mori* from Little Time: 'I should like the flowers very very much, if I didn't keep on thinking they'd be all withered in a few days!' (p. 316). Nevertheless, to borrow Lawrence's phrase (in the *Study of Thomas Hardy*), there is nothing 'necessarily tragic' in Hardy's tragedy. In a well-known pronouncement on Tolstoy's *Anna Karenina* and Hardy's Eustacia, Tess, and Sue, Lawrence asserts that these heroines 'were not at war with God, only with Society. Yet they were all cowed by the mere judgment of man upon them, and all the while by their own souls they were right'. As an observation this can be extended beyond these particular women; and, indeed, Lawrence himself generalises it to make it the distinctive 'weakness of modern tragedy'. What destroys Hardy's protagonists, despite their frequent tendency to complain against some hostile force that they seem to regard as inherent in nature, is their inability to adjust to the world in which they live. There is perhaps a level beyond this at which Hardy himself questions the rationality of a creation that permits of such mismatching between the individual and the world, and this may ultimately be a justification for the rhetoric of fate; but on a more immediate level of perception his characters are frequently seen to be the authors of their own undoing by the process of engaging in what Lawrence calls 'a war with Society' rather than the ultimate powers of the universe.

This is certainly the case with Sue and Jude. They are characters who in some respects may be regarded as neo-Ibsenites, seeking to live by a new individualistic code that puts them at odds with the insistent demands for conformity made on them by their Victorian world, and that keeps them in a state of perpetual tension with society. Sue ultimately collapses under the strain this struggle entails, and becomes a sort of 'tragic' figure in her perverse capitulation to convention. But her status as tragic protagonist is ambivalent: she may be seen either as a neurotic woman, vainly justifying her weakness by a set of spuriously advanced ideas, or as a genuinely heroic 'new woman', too isolated as yet to survive the hostility that her convictions attract. Hardy, it seems, chooses not to resolve this ambiguity; though he does offer the suggestion that she is a special type – a type likely to become more numerous in the future – for whom special conditions ought to be devised.

Jude, for his part, seems to grow in stature and become increasingly independent of the world's opinion, but he is ultimately defeated by the effects of Sue's collapse, which he, not quite unwittingly, helps to bring about by his obsession with Christminster. When the latter-day Sue develops extreme orthodox notions about the indissolubility of marriage, he partly realises that Christminster – for which in this context one can surely read 'the Oxford Movement' – is precisely the place that has fostered them; but he does not seem to remember that it was he, after all, who brought her back there against her better judgment. (If he is not quite the proverbial dog needlessly returning to his own vomit, he is rather like the venturer on a second marriage whose action, according to Dr Johnson, represents 'the triumph of hope over experience'.)

Such causes and effects belong to what Lawrence defines as the 'smaller system of morality, the one grasped and formulated by the human consciousness' as distinct from 'the terrific action of unfathomed nature' that is the background against which Hardy's tragic action is set in most of his novels. To argue, however, as Lawrence does, that this 'smaller system' is also a diminished system incapable of generating a true tragic effect is to ignore the fact that tragedy, especially in the novel, is itself a matter of 'the human consciousness'. There is no tragedy unless the characters' minds are influenced. Even the traditional tragedy that Lawrence finds in Shakespeare and the Greeks presupposes an ethos that is subscribed to by the audience, or is seen as powerful in its effect on the minds of the characters on stage, or, as frequently happens, is shared by both. The tragic reverberations are especially powerful when the latter condition obtains (i.e. when an ethos commands the assent of both characters and audience). An outstanding example is Sophocles's *Antigone*. The Greek audience was not only aware of Antigone's motive for insisting on the burial of her brother's corpse, but in all probability also accepted the idea of burial as a universal duty imposed by the laws of life. What she believed, and the way she acted on her belief, was seen not as a private and personal quirk, but as a sacred duty backed by divine authority. But, as the Hegelian interpretation of the play demonstrates, there is another view, inherent in the text, whether or not it was Sophocles's intended 'meaning', which sees the burial as the source of two potentially equal compulsions – that which operates on Creon as well as that which operates on Antigone. Creon feels compelled to forbid the burial because the brother had rebelled against the state. He is motivated by a sense of public, political duty that is every bit as strong as Antigone's private, religious duty. Once this point is perceived, the audience's response becomes a matter of balanced sympathies rather than absolute identification with one ethical mode, and with this balance creeps in the possibility of doubt. Creon may be seen as insecure in his tyranny, but Antigone may also be seen as extreme in her devotion. The modern condition of intellectual uncertainty is born, and the interpretation of the 'tragedy' becomes dependent on how the characters' actions are related to their convictions.

Jude the Obscure is a tragedy in which this process is still further advanced, and, indeed, much further advanced than in any of Hardy's own preceding work. The characters' underlying insecurities are brought nearer the surface, and the audience – now converted into the more reflective novel reader – is invited to judge them against a background that is presented as still more insecure. Education becomes a major, and necessarily ambiguous, force acting upon the minds of the central characters to detach them from communal values. The 'terrific action of unfathomed nature', which, as D. H. Lawrence rightly observes, plays such an important part in the Wessex novels, recedes in significance as the territory of *Jude* extends beyond the Dorset (or 'South Wessex') heartland to 'Mid', 'Upper', and 'North Wessex' and as its peripatetic characters migrate from Marygreen to Alfredston, Christminster, Aldbrickham, Kennetbridge, Stoke Barehills, Melchester, and Shaston with a restless movement even greater than that of Tess Durbeyfield's wanderings.

Christminster, the recurrent focus of Jude's odyssey, is itself a major centre of education, functioning as the nodal point of his illusions, while simultaneously offering the strongest contrast, and the greatest resistance, to them. To Jude's old acquaintance, John, it is merely a place of 'auld crumbling buildings, half church, half almshouse, and not much going on at that' (p. 132), but to Jude himself it is 'a unique centre of thought and religion – the intellectual and spiritual granary of this country', its apparent inactivity being only 'the stillness of infinite motion – the sleep of the spinning-top'. This exchange takes place in part 2, chapter 6. But in the same chapter, only a few pages later, Christminster, as reflected in the person of the Master of Biblioll – sole respondent to Jude's pathetic letters begging for intellectual assistance – becomes neither of these things, but simply an expression of the established social structure. The august academic's reply to Jude is couched in terms that embody the received wisdom of conformity: 'judging from your description of yourself as a working-man, I venture to think that you will have a much better chance of success in life by remaining in your own sphere and sticking to your trade than by adopting any other course' (pp. 136–7). The restlessness of his spirit, nourished, if inadequately, by his autodidact culture, urges Jude into motion, while society would have him be static. This stability, as seen by the self-educated Jude, is, however, merely another form of illusion. Within another two paragraphs he stands at the Fourways, a crossing point of thronging activity in the centre of the city, and senses that here is 'a book of humanity infinitely more palpitating, varied, and compendious than the gown life' (p. 137). Its range is wider, both geographically and historically ('men had stood and talked of Napoleon, the loss of America, the execution of King Charles, the burning of the Martyrs, the Crusades, the Norman Conquest, possibly of the arrival of Caesar'), and it includes the vital movement of the sexes as well ('loving, hating, coupling, parting'). And as he perceives this living, changing nature of the city, Jude also perceives the further irony that those who formally represent the processes of education, the students and teachers of Christminster university, 'were not Christminster in a local sense at all'. The Arnoldian stability of this fictionalised Oxford is itself an illusion; the reality is not academic, but popular, and partakes of the changing, fluctuating consciousness of men and women.

It is one of the many ironies of this novel that Jude, the young man 'on the move', should, initially at least, hitch his wagon to such a motionless and dully glowing star as static 'Christminster academical': and a still greater irony that when he is more truly enlightened by the intelligence of Sue, his education should crucify him on the cross of her insecure relapse into Christminster conservatism. To become a modern, individualised consciousness is to court this kind of disaster, since it is a process that necessarily involves uprooting and isolation. Jude and Sue's nomadic life dramatises their separation from the conformist world of their day. In one very obvious way it is their refusal to abide by the conventions of marriage that leads to Jude's loss of employment with Biles and Willis and to the gossip that subsequently drives him and his family away from Aldbrickham. By Lawrentian standards, this is a trivial basis for tragedy, something Jude and Sue ought to have been capable of rising above. It is not, however, as cause and effect that this social ostracism makes its chief impact on the reader, but as outward sign and symbol of the exposed and vulnerable state to which Jude and Sue are reduced. As 'free spirits' they are at the mercy of their own mental fluctuations, alienated from the unthinking support of an 'objective' social structure by the very freethinking nature of their own thoughtfulness.

That this liberated couple should ultimately move back to Christminster – the place of all places that, as Sue intuitively realises, they ought to avoid – is difficult to account for. But, again, explanation at the level of cause and effect is relatively unimportant. What Christminster represents for Jude is an overriding compulsion to find his home in an ideal community of learning – a 'university' town in the true sense of the word, where he could find a proper role by virtue of his innate worth and dedication. The yearning for such a Platonic society in which he might fulfil his aspirations is so great that it draws him despite the repeatedly discouraging lessons of experience. And, paradoxically, for Sue as well (despite her initial reluctance), Christminster becomes a transcendent goal, embodying for her, however, that conformity which exercises its emotional hold over her and dictates her conduct in defiance of her emancipated reason. Her rejection of traditional institutions and the traditional role of woman in the earlier parts of the novel may have its intellectual justification (there is little evidence to suggest that Hardy is adopting an anti-feminist stance), but her coquettish behaviour and her teasing perversity reveal how shallowly these

'advanced' ideas have taken root in her personality. Her intellec-
tualism is a wilful, hothouse growth, not a mature development;
it is brittle and always vulnerable to an emotional crisis. One of her
rare moments of true insight is when, having caught sight of her
divorced husband, Phillotson, in the streets of Christminster, she
feels 'a curious dread of him; an awe, or terror, of conventions I
don't believe in', which comes over her 'like a sort of creeping
paralysis' (p. 348). For her, as for Jude, the journey to Christminster
becomes a savage pilgrimage, with absurd and fantastic moments,
testifying to the inner compulsions of modern pilgrims of the
intellect.

Still, nothing in an artistically mature Hardy novel is as straightforward as that. The recurrence of such themes as rootlessness and
peripatetic wandering in *Jude the Obscure* cannot automatically be
equated with the tragi-comically insecure. Arabella, it must be
remembered, is just as much of a wanderer as either Jude or Sue – if
not more so, since her uprooting from the countryside takes her not
only to the same urban centres of Aldbrickham and Christminster as
Jude and Sue, but also to London, the metropolitan antithesis of
Wessex, and even as far away as Australia. Yet she remains firmly in
control of herself. She, too, is unconventional, not least in her
method of wooing, and quite unembarrassed by traditional sentiments of motherhood. The difference is that she knows herself
emotionally, and is clever enough to satisfy her instincts within the
appearances demanded by a conventional society. If Sue is the New,
and insecure, Eve, representative of the vulnerability of the immature avant-garde, Arabella is the Old Eve, secure in her power to get
what she wants by consciously manipulating conventions that have
no unconscious hold over her. Sue and Arabella can also be seen as
the embodiments of the Spirit and the Flesh respectively, which,
failing to cohere in the same woman, split Jude so that he becomes
dangerously divided against himself – exposed to destructive oscilla-
tions between intelligence and sexuality, heroic self-denial and
abysmal drunkenness. But neither Sue nor Arabella is a mere
morality figure. Each is a convincingly realised character in herself –
often, indeed, more acutely observed and plausibly portrayed than
Jude. Jude often seems like a projection of Hardy's own triple
preoccupation with class, convention, and learning; but Sue and
Arabella seem to be created from knowledge of actual women (Sue,
in particular, undoubtedly owes something to Tryphena Sparks).

They may still be a man's portrayal of woman, and the work of a man who is himself the product of Victorian values, even though rebelling against them. But Arabella in particular is a character who stands outside the ideals that Hardy derived from other men, such as Shelley and John Stuart Mill; and her downright earthiness brings the novel into contact with a world that is neither etherealised by intelligence nor frustrated by convention. In a comedy she might well be the heroine by virtue of her capacity to adjust to reality; in this tragedy, which so often verges on comedy, she embodies a female will that is reasonably good-natured when getting its own way, but untrammelled by conscience or guilt when dealing with opposition. She is ruthless and cunning in the ways of the world, so that she can use the sensitivity of others to her own advantage. Jude is thus putty in her hands precisely because he is unworldly and lacks her instinct for self-preservation.

It is also an element in the tragedy of Sue and Jude that they cannot live, as Arabella can, by instinct. Sue's original marriage to Phillotson is effected almost in violation of her physical feelings, as she admits when Aunt Drusilla says that he is one of those men 'that no woman of any niceness can stomach' (p. 210). Sue's own sexual appetite is not very strong – it operates negatively by making her unable to sleep with Phillotson, rather than positively in response to the virility of Jude. Jude, on the other hand, is a healthy sexual animal (in that respect, Arabella is his true partner), but his sexuality is so contravened by his conscious aspirations that it often seems to become merely a trap for him to fall into when blinded by his extravagantly high-minded notions. The animal in him takes revenge for being so neglected in the interest of the spiritual; and his thirst for drink functions in much the same way. Arabella, by contrast, manages to accommodate her instinct very successfully. Sue's dread of losing spontaneity by marriage – the formal process by which a woman is 'licensed to be loved on the premises' (p. 278) – is quite alien to Arabella, who is, ironically, both more calculating and more relaxed than Sue ever manages to be. Deceitful and exploitative as she is, Arabella can live spontaneously within the appearance of conformity (even though in one phase of her life she is actually guilty of the crime of bigamy), while Sue resists the chains of society only to live perpetually on edge and in a state of self-conscious anxiety.

It is thus impossible to pin down the tragic effect in *Jude the*

Obscure to one version of tragedy. Its very modernity consists in this
– that its episodes can seem both harrowing and ludicrous, and that
its two main characters can seem to be both self-consciously
perverse and the victims of a hypocritical, uncomprehending
society. If there is a central, unifying theme it is probably to be
found in the maladjustment associated with the struggle towards
liberation and modernity that makes tragically social misfits of Jude
and Sue. Education, in its widest sense, plays a major part in this:
Christminster deludes the hero and Melchester oppresses the
heroine.

Yet far from being a diatribe against the evils of education, *Jude
the Obscure* is, on the contrary, a passionate plea on its behalf. In his
1912 preface Hardy expressed a wry sympathy with the disgusted
'American man of letters' who bought a copy of the novel because
the reviewers told him it was a scandalous work, only (to his
disappointment) to find it 'a religious and ethical treatise'. Jude's
dream of self-improvement is his undoing, and Sue's inability to
bring her emotions into accord with her advanced opinions is fatal to
the happiness of both of them; but there is no moral to be drawn that
would support the status quo ante. Neither the Master of Biblioll's
advice nor Jude's dying repetition of the words from *Job*, 'Let the
day perish wherein I was born', receives the author's endorsement
or is expected to gain the reader's approval. Unlike, say, the ending
of *King Lear* – where there is a complete sense of exhaustion and
Kent's words on Lear, 'He hates him/That would upon the rack of
this tough world/Stretch him out longer' (V.iii. 313–15), command
universal agreement – the ending of *Jude* is one of unresigned
laceration. The cries from the Commemoration sounding so discord-
antly against Jude's biblical incantation still carry the burden of
discontent with the Christminster that is, as opposed to the Christminster that ought to be – the Christminster of Jude's imagination;
and this is a burden that has accompanied Jude throughout his
career. Similarly, Arabella's final words on Sue, 'She's never found
peace since she left his arms, and never will again till she's as he is
now!' (p. 428), operate to subvert the pious note of peace on which
Mrs Edlin would end Sue's story. The pulse of protest still throbbing
under these words reminds the reader of that refusal to conform
which gave Sue her vitality and charm in spite of all, while in Jude's
black chorus there still survives an energy of dissatisfaction that
focuses on the gap between the ideal and the real in Christminster.

It is this continuing impatience that especially distinguishes *Jude the Obscure* from traditional tragedy. There are hints that things might already be changing for the better so that a future poor scholar with the aspirations of Jude might not be left to rot in such embittered obscurity, and to this extent Jude's case might be felt as a provisional one only. But from within the circumstances in which he found himself, Jude has been struggling to affirm the creativity of the spirit, despite the inertness of established institutions. He has acted, albeit often quixotically and sometimes foolishly, in accordance with the novel's epigraph, 'the letter killeth'. So has Sue, until the point where her inner contradictions have suffocated her will. Although neither protagonist is given a traditionally tragic ending, in the form of Hamlet's 'the readiness is all' or Antigone's splendidly convinced defiance (indeed, it may be that Hardy deliberately parodies such endings in Sue's hollow resignation and Jude's final curse), the temper of the novel itself continues to deride the barrenness of conformity. The restlessness on which the novel concludes complicates its tone and perhaps aborts its tragic status; but such an ending keeps it nonetheless appropriately true to the instability that it has fostered throughout. And what certainly survives is the sense that Jude and Sue in their heyday were, after their fashion, sincere seekers for truth, and that, whatever the rights and wrongs, the folly and wisdom, of their actual accomplishments, they did make a heroic attempt to live not by the letter but by the spirit. The result is, generically speaking, a hybrid – a wild 'Polonial' novel, tragical-comical-historical-anti-pastoral-satirical, and even parodic – but nonetheless compelling and absorbing for all that.

SOURCE: 'Hardy's Comic Tragedy: *Jude the Obscure*', from *Critical Essays on Thomas Hardy: The Novels*, ed. Dale Kramer (G. K. Hall, 1990).

NOTES

1. Malcolm Bradbury, *Unsent Letters* (London: Deutsch, 1988), p. 96.

2. Thomas Hardy, *Jude the Obscure*, ed. Terry Eagleton, New Wessex Edition (London: Macmillan, 1974), p. 137; hereafter cited in the text.

3. Florence Emily Hardy, *The Life of Thomas Hardy, 1840–1928* (London: Macmillan, 1962, 1972), p. 272; hereafter cited in the text, identified by '*Life*'.

4. Robert B. Heilman, 'Hardy's Sue Bridehead', *Nineteenth-Century Fiction*, 20 (1966), 307–23; Rosemary Sumner, *Thomas Hardy: Psychological Novelist* (London: Macmillan, 1981); Rosemary Morgan, *Women and Sexuality in the Novels of Thomas Hardy* (London: Routledge, 1988).

FURTHER READING

Students are advised to consult the complete books from which extracts have been reprinted in this collection and, for Hardy's own comments, Harold Orel's *Thomas Hardy's Personal Writings* (Macmillan, London, 1967). See also *The Life of Thomas Hardy* below (under Biography). In addition, the following are also recommended.

BIBLIOGRAPHICAL

Draper, R. P. and Ray, Martin, *An Annotated Critical Bibliography of Thomas Hardy* (Harvester Wheatsheaf, Hemel Hempstead, 1989).

Gerber, Helmut E. and Davis, W. Eugene, *Thomas Hardy: An Annotated Bibliography of Writings About Him* (Northern Illinois University Press, vol. I, 1973; vol. II, 1983).

Taylor, Richard H., annual surveys of Hardy studies in *Thomas Hardy Annual*, ed. Norman Page (Macmillan, London), 1982 and each year subsequently.

BIOGRAPHY

Gittings, Robert, *Young Thomas Hardy* (Heinemann, London, 1975; revised and reprinted, Penguin Books, Harmondsworth, 1978).

Gittings, Robert, *The Older Hardy* (Heinemann, London, 1978; revised and reprinted, Penguin Books, Harmondsworth, 1980).

Hardy, Florence Emily [but in effect by Hardy himself], *The Early Life of Thomas Hardy, 1840–1891* (Macmillan, London, 1928).

Hardy, Florence Emily [but in effect by Hardy himself], *The Later Years of Thomas Hardy, 1892–1928* (Macmillan, London, 1930).

[The two volumes above were printed as one under the title, *The Life of Thomas Hardy, 1840–1928* (Macmillan, London, 1962).]

Millgate, Michael, *Thomas Hardy, A Biography* (Oxford University Press, London, 1982; reprinted as an Oxford University Press paperback, 1985).

CRITICAL STUDIES

General Books on Hardy including Material on the Tragic Novels

Boumelha, Penny, *Thomas Hardy and Women: Sexual Ideology and Narrative Form* (Harvester Press, Brighton, 1982).

Brown, Douglas, *Thomas Hardy* (Longman, London, 1954, revised, 1961).

Bullen, J. B., *The Expressive Eye: Fiction and Perception in the Work of Thomas Hardy* (Oxford University Press, London, 1986).

Butler, Lance St. John, *Thomas Hardy* (Cambridge University Press, Cambridge, 1978).

Carpenter, Richard C., *Thomas Hardy* (Twayne's English Authors Series). (Twayne, New York, 1964).

Cox, R. G. (ed.), *Thomas Hardy: The Critical Heritage* (Routledge, London, 1970).

Gatrell, Simon, *Hardy the Creator: A Textual Biography* (Clarendon Press, Oxford, 1988).

Goode, John, *Thomas Hardy: The Offensive Truth* (Basil Blackwell, Oxford, 1988).

Gregor, Ian, *The Great Web: The Form of Hardy's Major Fiction* (Faber & Faber, London, 1974).

Howe, Irving, *Thomas Hardy* (Macmillan, New York; Collier-Macmillan, London, 1976).

Ingham, Patricia, *Thomas Hardy* (Feminist Readings Series). (Harvester Wheatsheaf, Hemel Hempstead, 1989).

Kramer, Dale, *Thomas Hardy, The Forms of Tragedy* (Macmillan, London, 1975).

Miller, J. Hillis, *Thomas Hardy: Distance and Desire* (Harvard University Press, Cambridge, Mass., 1970).

Millgate, Michael, *Thomas Hardy: His Career as a Novelist* (The Bodley Head, London, 1971).

Morgan, Rosemary, *Women and Sexuality in the Novels of Thomas Hardy* (Routledge, London, 1988).

Page, Norman, *Thomas Hardy* (Routledge, London, 1977).

Vigar, Penelope, *The Novels of Thomas Hardy: Illusion and Reality* (Athlone Press, London, 1974).

Wotton, George, *Thomas Hardy: Towards a Materialist Criticism* (Barnes & Noble, Totowa, NJ, 1985).

Further Books and Articles on Specific Novels

THE RETURN OF THE NATIVE

Deen, Leonard W., 'Heroism and Pathos in Hardy's *Return of the Native*', *Nineteenth-Century Fiction* 15, no. 3 (December 1960), 207–19. (Reprinted in the earlier version of this Casebook.)

Fleishman, Avrom, 'The Buried Giant of Egdon Heath: An Archaeology of Folklore in *The Return of the Native*', in *Fiction and the Ways of Knowing: Essays on British Novels* (University of Texas Press, Austin, Texas and London, 1978), pp. 110–22.

Paterson, John, *The Making of 'The Return of the Native'* (University of California Press, Berkeley and Los Angeles, 1960).

THE MAYOR OF CASTERBRIDGE

Brown, Douglas, *Hardy: 'The Mayor of Casterbridge'* (Studies in English Literature Series). (Edward Arnold, London, 1962).

Draper, R. P., *'The Mayor of Casterbridge'*, *Critical Quarterly* 25, no. 1 (Spring 1983), 57–70.

Lerner, Laurence, *Thomas Hardy's 'The Mayor of Casterbridge': Tragedy or Social History?* (Sussex University Press [Chatto & Windus], London, 1975).

Maxwell, J. C., 'The "Sociological" Approach to *The Mayor of Casterbridge'*, in *Imagined Worlds: Essays on Some English Novels and Novelists in Honour of John Butt*, ed. Ian Gregor and Maynard Mack (Methuen, London, 1968), pp. 225–36. (Reprinted in the earlier version of this Casebook.)

TESS OF THE D'URBERVILLES

Claridge, Laura, 'Tess: A Less Than Pure Woman Ambivalently Presented', *Texas Studies in Literature and Language* 28, no. 3 (Fall 1986), 324–37.

Daleski, H. M., *'Tess of the d'Urbervilles*: Mastery and Abandon', *Esays in Criticism* 30 (1980), 326–45.

Hugman, Bruce, *Hardy: 'Tess of the d'Urbervilles'* (Studies in English Literature Series). (Edward Arnold, London, 1970).

JUDE THE OBSCURE

Heilman, Robert B., 'Hardy's Sue Bridehead', *Nineteenth-Century Fiction* 20 (March 1966), 307–23. (Reprinted in the earlier version of this Casebook.)

Ingham, Patricia, 'The Evolution of *Jude the Obscure'*, *Review of English Studies* 27, (1976), 27–37 and 159–69.

Jacobus, Mary, 'Sue the Obscure', *Essays in Criticism* 25 (1975), 304–29.

NOTES ON CONTRIBUTORS

KRISTIN BRADY. Associate Professor of English, University of Western Ontario. Author of *The Short Stories of Thomas Hardy* (1982) and *George Eliot* (1989).

JEAN BROOKS. Formerly Head of the Department of English, Rose Bruford College of Speech and Drama, Kent. Author of *Thomas Hardy: The Poetic Structure* (1971).

PETER J. CASAGRANDE. Professor of English, University of Kansas. Author of *Unity in Hardy's Novels* (1982) and *Hardy's Influence on the Modern Novel* (1987).

R. P. DRAPER. Regius Professor of English, University of Aberdeen. Author and editor of numerous books and articles, including *D. H. Lawrence* (1964), *D. H. Lawrence: The Critical Heritage* (ed., 1970), *Lyric Tragedy* (1985), *The Literature of Region and Nation* (ed. 1989), *An Annotated Critical Bibliography of Thomas Hardy* (with Martin Ray, 1989), and Macmillan Casebooks on Hardy, George Eliot, Tragedy, and The Epic.

DAVID LODGE. Well-known novelist; Honorary Professor of Modern English Literature, University of Birmingham. His critical writings include *Language of Fiction* (1966), *The Novelist at the Crossroads* (1971), *The Modes of Modern Writing* (1977), *Working with Structuralism* (1981), *Write On: Occasional Essays, 1965–1985* (1986), and a Macmillan Casebook on Jane Austen's *Emma* (1986, revised edition 1991).

JOHN PATERSON. Professor of English, University of California, Berkeley. Publications include *The Making of 'The Return of the Native'* (1960) and *The Novel as Faith* (1973). Editor of Harper & Row's Standard Edition of Hardy's novels.

ROBERT C. SCHWEIK. Professor of English, State University of New York College at Fredonia. Publications include *Hart Crane, A Descriptive Bibliography* (with Joseph Schwartz, 1972), *English and American Literature: A Guide to Reference Materials* (with D. Riesner, 1976), and various articles on Hardy and other nineteenth-century topics.

ELAINE SHOWALTER. Professor of English, Rutgers University. Author of numerous articles and studies, particularly of women's literature, including *Women's Liberation and Literature* (1971), *A Literature of Their Own: British Women Novelists from Brontë to Lessing* (1977), *The Female Malady* (1985), *The New Feminist Criticism* (1985), and *Speaking of Gender* (1989).

ROSEMARY SUMNER. Principal Lecturer, Goldsmiths' College, University of London. Author of *Thomas Hardy: Psychological Novelist* (1981).

TONY TANNER. Fellow of King's College and Professor of English, University of Cambridge. His numerous publications include *The Region of Wonder* (1965), *Three Novels by James* (1968), *City of Words* (1971), *Adultery in the Novel* (1979), *Scenes of Nature, Signs of Men* (1987) and various collections on American literature and Jane Austen.

RAYMOND WILLIAMS. Fellow of Jesus College and Professor of Drama, University of Cambridge until 1984; died 1988. Numerous works on literature and society, including *Drama from Ibsen to Eliot* (1952), *Culture and Society* (1958), *The Long Revolution* (1961), *Modern Tragedy* (1966), *The English Novel from Dickens to Lawrence* (1970), *The Country and the City* (1973), *Marxism and Literature* (1977) and *The Politics of Modernisation* (1989).

INDEX